the **juicy** guide

squeezing the best out of

brighton & hove

juicy books limited
13 Arundel Road, Kemp Town, Brighton
📞 **01273 672020**
📧 **www.juicyguides.co.uk**

CREDITS

written and compiled by Gilly Smith and Jed Novick

researchers from the University of Brighton's BA (Hons) Information and Media/Library Studies: Grace Haydon, Sian Guyton, Lucy Kamper, Andrew Murphy.

clubs: the Girls at Midnight and Louise Acford, clubbing editor at The Insight
gay: Lucy Kamper
shopping: Helen Paine Smith
teenage brighton & hove: Danielle Hayward (15), Hannah Potter and David Imms (16) Year 11 students at Patcham High School; Zenobe Reade (15) at Brighton College.
tweenage: Hayley Sensicle (10) at Balfour Junior School

contributors: Barrie Alderton, Anna Arthur, Marina Baker, David Barrington, Dave Bennett, Matt Blakestone, Dee and Paul Bonett, Simon Bradshaw, Alexi Cawson, Jeff Crosier, Rosie Davenport, Caraline Brown, Saul Dubow, Matt Evendean, Simon Fanshawe, David Hawker, Katy Gardner, Gavin George, Joanne Good , Madeleine Gregory, Fred Hasson, John Hinchliff, Julie Jennings, Emma Jowett, Viki Junor, Andrew Kay, Philippa King, Lucy McCrickard, Jeff Mead, The Midnight Girls, Bryony Mortimer, Amanda Sangorski, Adrian Sensicle, Peter Simmons, Paul Taggart, Louise Rennison, John Rowles, Lucy Shuttleworth, Emma Shuttleworth, Mike and Gilly Webber, David Whittle, Sue Willett, Lisa Wolfe and the people of Brighton and Hove via Opinion @ www.juicyguides.co.uk

photography: Paul Winter, www.paulwinter.co.uk
Fresh Agents Model Agency, www.freshagents.com

colour map: ARKA Cartographics Ltd

design: Adrian Sensicle of mole deign, *mole*design**@ntlworld.com**

CONTENTS

ABOUT THE AUTHORS

Gilly Smith left a career in radio and TV to write books - mostly on food - and features for the national press. Working with chefs such as Marco Pierre White, Jean-Christophe Novelli, and Pierre Koffman, on her first book, *The Mediterranean Diet* (Headline), and Australia's top 22 Chefs in her last book, *Australia, New Food from The New World* (Andre Deutsch), she has developed a critical edge to her love of good food. She moved to Brighton in December 1997 after 17 years in London when she and husband, Jed Novick wanted a better quality of life for their children while refusing to compromise on the coffee. They live in Kemp Town with their two daughters, two dogs, two cats, six goldfish and much of their extended family.

Currently music critic and feature writer at *The Daily Express*, **Jed Novick** worked as arts editor for *City Limits*, *The Observer*, *Time Out* and *The Guardian*. He is also the author of seven books on popular culture and TV heroes including Tommy Cooper, Morecambe and Wise, Benny Hill and Michael Palin's first authorised biography, *The Life of Michael* (Headline). A former sports reporter he is also the author of two books on football, *Winning Their Spurs* and *In A League Of Their Own* (Mainstream).

PUBLICATION DETAILS

First published in Great Britain in 2002 by Juicy Books Ltd

Copyright © Juicy Books Ltd, 2002

The right of Gilly Smith & Jed Novick to be identified as the author of this work has been asserted by them in accordance with the Copyright, Designs and Patents act 1988

A catalogue record for this book is available from the British Library

ISBN 1-903320-02-X

cover, text & juicybooks logo designs © 2002 Adrian Sensicle / mole design

printed in England

00.1

As we send the third edition of *The Juicy Guide* to the printers, the sun is shining, the sky is blue and we've spent the day cycling with the kids in Seven Sisters Country Park – what do you mean "deadline"? It's the Easter holidays. Like the thousands of people who moved here for the quality of life, we spend the sunlight hours on the beach and then half kill ourselves by working around the clock. Anyway, the point is that right here, right now, there's nowhere that we'd prefer to be.

Much as I'd like to think that we're individuals, that there's no such thing as homogeneity, the truth is that Brighton in the sunshine is enough to seduce a staggering 40% of the thousands who fled London last year in search of a better lifestyle. Once they get here and find themselves blown off their feet in the January storms or braving the mad rains which almost swallowed the surrounding countryside in seconds again this year, it's a different story. But when the sun comes out again and lights up the gleaming white crescents and terraces from Kemp Town, it's like it's never been away.

But what does it feel like to be part of that zeitgeist, the thing of the moment, the most exciting new City in the UK? Well, let's get a bit of perspective here - when the Prince Regent, probably out of his box on laudanum, packed his bathers, gathered his courtier chums and decamped to an old farmhouse in the Old Steine, shipped in a load of Chinese dragons and Indian minarets and proclaimed Brighton fit for a Regency prince, he was way back in the queue of out of towners who set their sites on this fine old seaside town. And I hate to say it, but anyone who watched what Tony Wilson and Factory Records did to Manchester in the late 1980s or watched the spin doctors of SW1 reinvent The UK of the 1990s as Cool Britannia, will know that it's hard sometimes to work out whether life imitates art or whether it's the other way around.

Whatever the hype, apart from the effect on the house prices, it's mostly in our interests. Let's remember that we're a nation of shopkeepers and of that 40%, a fair few brought their traders' agreements and international menus with them. They teased us with their new designs and tantalised us with their soul food, and still we beg for more. Never before have we had so many fabulous places to shop or bars, pubs and restaurants to delight our senses.

And never before has a guide book so completely tapped into the needs of a local readership. "A guide book? What do I need with a guide book? I live here"; it was a common cry two years ago. Now, as the only reference guide to just about everything you need in your life - and with no ads to prejudice what we say in our review section - *Juicy* has become the *Time Out*, the *Lonely Planet*, the *Rough Guide* of the south coast, an essential read for anyone who needs to get out more.

Over the past year, Juicy's website has been besieged with questions about everything from work, health, community, arts, kids - and we've tried to deliver. A free monthly newsletter keeps subscribers up to date with the endless number of bars and shops opening and closing, arts reviews and restaurant write ups - all seeringly honest. Without the support of advertising in the review section we may be poor, but at least we don't have to pay lip service. And perhaps because the Opinion button on the website has almost been rubbed away with over use, we tell it how it really is, how the city sees itself by asking readers to feed back on what they've been fed, where they've been shopping and where the best nights out are to be found.

The Juicy Awards at The Dome on June 24th will celebrate the spirit of Juicy by showing how much talent is under our noses in a party for 1500. Listen in to Juice 107.2 Fm for more details or visit the website at ***www.juicyguides.co.uk*** and come and join us. And until the next edition, have a great year whether, like some of Juicy's new readers, you're relocating from Israel or whether you've lived here all your life. We reckon that Dr Johnson was misquoted when he said that when you're tired of London, you're tired of life. Either that, or he'd never been to Brighton.

01

● PLANES, TRAINS & AUTOMOBILES

● BRIGHTON BOUND

● FROM LONDON

NEVER EVER take the A23 out of London unless you're coming from Croydon. And if you're coming from Croydon, then take the train. The A23 is still a car park. Drive back late at night and you'll still hit traffic. Signs from Brixton and Holland Park may seduce you with the promise of a straight road south, but remember: the M25 is there for a reason.

● RAT RUNS

● FROM BRIGHTON TO LONDON

TO SOUTH WEST LONDON
A23
M23
M25 (Heathrow direction)
Junction 9 (Chessington World of Adventures).
Third exit off first roundabout - A233 to Esher
A244 at next roundabout to Oxshott all the way to A3 into London, picking up signs for Fulham and Hammersmith or straight on for Wandsworth.

● TO WEST AND NORTH WEST LONDON
A23
M23
M25 (Heathrow)
M40
A40

● TO NORTH, NORTH EAST, SOUTH AND EAST LONDON
M23
M25 anticlockwise to the Brands Hatch exit off the M25

To cut up through SE London into central London in about one hour 50 minutes:
A23
M23
M25 (Dartford) to junction 3 A20 (Brands Hatch)
A2 for East London
Turn right into Kidbrooke Rd (A2213)
Sun in Sands roundabout to Blackheath
Right into Greenwich High St towards Surrey Quays and Rotherhithe, Tower Bridge and the City, or Blackfriars and Kings Cross.

For Dulwich, Brixton Clapham and routes off South Circular, take the A205 off the A20 at Eltham.

● FROM LONDON TO BRIGHTON

FROM SOUTH WEST, WEST OR CENTRAL LONDON

A3
A243 Chessington turn-off
M25 to Gatwick
M23

FROM SOUTH AND EAST LONDON

A20 from New Cross and Blackheath
M25
M23

FROM NORTH EAST LONDON

Cross the river via the Blackwall Tunnel to A102(M). You'll see two signs for the M25; one directs you straight on down the A2 to the M25, while the other, shorter route takes you off the A2 via a right turn. Keep going straight through the lights until you see signs to the A20. Then M25, then Gatwick and the M23.

● TRAIN

National Rail enquiries:
08457 484950
Connex customer service:
0870 830 6000
South Central Disabled Assistance: *0845 123 7770*

Thameslink customer service:
0207 620 6333
Thamesklink disabled:
0207 620 6376

Trains from Brighton to London run every 20 minutes.

50-minute trains leave Brighton for Victoria from 09.50 on a weekday and then at 20 and 50 minutes past the hour until 21.50.

From Victoria, the 50-minuters start at. 06 and 38 past from Victoria from 0838 until 1806 ten 1908, 1937, 2008, 2038, 2308

The Thameslink route travels to Bedford via London Bridge, Blackfriars, Kings Cross and Luton. It also runs plenty of fast trains, averaging just over an hour to Blackfriars.

The last trains home are 01.00 from Victoria arr 02.30 (unless you can deal with the milk train at 04.00), or the 23.04 from Blackfriars. Allow 10 minutes earlier from Kings Cross Thameslink and 10 minutes later from London Bridge.

If you don't want to cross London by Tube, jump on either line and change for the faster train at East Croydon or Gatwick. The same applies if you're coming from London and want to get home as soon as possible.

Sunday trains are a nightmare, what with repairs to tracks and leaf sweeping and so forth, so avoid the headache and come on a Saturday. Different rules again apply on Sundays. You might end up where you want to go, but then you might end up in Littlehampton, having visited every town between here and Bournemouth.

● COMMUTING

If the trains are running, commuting is an attitude; if you think of it as your daily meditation, opportunity for a nap, or the only part of the day when someone doesn't want a slice of you, it can be a delight. Leaving London through south London and rolling into the green and pleasant land of Sussex before driving home along the seafront is a particularly welcome reminder of what life is all about. If the trains are offline, get online - if you can and let the internet take the strain for a bit.

The stopper trains serve mid-Sussex via Burgess Hill, as well as Gatwick. Long-distance services also link Scotland, the north and Wales without the need to go into London.

There are plenty of stations for you to choose from: Brighton, Hove and Preston Park serve the central towners, with Hove offering a last-minute option from Victoria if you can see your Brighton train heading off without you. London Road Station feeds the East-West route to take you to the seaside towns along the South Coast.

● PRICES

£15.20 day return with the condition that you arrive in London after 10am.

A weekly travelcard allows you to travel at any time of the day for £65.50 return, or £76.50 if you buy a ticket which covers all Tube zones. A monthly costs £251.60, or £293.80 including the Tube pass. You won't have to queue and it works out cheaper than buying daily tickets. You'll need a passport photo for your travelcard.

If you can leave after 10am, you can get a third off with a Network card that costs £20 a year; a £15.20 day return then becomes £10.05. There are also special deals to Victoria or London Bridge at £10 as long as you don't come back with the evening rush-hour crowd. If you're leaving your car at the station car park, it will cost you £3.50 for the day. Presumably someone will notice if it's been there a week, but it's still one of the best bargains in town.

● COACH

National Express (08705 808080, www.gobycoach.com) has coaches leaving for London Victoria every hour from Pool Valley with stops at Stockwell and Streatham. Day return tickets cost £8 and the journey takes two hours.

● LEFT LUGGAGE

Travelite
164-166 Kings Rd Arches, Brighton
01273 773776

● PLANES

Gatwick is 30 minutes away on the fast

train, 50 minutes or so if you get the Hassocks hopper, and a taxi is also an affordable option.

Long Distance Cars (01273 581581) will pick you up from your terminal if you pre-book and give them your flight number. They charge between £40 and £50 depending on which airport you're going to and an extra £3 for an estate car. The M25/M23 route is extremely easy,

Jetlink (08705 808080, www.gobycoach.com) runs to and from Heathrow and Gatwick and take one hour and 50 minutes respectively. Allow for traffic jams on the M25 at busy times though. Also try One Stop Travel Shop (01273 700406) or Brighton and Hove Buses (01273 886200). The Council also runs a travel information line (01273 292480).

Luton is easy with the Thameslink service, but Stanstead involves a train to Liverpool St and then a tube to Farringdon to connect with Thameslink. You can also try Jetlink (number above).

TraveLine (0870 6082608) for buses from Brighton across the country. Shoreham Airport (01273 296900) offers a myriad of treats from flying lessons to day or weekend trips, all pre-arranged.

● TAXIS

01273 204060; 747474; 205205 (Brighton)
01273 202020 (Hove)
01273 414141 (Portslade)

Proof that Brighton is a small city comes in the form of a cab receipt. From the end of Hove to the end of Kemp Town, any of the blue and white cabs will charge you around £10, with hops into town from either end at around £6 or £7.

You can now hail any Council-endorsed cab anywhere in Brighton and Hove as long as they've got Brighton, Hove or Brighton and Hove writ large upon their roof or side. Or pop along to one of the many cab ranks in town (ring 01273 202020; 747474; 204060), or just hop on one of the many buses (see section below).

If you're coming off the train though and you're queuing for a cab, let's get a little cab sharing part of the local culture. Stand tall and ask if anyone else is going to Seven Dials or Kemp Town. Listen, they do it all over the world, so why not in Brighton? Think about the environment and save yourself a few bob too.

● BUSES

Rumour has it that Brighton's bus service was used as the blueprint for Auckland's revamped transport system and is deemed to be the best in the world. Brighton must be the only place in the world where buses are named after its celebrated locals, as well as boasting the longest commitment to an environmental policy in the country. While the rest of the UK mutters about pollution and makes New Year resolutions to use the bus more, Brighton and Hove folk have changed their travel habits substantially. Bus usage here has gone up by 25 per cent in the past couple of years compared to a decline or static usage everywhere else in the country.

The environmental message is clear with pedestrians, cyclists and buses welcome in Brighton's fair city and cars barred from the city centre until 6pm. Car parks surround the main arteries, giving you little reason to clog up local lungs with carbon monoxide. And with asthma a serious concern in Brighton's basin, we need to do whatever we can to limit pollution.

The inequalities of the central fare system which penalised the less well-off have now been tackled with everyone from Newhaven to Shoreham now paying the flat fare of £1 (50p concessions) once saved for the Whitehawk pockets. The inner cityers are not quite so happy since they too have to pay the £1 for their two-stop trip, but hey, they can always walk. Apparently the rise paid for the 23 new buggy/wheelchair-friendly, double-deckers, which joined the 5a and 5b route this year serving Hangleton, Hollingbury and Patcham.

● TICKETS

£12.50 pack of five-day passes; £13 for a weekly saver. Both are available from the Post Office, newsagents and One Stop Travel Shop at the Old Steine.

£2.60 (£2.20 central area) all-day pass (available on board).

● CARS

Parking vouchers can be bought from shops displaying a green 'V' sign and come in books of £5 or more. A couple of £1 vouchers will enable you to park in the few bays around town while you drop back your library books, or get a couple of extra bits and bobs without going through the whole rigmarole of a multi-storey. To help visitors there are huge neon signs on the main routes, which tell you, how many spaces are available in the various car parks. There are a few available bays towards Hove where you can park for two hours as long as you don't return while the traffic warden has still got your number. From June 2001, the council is stepping up its enforcement of on-street parking.

● BIKES

This city loves to cycle and the cycle lanes (almost) allow cyclists to get around without fear for their lives. As a result, it's rare to see the face-down, flat-backed and helmeted cyclists that duck and dive through some of our other cities. Instead, if you're driving in Brighton and Hove, beware the head-in-the-clouds, hair-flowing-in-the-breeze-type of cyclist who doesn't notice when the cycle paths have run out into the main road because the sea looks just so lovely up ahead.

The Council has promised that it will eventually extend the track that starts past Sainsbury's on the Lewes Rd and leads down to the cycle tracks, which pick up at The Level. It also plans to extend the seafront cycle track east from Brighton Pier to the Marina and to continue the cycle planes north from Preston Park along the A23.

The cycle paths between Brighton Pier and Hove Lagoon can be cluttered with tourists, rollerbladers and children learning to ride their own bikes, but when the crowds have gone home, there's nothing finer than a ride beside the seaside on an out-of-season morning.

Do remember that Brighton and Hove is a city on a big hill, and if you've just moved into Hanover or Fiveways, and you're considering ditching the car in a bid to go green, you're going to get good and fit. The South Downs, too, is a curiously deceptive learning curve; most mountain-bikers can be seen pushing their multi-geared, techno cycles back from what seemed like a good idea at the time. The gentler slopes of the South Downs Way, a long-distance bridle track which runs along the back of Brighton and Hove, is a better bet.

The number of cycling shops reflects Brighton's interest in this mode of transport. Prices vary enormously for repairs and maintenance, so shop around. One of the best finds is Baker St Bikes (01273 675754) where the price of a puncture repair is about half that of anywhere else in town and where they can usually do it while you wait. Planet Cycle, to the Kemp Town side of Brighton Pier (01273 695755) is a very friendly place, full of cheap-ish bikes, good advice and plenty of rabbit. Their other branch, just under Alfresco's by the West Pier, hires bikes for summer-trippers: £3 for one hour, £5 for two hours, £8 for four hours, £12 all day. You'll need a £20 deposit and some ID.

Contact Roger Simmons, the Council's walking and cycling officer (01273 292475) for information on cycling and cycle routes.

● LIMOS

The stretch limos littering the seafront throughout the summer are more likely to be full of wedged-up holidaymakers than local glitterati, most of whom don't realise that you're not supposed to open the windows. Definitely for those hoping to impress their mates, a limousine service seating eight people costs about £100 for the evening; a turbo Bentley will set you back about £45 an hour.

● FERRY

Newhaven to Dieppe is a two-hour hop on the Seacat. Phone Hoverspeed (08705 240241), or check the Net or Teletext for special deals, or try its website: www.hoverspeed.co.uk.

02

● Brighton and hotels. The very thought inspires fantasies far too racy for these pages. But it's not just a city for lovers; Brighton and Hove has to find pillows for all sorts of people who bring their business and their credit cards to town. Model Railway enthusiasts, Methodist preachers and experts on skin disease have all been seen traipsing through the revolving doors of "Conference Central", The Brighton Centre. And then there's the festival types, high art fans coming down for the weekends of May, performance artists over from France, whole symphonies sharing hotels with acrobats and pyrotechnic artists and all of them wanting a breakfast to suit their own dietary requirements.

Tourists, hen and stag-nighters, potential relocators looking for their dream home and sexy locals who've left the babysitter in charge back in Seven Dials, this chapter is for them. It gives a peek behind the net curtains to show what Brighton's really like, from the urbane, genteel Victorian city by the sea to the blatantly ostentatious sex kitten of a city. The Regency and Georgian styles reflect the decadent and exotic character kick-started by the Prince Regent and his gang while the New Bohemians of The Pelirocco and Blanch House, with their pop-star designed rooms, take Brighton into a new chapter of arty indulgence.

This time next year, a bunch of new hotels will have come to town, The 74-bed Waterfront Hotel offering oysters and champagne to shoppers staggering back from the knock down designer outlets at the Marina, and the gorgeous Hotel du Vin chain pitching camp at the old Bar Centro in Ship Street. If the Bristol Hotel du Vin, a grade II listed derelict sugar mill turned boutique hotel with a huge iron staircase sweeping up to New York loft style pads, is anything to go by, it'll set a new standard in Brighton and Hove.

● BUDGET

Even the most splendid of Brighton's old hotels offer mid-season, midweek cheapies and you can often find a room for £40 or even less. For instance, The Hilton will give you a seafront room for £50 if it needs to fill its rooms, so if the wind is up and Brighton's looking empty, haggle! All the prices quoted are per person, per night, unless otherwise stipulated.

Colson House

17 Upper Rock Gardens, Kemp Town
Tel/Fax: 01273 694922
info@colsonhouse.com

Ignore the slightly shabby front of this hotel because as soon as you walk inside it is clean, airy and spacious. This continues throughout with its eight en-suite rooms all perfectly coordinated and comfortable. This modern, gay-friendly hotel offers a great location - near to the sea and town - with welcoming young proprietors. Prices are between £25 and £30 per person per night.

Cosmopolitan

29-31 New Steine, Central Brighton
01273 682461 Fax: 01273 622311
reservations@cosmopolitanhotel.co.uk
www.cosmopolitanhotel.co.uk

Not one for the style guru, but there are two very good reasons why The Cosmopolitan is listed: it offers one of the cheapest views of the sea and Brighton Pier available, and it has a chintzy Sixties bar which often stays open all night. Prices range from £35 to £85, depending on the time of year and size of the room, a full English breakfast is included and rooms with a sea view are also available.

Lichfield House

30 Waterloo Street, Hove
01273 777740 Mobile: 07970 945464
feelgood@lichfieldhouse.freeserve.co.uk
www.lichfieldhouse.freeserve.co.uk

About 15 minutes walk from the centre of Brighton, this small guest house caters for a clientele which wants modern, well furnished but individual style rooms. Try the French Lavender room or the Mulberry Georgian room and book yourself an aromatherapy deep tissue massage or reflexology session in the on site treatment room. The service is friendly and efficient and there is a communal breakfast room, which houses a fabulous old jukebox - which you can check out on their website. Although not situated in the heart of Brighton, there are plenty of bars and restaurants nearby, and parking is much easier. Prices start from £20 per person.

Penny Lanes Hotel

11 Charlotte Street, Kemp Town
01273 603197
pennylanes@pscience.net

Romantic, Victorian and specialising in comfort, Penny Lanes offers four posters, shaggy rugs and a sumptuous Eggs Benedict for breakfast. Vegans, vegetarians and carnivores come back for more from this tasteful little seaside guest house. Prices start from £25 per person and children go half-price.

Sea Spray

25 New Steine, Marine Parade
01273 680332
seaspray@brighton.co.uk
www.seaspraybrighton.co.uk

Contemporary, friendly boutique hotel with oriental rooms and four poster beds, all with sea views and not a hint of chintz The modernity and enthusiasm of their website is reflected when you visit this hotel. The staff are friendly and more than happy to help and the rooms are immaculately decorated in bright colours and spacious. Breakfast is made to order, vegetarian and vegan options will be cooked up on demand and all included in the price of £65 per night per room at the weekend.

Valentine House
38 Russell Square, Central Brighton
01273 700800 Fax: 01273 707606
john@valentinehousehotel.freeserve.co.uk
www.valentinehousehotel.com

This Georgian terrace house is very cute from the outside, small and covered in flowers throughout the spring and summer and this theme continues inside with cosy little en-suite rooms and an awful lot of chintz. It is located on a really nice little garden square but couldn't really be more central being two minutes from the sea and two minutes from the town. With rooms as reasonable as £45 for a double per night, it's a great base for those wanting explore the local area.

Walkabout Inn
79-81 West Street, Central Brighton
01273 719364

Central place to stay until you move on or get your own place. It can be noisy but the atmosphere is friendly and it's cheap. Doubles cost £70 per person per week, triples and quads are £60 and dorm beds are £55 per week. All the rooms have individually controlled radiators, washbasins and lockers, although the word is that sometimes the hot water can run out. The kitchen is too small and the TV is temperamental, but it's a good place if you're new in town and your budget is tight.

● AFFORDABLE TREATS

Brighton Pavilions
7 Charlotte Street, Kemp Town
01273 621750 Fax: 01273 622477
sanchez-crespo@lineone.net
www.brightonpavilions.com

A perfect example of the boutique hotels Kemp Town is famous for. Roman busts and oriental statues, ochre and Pompeii Red décor and classic design features in themed rooms like the Royal Pavilion (with its gold silk draped four poster) make this little hotel a Kemp Town gem and some say it's better value than The Grand. Prices vary between £36 and £52 per person.

Cavalaire Hotel
34 Upper Rock Gardens, Kemp Town
01273 696899 Fax: 01273 600504
cavalaire.hotel@virgin.net
www.cavalaire.co.uk

One of Kemp Town's finest finds, this friendly and stylish little guest house is also a haven for non smokers. The owner is passionate about Brighton and this is reflected in his local knowledge and the many pictures, which cover the downstairs walls. There's even parking for residents which is unheard of in

Kemp Town. Prices start at £25 and go up to £80 for a superior double en-suite

Dove Waldorf Hotel

18 Regency Square, Central Brighton
01273 779222 Fax: 01273 746912

This Polish-owned, family-run hotel is an oasis of calm, which you probably won't ever want to leave. The double beds are huge - as, happily, so are the rooms. Most can convert into family-size rooms and the front-facing ones also have a sea view. The minimalist and cosmopolitan décor is in neutral and light colours, complimented by wooden furniture and palms, while the plush pile carpets will ensure you'll return home vowing to redecorate. The owner is charming and helpful and has created a genteel guest house, which is atreat. Prices vary according to size of room, but expect to pay between £40-£60.

The Genevieve

18 Madeira Place, Kemp Town
Tel/Fax: 01273 681653
info@genevievehotel.co.uk
www.genevievehotel.co.uk

Big beds are the hallmark of the Genevieve, namesake of one of Brighton's most romantic films, with luxury 4 poster beds & a super kingsize bed from £80. Non smoking rooms are available, as well as Continental and veggie breakfasts.

Granville Hotel

124 Kings Road, Brighton seafront
01273 326302 Fax: 01273 728294
granville@brighton.co.uk
www.granvillehotel.co.uk

A runner up in the Juicy Award for hotel of the year in 2000, The Granville is quality. This is smaller than many of the seafront hotels but easily as elegant and indulgent for those who stay here. Each of the rooms is individual and if you really feel like treating yourself why not stay in their Grand double room, relax on the antique four poster bed and have a relaxing soak in the jacuzzi spa bath before taking in the intoxicating views of the West Pier by night whilst eating in their organic restaurant that specialises in vegetarian dishes. Double room prices start from £85 per night but you'll pay a little more for the Grand Room at about £145.

The Lanes Hotel

70 Marine Parade, Kemp Town
01273 674231 Fax: 01273 674230
www.laneshotel.co.uk

This old traditional seafront hotel is a fair size but still small enough to offer a personal service. The rooms are reasonably sized and tastefully presented, with just enough facilities without being cluttered, despite the garish patterns in the carpets and curtains of the lounge areas and reception downstairs. The obvious attraction of this hotel is the sea views available from many rooms, even those not directly at the front, and the front lounge, but the late night residents' bar also offers a slight incentive. Prices vary greatly from room to room and also reduce by nearly half during the week compared to the weekend, but start at around £50.

Marine View Guest House
24 New Steine, Central Brighton
01273 603870
mvbrighton@aol.com
Brand new to the business and full of enthusiasm for the best of Brighton and Hove including clubs, restaurants and the greatest places to visit. Prices start at £30.00 per person per night.

The New Madeira Hotel
19-23 Marine Parade, Kemp Town
01273 698331 Fax 01273 606193
info@newmadeira.co.uk
www.newmadeira.co.uk
Fifteen of the 35 rooms here look right over the sea and the pier with all providing en-suite and all mod cons. Prices start at £45 for a single and £75 for a double.

New Steine Hotel
12a New Steine,
Central Brighton
01273 681546 Fax: 01273 679118
newsteine@hotel-brighton.fsnet.co.uk
www.newsteinehotel.com
Hervé, Georges and Stephane earned their four diamonds for their friendly service and mix of modern and quaint bedrooms. Dinner is French and open to the public (but booking is mandatory), and there's an internet kiosk too. Breakfasts are English, vegetarian, vegan or continental.

Paskins Town House
19 Charlotte Street, Kemp Town
01273 601203 Fax: 01273 621973
welcome@paskins.co.uk
www.paskins.com
Farm-fresh organic traditional and veggie breakfasts, fluffy towels, fresh flowers and four poster beds make Paskins one of the most famous town houses in Brighton. All the rooms are spacious and tastefully decorated, including their four-poster bedrooms for those looking for a romantic break in Brighton. Prices range from £60 per room per night for a standard room without en-suite to £90 for the four-poster. Find time to have a chat with the main man, Roger Marlowe; as chair of the Hoteliers Association he is one of Brighton's movers and shakers and knows all the gossip that makes this city tick...

Hilton West Pier
Kings Road, Brighton seafront
01273 329744 Fax: 01273 775877;
Freephone: 0990 515151
This is, as the name suggests, a large hotel, which forms part of the countrywide chain. As such, it doesn't have any character pertinent to Brighton, hence the rooms are what you'd expect from this type of business hotel. However, the staff are very friendly and the sea-facing balcony rooms boast undoubtedly the best view of the West Pier. You can use the facilities of a health club, which is 200 yards up the road, although once you've

done the walk that may be enough exercise! Prices vary greatly and deals are always available. Expect to pay from £40 per person, with a seaview supplement.

Strawberry Fields

6-7 New Steine, Central Brighton
01273 681576 Fax: 01273 693397
strawberryfields@pavilion.co.uk
www.brighton.co.uk/hotels/strawberryfields
If it's good enough for the Minister of Tourism who chose to stay here during a conference, it's good enough for us. Overlooking a garden square right next to the sea front it is hard to fault the location of this hotel. Inside, although the décor is far too busy and leaning on the chintz side the rooms are comfortable with good facilities and the family who own it are friendly and efficient. Many rooms are en-suite with sea views and at £35 per person per night it is about the average price for this area of town but offers an exceptional service, especially for families, with reduced rates for children, a play area a baby listening service with NNEB qualified supervision and qualified child minders.

Sussex Arts Club

7 Ship Street, The Lanes
01273 727371
The five double bedrooms (£80), one single (£50) and the Arts Club suite (£100) with its four-poster bed make this one of the best small hotels in central Brighton. Mary and her staff care not a jot for a famous face, which is

probably why Julie Burchill made it her home for a year before she moved to Hove. Residents are free to mingle with Sussex's Bohemian set in the late bar.

● INDULGENT

The Belgrave

64 Kings Road, Brighton seafront
01273 323221 Fax: 01273 321485
thebelgrave@cwcom.net
www.thebelgravehotelbrighton.com
Run by the former House Manager at The Metropole, the service is quality but less corporate than most. Understated and simple but certainly elegant, this hotel has the views of the sea but is also situated on the main road leading up to the town. The rooms are newly refurbished which was successfully and tastefully done, they are spacious with en-suite and contain all the necessary facilities. The Hotel also boasts a relaxing lounge bar and their own contemporary restaurant which serves international cuisine and is available for private hire. Prices for a double room for a weekend by the sea start at about £130.

Blanch House

17 Atlingworth Street, Kemp Town
01273 603504
www.blanchhouse.com
Nominated for the sexiest hotel at this year's Juicy Awards at The Dome, this is the hotel of hedonism. Sip complimentary champagne in a Victorian free standing bath in the

Perrier Jouet suite (£220 including free bottle of PJ), get romantic in the blood red fabrics of the Decadence suite (£190) or dream of far away lands in the Morocco, India or Snowstorm rooms (£100-125). On site reflexology and late breakfasts for nightbirds (for an extra tenner), sumptuous restaurant and the coolest bar in town all add up to a treat of treats. The stair carpets may be a bit shabby, some of the rooms may be on the small side and the ambience can be charmingly chaotic, but this is an original and genuinely Bohemian refuge from the corporate nightmare of hotel-land.

The Grand
Kings Road, Brighton seafront
01273 321188 Fax: 01273 224321

Every film or TV series that is worth watching has a chase scene, a balcony-dangling scene or just a 'bus going past the front of the building' scene that shows The Grand. It is an impressively ornate building, which has housed more presidents than the White House, more Prime Ministers than Number 10, and more celebrities than the Priory. It's worth saving up just to pop in for a drink if you can't stretch to an overnight stay. The staircases, which run through the building, are bigger than most people's houses and the bedrooms are equally spacious and indulgent. Prices start from £275 per room for a sea-facing double; deluxe doubles, which offer access to a balcony and include the use of the gym.

Hilton Metropole
Kings Road, Brighton seafront
01273 775432; Fax: 01273 207764;
Freephone: 0990 515151

This hotel is situated on the seafront next to the Grand Hotel and although lacking its neighbour's history or grandeur, is more than a match for many of the other big hotels on the front. There is a bar and restaurant with a covered conservatory looking over the Channel, and a downstairs nightclub for those of you with the stamina and stilettos required. Obviously it lacks the character of the smaller guest houses, but who needs character when you have a sauna, steamroom, spa and on-site beauty consultant? Prices vary greatly and deals are always available. Expect to pay from £90 per person for a seaview room.

Hilton West Pier
Kings Road, Hove seafront
01273 329744

Corporate twin of Brighton favourite, The Metropole. While other chain hotels in town will insist on inflicting their appalling taste on their guests, the Hilton's more subdued style is much appreciated. The ylang ylang body lotion and lavender-scented 'relaxing water' is another nice touch, displaying an understanding of what a night in a hotel should all be about. The balconies overlooking the English Channel could do with a lick of paint though and the much-hyped Hilton health club is a rainsoaked dash down the road to the

Metropole. A twin is £170, double £190 and the really swish suite is £395. Prices come down according to demand and you can get a room here for £50.

Montpelier Hall
Montpelier Terrace, Montpelier
01273 203599 Fax: 01273 706030
If you're looking for a traditional, antique filled stay near the town but just tucked away, this is the place for you. This regency villa is impressive and elegant from the outside and the dining room and lounge are suitably crammed with a mixture of ornamental antiques and chandeliers but retain that sense of grandeur. There is a walled garden with a pond and an abundance of exotic plants where they host barbeques in the summer and private parking for guests. Prices start from £25 to £40 per person for a single room and a full English breakfast. It's a shame that the place is run by a charmless version of Basil Fawlty though.

Nineteen
19 Broad Street, Kemp Town
01273 675529
info@hotelnineteen.co.uk
www.hotelnineteen.co.uk
Minimalist chic off the seafront with soothing Zen white walls, vast beds - three of which are on plinths of blue glass bricks - and local art and architectural flower displays making the place a feast for the senses. Another of Kemp Town's cool boutique hotels which has added to the neighbourhood's

reinvention over the last couple of years. Sunday morning breakfasts are a complete treat as you help yourselves to chilled champagne. In the summer, you can take your bucks fizz and breakfast in the privacy of the stunning walled garden. Prices for a double room start are from £95 to £135.

The Old Ship Hotel
Kings Road, Brighton
01273 329001 Fax: 01273 820718
oldship@paramount-hotels.co.uk
www.paramount-hotels.co.uk/oldship
The outside of this sea front hotel is slightly deceptive; as it doesn't make it stand out as it possible should. When you walk through the door the sheer size of this hotel is a surprise and the vast expanses of deep red and dark wood finishes show that it is very well looked after. The rooms are stylish but still comfortable, all en-suite and many with sea views. The size does mean that there isn't so much of the personal touch but the staff are still friendly and efficient and with Redz Brasserie (which you should avoid) and Bar next door and plenty of room to host conferences but with mixed reviews in the past it might be one you only try once.

The Oriental
9 Oriental Place, Central Brighton
01273 205050 Fax: 01273 821096
info@orientalhotel.co.uk
www.brighton.co.uk/hotels/oriental
Two years ago the Juicy award winning Oriental with its individually designed

rooms, ornate furnishings and moody lighting was the place to hang out for Brighton's creative and artistic types. Two minutes from the sea this small but perfectly formed hotel is immaculately decorated with wooden floors and dark blue velvet. The front room looks like many of the funky cafes in town and the bedrooms are small yet bright and airy and each are individually decorated. The double rooms are en-suite and the friendly owners make sure all the rooms contain a plant and oil burner to ensure any visitors can relax. In the summer you can sit out on the balconies on the front bedrooms, though the calm atmosphere of the hotel alone is enough to attract an artistic clientele that just keep coming back. Prices start from about £60 per room in the week.

Pelirocco

10 Regency Square, Central Brighton
01273 327055 Fax: 01273 733845
info@hotelpelirocco.co.uk
www.hotelpelirocco.co.uk

This is easily the coolest of all the hotels in Brighton, and if you're looking for something a little bit different, a little bit rock'n'roll, you've found your bed for the weekend. With 18 individually styled and decorated rooms there's a theme for everyone, sponsored by products such as Playstation 2, Smint and Absolut Vodka and with inspiration from artists and fashion labels it is the hotel to stay in. Even the names of the rooms and the leaflet ooze style and personality and the place itself doesn't

let you down. Prices range considerably depending on what room you fancy but start at around £50. Breakfast is included in the price and you can enjoy it to the beats of chilled out music and the sounds of the sea.

Prince Regent

29 Regency Square, Central Brighton
01273 329962 Fax: 01273 748162
Freephone: 0800 0199332
reservations@princeregent.com
www.princeregenthotel.co.uk

This has all the grandeur and elegance of the larger traditional hotels but wrapped up in a smaller package with really friendly and personal service. The halls and rooms are draped with paintings, there are antiques everywhere you look and the carpets are a deep luxurious red. If you're after a romantic trip back in time where you can sit back and pretend you're royalty, book the grand balcony room. For £150 you get en-suite, a magnificent antique four-poster bed, and a bay window and balcony with incredible views of the square, the sea and the West Pier. Other double rooms are slightly less over the top and prices start at about £95.

The Regency

28 Regency Square, Central Brighton
01273 202690 Fax: 01273 220438
enquiries@regencybrighton.co.uk
www.regencybrighton.co.uk

If Joan Collins ran a guest house, this would be it. Unashamedly exploiting Brighton's heritage this hotel offers the

Regency Suite, an ostentatious, canopied four-poster room with all the trimmings - gold brocade, velvet tassels, heavy rococo drapes and a view of the Square and the West Pier. Although this room is the piece de resistance, there are other comfy doubles and singles available. The bar and lounge are decorated in a similarly ornate fashion, and the one careful lady owner is herself a vegetarian so all breakfast tastes are catered for. Regency Suite costs around £125; other rooms between £50 and £90 depending on time of year.

● OTHERS TO TRY

Alpha Lodge
19 New Steine, Central Brighton
01273 609632

Ashley Court Guest House
33 Montpelier Road, Montpelier
01273 739916

New Europe Hotel
31-32 Marine Parade, Kemp Town
01273 624462

Shalimar Hotel
23 Broad Street, Kemp Town
01273 605316

● SELF-CATERING

Best of Brighton and Sussex Cottages
Windmill Lodge, Vicarage Lane,
Rottingdean BN2 7HD

01273 308779; Fax 01273 300266
brightoncottages@pavilion.co.uk
www.bestofbrighton.co.uk

Contact Susannah or Heather. This company lets and manages many properties in Brighton and the surrounding area and is continually adding to its list, so phoning for a brochure is recommended. There's a good selection of properties - all sizes to suit all pockets. All the properties inspected by The English Tourism Council and given a Star grading.

They've got a luxury three bedroom/two bathroom balcony penthouse above the Metropole Hotel with excellent views both in an Easterly and Westerly direction which sleeps 6/8 people (and costs between £575 a week for four people up to £925 a week in the summer for up to six people, a town house in Kemp Town and a maisonette in Arundel Terrace other cottages in villages further from Brighton, and a Tudor Manor House in East Sussex which sleeps 18 people...the list goes on.

Try the following cottages for the best of what is on offer and expect the prices to rise in the summer and supplements for extra people. Prices include electricity, gas, linen and cleaning.

Horseshoe Cottage in the village of Rottingdean sleeps four in one double and two single rooms. The village is on the seafront about three miles from Brighton and has maintained its olde worlde charm, and is near the pond on the green and the beach. The cottage is very old and its size and steep staircases reflect its grand old age, but it is mod in all its cons and only a 10-minute bus ride from town. Costs range from £360 to £535 per week.

Seapoint Cottage is situated nearby Roedean School with panoramic views across the golf course to the sea and Marina. About five minutes' drive from Brighton, it has direct access to rural walks and is peacefully set back from the coast road. It sleeps seven, with two doubles, one twin and a single and costs between £375 and £600 per week.

Brighton Holiday Flats
50 Kings Road, Brighton, BN1 1NA
01273 260100
bookings@brighton flats.co.uk
www.brightonflats.co.uk
You can't get more Brighton than these 22 self-catering apartments, situated on the seafront in the heart of all the rock and souvenir shops.

They have all been recently refurbished and the larger flats have a panoramic view of Brighton's beach nightlife - so when you are sitting in your spacious lounge with a G&T you can watch your friend queuing for a nightclub. The flats are booked up very quickly in the summer so be warned. Prices for a studio which sleeps two are between £180 and £280 per week; four-person apartments start from £210 per week, and the larger apartments with sea views which sleep five start from £320 per week.

Prices rise in peak season.

Brighton Lanes
14a Ship Street, Brighton, BN1 1AD
01273 325315 Fax: 01273 323882
intermkt@pavilion.co.uk
Contact: Gordon House. This company owns two adjoining fisherman's cottages built in 1562, which are situated in Brighton's Lanes. They are furnished with original oak and pine furniture and retain the old stairwells and doorframes. Ideal for families, the cottages comprise a lounge, kitchen, double bedroom on the first floor and two small bedrooms on the top floor. People were smaller in the 16th century, so unless you're Ronnie Corbett or Lulu it's going to be a tight squeeze, but the history of the houses makes it worthwhile. Two modern apartments are also available in Ship Street which sleep four. Spacious and comfy they may be, but these lack the character that the cottages have. Cottages cost between £400-£500 per week depending on season. Apartments cots between £220-£350 per week. Day rates available.

Metropole Court and Cliff Edge Cottage
Cliff Edge, 28 Marine Drive, Rottingdean
01273 302431 Fax: 01273 307744
Contact: Harold/Valerie. The Metropole Court apartments are situated above the Metropole Hotel on Brighton seafront. Part of the accommodation deal is the free use of the Metropole's health club facilities and entry to the Metro nightclub. One-bedroom flats, most have twin beds in

the bedroom and a sofa bed in the lounge. Recently refurbished, two of them also have a glorious seaview. More expensive, the penthouse sleeps three people and also has a seaview. All the apartments have a kitchen, dining area, lounge and bathroom. The furnishings are rather pink and frilly (think Laura Ashley meets Barbara Cartland), but if you're just using it as a base to sightsee and enjoy the view, it's not too distressing.

Also available during the summer season is Cliff Edge Cottage which, as its name suggests, is on the edge of a cliff. Situated in the village of Rottingdean, about six miles along the coast from Brighton, the cottage sleeps two people and offers amazing views over the Channel. Off-season prices for Metropole apartments from £260 per week, Penthouse suites from £300 per week, rising to £420 in summer. Cliff Edge Cottage costs between £260-£330 per week and is not available for single nights.

● BACKPACKERS

Baggie Backpackers
33 Oriental Place, Central Brighton
01273 733740

Brighton Backpackers
75-76 Middle Street, Central Brighton
01273 777717

Fries Green Backpackers Rest
20 Middle Street, Central Brighton
01273 747551
Dormitories only.

● CAMPING

Sheepcote Valley
Off Wilson Avenue, east of Kemp Town
01273 626546

● *I first came to Brighton in 1947 and after 55 years, I still don't regret it. To me Brighton is the centre of the universe from where you can travel anywhere in the world from Australia to Alaska. I moved here like so many of my fellow writers and theatrical artists, because I could get home from London after midnight. I have sweet memories of the Brighton Belle service to Victoria that ran several times a day right up to the Sixties, but is now part of the Orient Express. That's what brought me to Brighton but its only in the past few years since I stopped travelling so much that I have been able to know the place and its people and surroundings. And that's why I chose to stay.*

Edward Murray, *80 year old foreign correspondent, lives in Seven Dials*

03

● As soon as the sun shines, the South East packs its buckets and spades and heads to Brighton, looking for espressos and candyfloss in the place they call London-by-the-sea. London should be so lucky. The mix of chrome cafes, hip bars and Brighton rock is unique to this city; compared to Eastbourne, Clacton and Margate and, no disrespect, but there's no comparison. This is the seaside, 21st century style.

There are clubs and pubs, cafes and bars, stalls selling rings and books and sarongs. There's basketball, a kiddies playground with paddling pool, bungee jumping, crazy golf and a Mary Poppins carousel. If you can't find something here, I'd go and see a doctor and get them to check your pulse. See if you're still alive.

The seafront, the peeling balustrades stretching back from the Brighton Pier against the shimmering whiteness of the Regency squares on Marine Parade, the Volksrailway, deckchairs, pebbles and naturist beach give off the mixed signal of decadence and decay which is Brighton's charm. The fish and chip bars on Madeira Drive are a glitch in the Council's plan to create a San Francisco in Sussex, but somehow a perfect reminder of what British seaside towns should be about. In a city where the best summer clubbing tips straight out on to the beach at dawn, fish and chip caffs like The Madeira Café also provide an important service: breakfast starts from 3am. It even does a vegetarian breakfast in this veggie capital of the UK.

● BRIGHTON PIER

It is the quintessential joy of Brighton that you can go from a chic café to the tacky pier in just a few steps. One minute you can be sipping an espresso discussing that arty something you saw last night at The Duke Of York's, the next minute you're rolling balls in the Dolphin Derby desperate to win a fluffy alien key ring.

Everyone goes to the pier. If you visit, you go to the pier. If you live here, you wait for your mates to visit so you can take them (and yourself) to the pier. Somehow, it straddles that divide between being irredeemably naff and wonderfully entertaining.

The Pier with its palm readers (invariably out to lunch) and candy floss and fudge (don't do it. It doesn't matter how much the little ones bawl - don't do it) has mercifully enclosed its brain-shattering arcade in a noise-proof bubble, leaving you free to wander out to sea, or take a quick ride on the Waltzer or the trampoline that can be found in a cage on the edge of the pier. Gaze in wonder at the Rollercoaster and exclaim "Who on earth would want to go on that?" before stopping for lunch at the fish and chip restaurant standing grandly in the middle of the Pier is also a must, with its offer of a glass of champagne accompanying your mushy peas.

● THE WEST PIER

Along the promenade towards Hove is the 130-year-old, grade one-listed West Pier, floating like a ghost ship as the starlings mass above at sunset, dancing in formation for the meditative seafront traffic. Its decline began after the Second World War from lack of investment and it closed in 1975 when it finally became unsafe for the public. But its shell remains unchanged since 1916, and its concert hall and theatre are the best surviving Victorian and Edwardian entertainment buildings in Britain.

Whether or not it will regain its glory is one of those soap scripts which plays out in the readers letters page of The Argus. In the meantime, the hard hat tours of the West Pier have been put on hold, but with any luck they'll be up and running again by the time you read this. As we speak, remedial work is being carried out to make the pier safe for the tours and if they can get the proper insurance, all will be well. Ring 01273 207610 to find out the latest.

What's the story with the West Pier, long term? Now there's a question. In 1998, it was given a Lottery grant to repair and renovate with the plan being to "restore it to its former glory". What this means in the real world is that there'll be "performance space" though not as it was because it wouldn't be commercially viable to re-create it as it was in the 1920s. There will also be shops and cafes, but that of course is all still under wraps. "We're still working on the uses of the Pier" a spokesperson told us. "It's a unique opportunity and it would be silly to rush into anything. But we're consulting with restaurateurs and also people like Norman Cook because it's for everyone and has to appeal to everyone."

There is, though, a blockage. The legality of the Lottery grant has been challenged by the Brighton Pier and the case has been referred to the Bermuda Triangle that is Brussels.

What's it to do with the Brighton Pier?

"They've enjoyed a monopoly for so long and they don't want it threatened" said the spokesperson.

But it's not as if you want to set up a Dolphin Derby is it.

Pause.

"No."

● BETWEEN THE PIERS

Lottery money has also reached the shores of the beach between the piers. A flurry of activity has transformed what was a tacky line of fish and chip booths into an alfresco pleasure dome. From the Mary Poppins carousel to the children's playground beyond the West Pier, the seafront has enough to keep the kids happy, while a stretch of cafés serves the grown-ups. The sandy volleyball court gives the girls something to watch as the sun goes down, and the town's best clubs, The Beach, Arc, The Zap and the Honey Club entertain sun-drunk, pre-clubbers on terraces leading out to the sea. Even the hippies have got wise and in summer the beach towards Hove is littered with Thai trousers, sarongs, ankle bracelets and fruit stalls. If the beach were sandy, we could be in Goa.

● THE PEACE STATUE

Above the bartering and the basking, the evening rollerbladers glide towards the manicured lawns that separate Brighton and Hove. It is here that you will find the peace statue of the angel, as it smiles down at the mini-shorts and crop tops which make The Ellipse - where the boys play basketball - more Venice Beach than hippy India. For a great way to take in the seafront, hire a bike for all the family, and head down the cycle track all the way to Rottingdean. You can hire bikes from Sunshine Bicycles (under The West Pier) - £3 for one hour, £5 for two, £8 for four, £12 all day. You'll need £20 deposit and some ID. They also do family bikes with all the seats and buggies and things. If rollerblading's more your game, you can hire them from Pulse (23 King's Road Arches, just under Alfresco's - 01273 720788) - £3.50 an hour, £5 for two hours or £10 all day.

● THE FISHING MUSEUM

The fishing museum celebrates what Brighton used to be (and still is to the tiny minority of fishermen pushed out of town to Moulsecombe's housing estates). The museum strews its fishing nets and boats across the beach in a bid to catch the tourist trade if the cod is less willing. The fish shop next door sells fish straight off the boats (Rick Stein swears by it), while another sells smoked fish which it will sandwich up for you if you fancy eating it right then and there. The availability of fish depends on the catch, but the museum is open throughout the year. Look out for the Blessing of the Nets as part of the Brighton Festival in May (see The Season chapter) when the first mackerel catch is barbecued and sold to a salivating crowd. If you fancy hiring a fishing boat, ask at the museum for a list of skippers who are willing to take you out.

● BLACK ROCK

East beyond the buzz of the beaches between the piers the mood changes. The cosmopolitan feel gives way to something much more rooted in Old England. The harsh would call it shabby, the romantic would say it's a throwback to the days of Donald McGill postcards and Carry On films. Here, it's a universe away from ideas like City Of Culture and any pretensions of Eurochic. Even in the height of summer there are less people here - still loads, but less. There are playgrounds and seaside entertainments that have fallen into disrepair, rides that have made good friends with rust. In the summertime the caterpillar emerges from its winter hibernation to take screaming four-year-olds through its giant apple. The pitch and putt, Peter Pan's playground and an new assortment of hair-raising rides provide a quieter amusement away from the Pier and is largely aimed at younger children.

One of Brighton's best clubs, Concorde 2, has risen from the ashes of the original Concorde - once the coolest and hippest of all clubs - and is now Kemp Town's home to gigging and drinking. Apart from the very fine Volks Tavern (see Clubs for details), until the new development reinvents this part of town, it's the only reason why anyone would go down by night unless you're going to sit on the beach and look at the stars. By day, Planet Cycle and various kayaking shops hire out bikes and boats.

Further along, Black Rock originally marked the boundary of Brighton, although the Marina now lies beyond it and calls itself part of the city. Back in the Thirties it was the site of an open air swimming pool built on the site of a terrace garden, but it closed in 1978 and only now has its redevelopment been put out to tender. Former ice-skating star, Robin Cousins has a plan to make it into a huge ice rink, and there are bids for a whole host of cafes and restaurants on the site. It couldn't come too soon for those at the end of Kemp Town; the area is currently disused except for a car and coach park for tourists who can take the Volkstrain up to the Pier. In the summer, the little train runs every 15 minutes and is a particular treat for younger kids.

● THE NATURIST BEACH

The Naturist Beach at Kemp Town is awash with deep-sea swimmers, kayakers and naked bodies (mostly men) throughout the year. As soon as the sun shines, they're out, making a stroll on a balmy February afternoon a surreal experience. Brightonians turn the other cheek as naked men parade their wares, sometimes a little too close for comfort, but those of a nervous disposition should stay well away. Brighton Belle (Hove, actually), Julie Burchill refers to it as "Ghost Brighton. The one part that could happily have played host to one of those arch-miserabilist Eighties videos by The Smiths or Pet Shop Boys". The built-up shingle is a thoughtful gesture by the Council to shelter the naturists from the stares - or maybe that should be the other way round. Duke's Mound is a dirty scrubland that tries to keep itself respectable with its climbing plants and bushes, but is more of a cruising haven for the local gay community. Not a place to visit after dark.

● THE MARINA

Beyond the meditative fishermen lined up on the sea wall, lies the extraordinary expanse of Brighton's Marina, a world unto itself that looks like something out of The Prisoner, a south coast Portmerion of almost spooky box-like conformity where nothing is quite as it seems and there's the feeling that if you scratch the surface... who knows what you'll find.

What you actually find are million-pound Princess yachts moored outside box flats, a floating Chinese restaurant with roof tiles shipped all the way from China, McDonalds, an enormous bowling alley, a swanky David Lloyd health club with café/bar looking out to sea, an eight-screen Virgin cinema complex and a casino. The locals get as far as the gym, bowlplex, cinema and the huge Asda superstore, while visitors head for the collection of designer factory outlet shops that make up the town square. The pubs and restaurants perch seductively on the water's edge, but fail to persuade Brightonians to call it their own.

As we write, the Marina is having a bit of a facelift. Its fortunes have changed since the Brent Walker Group bought it in 1985 and then backed off a massive investment plan leaving a cold, soulless kind of place. But then the rich kids moved in with their yachts and their wallets and The Money Men finally noticed its potential and a 74-room hotel, oyster bar and plethora of theme bars and cafés is about to serve its growing community. Holidaymakers Neilsens have moved into an office on the new waterfront that can accommodate its 100 new staff, and it's still a buzzing place for the foreign postings attached to giant employers such as American Express. Word has it that the bijou residences and super-smart facilities are even attracting the boyz from Montpelier. We wait with open minds even if the Feng Shui experts claim that it's doomed...

For seagoing folk, it offers much more (tel Marina enquiries: 01273 819919). For those popping in from Barbados en route to France, there's a boatyard (01273 609235), with a 60-ton travel hoist and separate crane to deal with those essential repairs, as well as storage facilities, direct sea access and berthing for 1,300 craft. There's also a launderette, showers and washrooms for berth-holders and 24-hour security, which covers the Barrett complex. Apparently in its 20-year history there's never been a single burglary.

The Marina's very friendly yacht club bends over backwards not to be 'snotty yachty' (01273 818711 for membership details). The club offers sailing courses to newcomers in its Club Class in an attempt to lure new folk into the sailing fraternity, in which Club members take novices out in their own yachts on six Saturdays in spring and another six in autumn. The Cruising and Motor Boat sections also take non boat-owning members out on trips. There's also a Diving section which meets every Tuesday for training. RYA recognised sailing lessons for children and adults are also available at the Marina from Neilsons whose fleet of identical Sigma 8ms sits on the West Jetty. Neilsons also do pre-flotilla training courses on a Moody 31.

If you want to charter a boat for anything from a stag or hen party to a wedding, corporate do or ash scattering, Mike Snelling (07973 386379 or 01273 585000) is a local skipper who will put you in touch with charter-licensed boat owners. Some of the boats are wheelchair-friendly too. He's also the man to call if it's a beautiful evening and you fancy a trip out to sea to watch the sun set. Nick Light, the skipper of The Aquamanda (01483 417782), a twin, 6.3litre-engined Aquastar, is also available if you want to book his boat for a little corporate venture or sightseeing trip. During the festival, you can take a trip from the West Quay at 6pm every night (6pm and 7.15pm on weekends) for a tenner. Book at the Dome Box Office (01273 709709)

The average price of hiring a boat is £40 per hour, but as it's just a matter of chatting to the boat owners, it's all open to negotiation. Each boat can take up to 12 people, and some skippers are happy to do a last-minute, four-hour trip up and down the coast on a nice evening for about £150, provided they haven't got anything on. Mike warns that if you want to book a boat for the day in mid-July, you'll have to book six months ahead, but if you fancy a sunset trip in February, five minutes notice will probably be enough! Of course, you can always splash out on your own Princess Yacht, or pop down to the harbour to dream; the Marina is home to the largest sales office in the UK (01273 686368). Prices range from £140,000 to more than £1million.

Mike Snelling will also organise fishing trips and anglers will be pleased to know that there are several wrecks in the area where a host of specimen cod, pollack and conger gather. Ground fishing offers more in the line of cod and whiting in the winter; and tope, dogfish, bass, black bream and skate in the summer. The Marina's fleet can take up to 120 people out at one time which has encouraged Brighton to become a popular venue for angling competitions.

● THE UNDERCLIFF

Since the landslide of the cliff between Asda and the Marina beaches, one of Brighton's best-loved walks has been cut short. The section behind the Marina - from Black Rock to the Marina's boat yard - is still closed, but you can go up to ground level and walk that bit along the road before going down the path to the sea path on the far side of the Marina. This is where the surf boys hang out, looking like awkward seals flapping around in the waves. The Undercliff walk is open from here through to Rottingdean and, landslides aside, it's a beautiful walk.

In the summer, this stretch is where you'll find the locals playing in the rock pools with their kids, swarming around the café in the cliff wall at Ovingdean Gap, and cycling or jogging along the neat little groynes which partition off the stretches of sandier beach. They also serve the purpose of encouraging a more secluded, private kind of sunbathing in summer, away from the overwhelming activity of the beaches between the piers.

● *Why do I live in Brighton? Where else could I encounter giant jelly fish gliding on the low tide on an otherwise uneventful Sunday morning, accompanied by a string quartet, and presided over by our own resident mermaid? Where else could I take the children on the beach every day in the summer until the sun sets, and watch the herons and dolphins, or feel the thrill of the race course on race days in my lunchtime. Here I can sip my tea in the Meeting Place Cafe, and wonder if those four elderly ladies sitting opposite you in identical twinsets, pearls, ill fitting wigs, and large snap shut handbags are really bank managers from Surbiton.*

Julie Jennings, *39, single parent and ceramicist, lives in Elm Grove.*

● *My first taste of Brighton came as I walked out of the train station. It was a beautiful sunny day, and catching sight of the blue sea at the end of the road, I was taken. When I had the choice between moving back to London or moving to Brighton - well, no contest. My first home was a fantastic garden flat in Tisbury Road just up from Hove Town Hall. Owned by two women artists, it had a gallery bed which could only be reached by a ladder. With huge rooms, high ceilings, wooden floors and large oil paintings everywhere - it fulfilled my expectations of Brighton as a crazy, creative place. I used to get up for an early swim at the King Alfred Centre, take a brisk windswept walk along Hove promenade followed by breakfast outside my back door, if it was sunny. Since then I have always lived in Hove. With its wider streets and less frenetic atmosphere, it's the perfect place to live in this city. Taunts that it is populated only by OAPs are patently untrue - nowadays Hove is increasingly trendy, there are great places to eat (including Oki Nami and La Piazza), and great places to shop. Unattached? Check out Waitrose. Cullens is for celeb spotting, and since the pedestrianisation of George Street, an influx of trendy bars and coffee shops means it's no longer just charity shop city. Forget the tourist ridden streets of the town centre, Hove is on the up, although with that parking has become a nightmare!*

Nigel Berman, *editor,* The Insight

04

● Brighton (and less so, Hove) is an arty tarty glamourpuss of a city which likes nothing better than to show its knickers in public. Can you imagine the joy on the face of its councillors then when they heard about the Capital of Culture campaign? Like an eight year old ballerina, Brighton donned its tutu and Doc Martins and, stroked by its adoring uncles and aunties in Kings House, pushed itself into the limelight and took a deep curtsey. Capital of Culture! If a quick skim through the next few pages doesn't persuade you of its place on the podium, have a look through the previous two editions of the Juicy Guide to see how art and artiness is etched into the paintwork. It won't get the medal of course. Bradford and Newcastle need the accolade much more than we do, but who said anything about winning? The Where Else campaign, Brighton's golden opportunity to show off to the world, is a startling programme of arty events, some especially commissioned, others, like the thirty six year old Brighton Festival, already part of Brighton's history. At worst, it will have the Argus letters page rattling with indignation and at best it will attract more tourism, bring new money to a city where culture is the air we breathe and persuade the locals to get out more.

● THE FESTIVAL

A carnival to match the likes of the Edinburgh Festival, Brighton's starts on May 4th when the city's 45 schools parade along the seafront into town decked out in fancy dress. Now in its 36th year, the Festival runs through to May 26th with more than 800 performances, including free ceilidhs on the beach, high-tech multi-media performances in dance and theatre and live world music and jazz, pull in the crowds from in and out of town, while the local cafes and restaurants go alfresco to accommodate all the extra punters.

Nick Dodds is the new Festival Director and has left the helm of The Edinburgh Festival to steer Brighton into a more appropriate recognition of what goes on down here in the heady month of May. With £22 million ploughed into the Brighton Dome, the festival has come home to roost here and will play host to eleven world premieres (including eight commissioned by the Brighton Festival) and eight UK premieres.

The programme is salivatingly good; The Royal Philharmonic Orchestra, Scottish Opera, The Brighton Festival Chorus, New York jazz salsa legend Eddie Palmieri, South

African pianist Abdullah Ibrahim and Juicy's favourite lullaby, the hugely hip Lambchop. They've even booked Johnny Depp's favourite Romanian gypsy band Taraf de Haïdouks and paired them up with the Lebanese Oud player Rabih Abou-Khalil. Renee Harris's Rome and Jewels is a black street-dance take on Romeo and Juliet, and can you believe the names they've mustered for the Book Festival? Terry Jones and Terry Pratchett on stage together for the first time, Louis de Bernières, William Boyd, Hanif Kureshi, Andrew Motion, James Fenton, Edmund White, Catherine Millet, Mo Mowlam, Margaret Thatcher (hmm, maybe not) and Jonathan Meades.

The second weekend is when art takes to the streets with stilt walkers and full scale choirs, acrobats and salsa bands around just about every corner. Make sure you get to Preston Park for A Little More Light by Groupe F, with the world's leading pyrotechnician Christophe Berthonneau who was responsible for the Eiffel Tower Millennium display. And it's all free.

The third weekend, The Brighton Circus Festival featuring dare devil acrobat, Circus Baobab from Guinea are an option to The Moscow State Circus and the festival's own children's circus Short Circuit. On the Sunday (19th May), Dieppe's best food producers sell their wares in Bartholomews at the Dieppe Market. Brighton, meanwhile, goes back to its roots as the first mackerel catch of the season is paraded on the beach for a massive lunchtime barbecue outside the fishing museum.

The blessing of the nets, an old Pagan custom, is little more than an excuse for a party for the local fishermen and their families, but this year will again revive the Christian interpretation with a blessing of the catch by Brighton's community vicar, Canon Michael Butler. Brighton's and Dieppe's mayors join in with the sea shanties, hymns and readings, and as the mackerel is thrown on to the barbecue, a Punch and Judy show reminds us of what the seaside is all about.

By the fourth weekend, you'll think you're in Rio. Brighton's coolest samba drummers, Carnival Collective lead bands from around the UK and Europe in the first ever Brighton Samba Encounter which includes an evening show in the Corn Exchange, and a mass procession along the seafront the following day.

The Open - formerly known as the Umbrella - includes one of the most celebrated parts of the Brighton Festival, the Open Houses, in which Brighton's artists open their homes and studios to visitors. For details of the Festival Open, see the Open brochure.

For information about the Festival, phone the Brochure line 01271 336023 or check the website www.brighton-festival.org.uk. Events at the Dome can be booked via their box office: 01273 709709 or by e-mail tickets@brighton-dome.org.uk

● GLYNDEBOURNE

For opera fans, Glyndebourne offers its theatre space for the Festival line-up.

Glyndebourne itself is only open during the summer, with its own festival running from May to August, so it's a fabulous sight to see the succession of DJs, evening dresses and picnic hampers all heading through the gates of the Glyndebourne Estate on a hot summer's day. The information line (01273 815000) is open all year.

● OPEN HOUSES

If you're one of those people who feel stifled and put off by the oppressive silence of art galleries, but still like to gaze wistfully at other people's creations, this is for you. The Open House season is a unique idea peculiar to Brighton, which has grown and grown over the past 19 years. Local artist Ned Hoskins had the original bright idea to exhibit what his work looked like in the real world - in other words in his own home. The aim was that visitors could have a chat while they gazed, or a glass of wine, and the chance to be a sociable human in a warm home rather than some isolated being in a cold gallery.

Across town, other groups copied Ned's idea and it has now become the biggest show of contemporary art in the South East, attracting 15,000visitors a year and a wealth of international art collectors and critics. This year, more than 200 homes across Brighton and Hove will be exhibiting paintings, stained glass, sculptures, ceramics, photography and furniture. Everything is for sale and it's great fun, whether you want to buy, chat, or just have the opportunity to nose around other people's homes!

The Fiveways Group of artists is one of the most organised among the participants, with Ned Hoskins now taking a back seat to new chairperson, Lucy Parker, the proud owner of the most glamorous garage in Cleveland Road. Some of the Open Houses even welcome you into their gardens - or in most cases, their backyards, which have become famous for displaying amazing creativity in such confined spaces. Make a date to nose around Chesham Street in Kemp Town and Upper North Street in Montpelier. Both streets open up their gardens and homes during Festival weekends, and the idea is simply to walk in and look around.

To join the house or garden artist's scheme, either contact one of the groups or approach the Festival office (01273 700747). The benefits of being in a group come down to cost. The Fiveways, Beyond the Level, Kemp Town and Seven Dials groups are well established, can attract sponsorship, and have mailing lists which will save a fortune in postage if you're serious about selling your work. Newer groups include Rottingdean, Hove and Montpelier.

● CHARLESTON

The Charleston Literary Festival rounds off the springtime feast of culture with a host of luvvies discussing their respective oeuvres in the grounds where Vanessa Bell hung out with her sister Virginia Woolf and their Bloomsbury chums. Charleston is a treat of a literary festival, not least because of its extraordinary setting. The garden is one of the gems that studs the Sussex landscape and much of the festival takes place in a marquee on its lawns. Visitors are encouraged to take tea in the grounds and breathe in the spirit of an era that still lives on in the farmhouse's museum. A recent successful exhibition of Bloomsbury art at the Tate and other galleries has given Vanessa a posthumous stamp of approval, so Charleston's literary festival should be awash with new fans this year.

Open from April to October, Charleston itself houses the astonishing collection of artworks that Vanessa Bell and Duncan Grant, her lifelong partner, amassed throughout their lives. Look out for Gouache table tops, experimental painting on the backs of doors and picnic plates, Picassos and Matisses abandoned in dark halls, and some of the first post-Impressionist work casually scattered throughout the house, illustrating the spontaneous creativity, which characterised their lives.

The Bohemian complexity of the relationships within Charleston's walls, and the creativity that spun from them, is almost tangible. When Vanessa and Duncan first moved into the rented farmhouse in 1916 as conscientious objectors working the land instead of fighting for their country, David "Bunny" Garnett (Duncan's friend who was later to marry Duncan and Vanessa's daughter, Angelica), moved in too. While Vanessa's brief affair with Roger Fry, apostle of Cezanne and the Post-Impressionists, also earned him a room in the house until his death. Angelica had grown up believing that her real father was Clive Bell, father of Quentin and Julian. At that time, Clive was living with the flamboyant patroness of the arts, Lady Otteline Morrell, and would often visit with his long-term love, the socialite, Mary Hutchinson. He moved in during the Second World War and lived happily in the unconventional family unit, staying on to live alone with Duncan after Vanessa's death in 1961.

Virginia Nicholson, Quentin's daughter, remembers Charleston as a place where "messy creativity was a way of life". In her sumptuous coffee-table book, Charleston: A Bloomsbury House And Garden, Virginia describes "the wonderfully uninhibited, irreverent quality to the decoration of the house which is that of a child let loose to experiment".

● MEANWHILE, BACK IN BRIGHTON.

● RALLIES

Every weekend sees some sort of rally along Brighton's popular Madeira Drive, from time trials for exciting sports cars to Beetle maniacs and Mini obsessives parading their motors, through to the simply odd, like the rally for coach-spotters! The Classic car run is on June 9th this year with the London to Brighton bike ride on the 16th.

● PARTY IN THE PARK

Southern FM's pop extravaganza is on June 23rd this year from 12noon to 4pm.Last year more than 60,000 fans turned out to watch Steps, Hearsay and A1among others, entertain the crowds - and what's more it's all free.

● THE JUICY AWARDS

Part of the Capital of Culture's Where Else campaign, the Juicy Awards will be celebrating the best talent from our own backyard on the stage of the newly refurbished Dome. At a party for 1500 broadcast on Juice 107.2FM and presented by the sexiest celebs in the city, awards will go to the best restaurant and sexiest hotel as well as the most innovative business and the most outstanding contribution to the local people (my money's on Fatboy's Big Beach Boutique). Details from the Dome box office (01273 709709) or e-mail: gilly.juicy@btopenworld.com

● OCEAN CARNIVAL

The last weekend of June sees the English Channel get its chance to join the fun. Considering how much time we all spend staring at it, the sea is rather under used, but this weekend, it becomes the focus as Ocean Carnival does on the waves what the festival does on the streets.

● THE PEACE FESTIVAL

7th July on Hove Lawns from 11am till late. A cross between Womad and Glastonbury, with enough tents full of kids activities and live bands to keep you thinking about Peace all day long.

● BIG BEACH BOUTIQUE

As the sun set on the thousands who watched The Fatboy spin his discs last year, something strange happened on Brighton beach. It had been a great gig with Lord Slim's big smile and big heart turning up the bliss gauge of the widest cross section ever to turn up for a dance night. But as Fatboy lost the back beat on "Bird of Prey" and Jim Morrison's ghostly lyrics hung in the heat of the night, the boats became still and the crowd looked around in awe and realised that they were right there, right then, in the best place in the world. He loved it too and plans to do it again on July 13th.

● STELLA MOVIE CLASSICS

On July 26-27, the beach fills as those very nice people at Stella Artois erect an enormous screen, hand out the bevies and show a few thousand people a couple of very cool movies as the sun sets past the West Pier. Of course you can't hear a word but that's really not the point; it'll make you weep to be part of such a chilled community.

● PRIDE 2002

Just after the Gay and Lesbian Film Festival at the Duke of Yorks, Brighton and Hove celebrates its title as Britain's Pink Capital as 10,000 of the town's most flamboyant residents parade from the seafront through the town centre to Preston Park on August 10th. Pink In The Park is where the floats come to rest, offering seven hours of dance, champagne, performances, as well as funfairs and market stalls.

● AUTUMN IN THE CITY

The festival and the summer done, the city's Where Else campaign gets even more arty as buildings are dressed with piercings and jewellery, the Sacred and Profane hits the newly refurbished Brighton Museum & Art Gallery and a parade of cows makes its way from New York to Brighton. The sponsored cows are life size hand painted works of art and have been bringing major cities in America to a halt as Tutancowmoon, complete with gold head-dress and Vincent Van Cow adorned in sunflowers perch outside their sponsors' buildings. Shame the Twin Cowers had to go though.

For those who missed the Open Houses during the Festival, there's another chance to nose inside other people's houses in the Brighton Arts Trail from October 5th - 20th. The Autumn Dance Festival and a City Jazz Festival continue to make us feel like the summer is about to start all over again before The Jewish Film Festival reminds us that it's time to hibernate again at the Duke of Yorks.

● LEWES FIREWORKS

It must be something in the Sussex air, but the wild party spirit spreads even to the gentle suburban town of Lewes - once a year anyway. Lewes has an underbelly still gurgling with the dissension of its Pagan days and violent history. On November 5th, unhealed memories of religious persecution and war are ripped open to fuel a fire that burns throughout the town in a terrifying display of tar barrel races and pyrotechnics. Effigies are even erected and burnt at the stake. Everyone goes to Lewes on Bonfire night so if big crowds in small spaces make you feel uncomfortable, steer clear. Street crime, such as bag-snatching, is also a problem, so we recommend a picnic high on the hill above the town where you can watch the entire proceedings in safety, or wait until the following weekend and take the kids to see the tamed-down version of the same procession in the neighbouring East Hoadley.

● WINTER

As autumn freezes over into the bleak mid-winter, Brighton gets its skates on and heads off to the Brighton Centre. Thanks to a brainwave by ex skating champ and Lewes Crescent resident, Robin Cousins, is now going to be iced over every December until Holiday on Ice takes over in January. Last year a city full of mums, dads, wobbly six year olds and Wild Fruit transvestites were all grooving to Kylie in a truly Brighton mood.

● NEW YEAR'S EVE

The Old Steine becomes the focus for Brighton and Hove to get truly soppy about how lovely life is down here. Early evening sees an enormous family-friendly crowd gather to watch bands on the stages at the Old Steine and Victoria Gardens, as fire-eaters, jugglers and a wild variety of street artists crank up the euphoria gauge before the fireworks welcome in the New Year. The festivities kick off with Burning The Clocks, a kind of Burning Man Festival of Brighton. It's a mix of Pagan celebration and pyromania in which lantern clocks representing the old year are cast on to a sculptural bonfire to bid the year goodbye. Normally celebrating the winter solstice, Burning The Clocks was moved to New Year's Eve two years ago when a storm meant that of the 75,000 expected visitors, only the (fool)hardy and drunk actually made it! But while the fireworks fizzled and the limp lanterns drifted off, Brighton dusted itself down and got on with the party. It's a seaside thing.

For a full events listing, call the Council on 01273 292711/292712, or obtain an information leaflet from the Tourist Information centre at Bartholomews.

● *Typical Day of a writer and performer living in the Montpeliers ...*

Get up at the crack of midday and walk along Clifton Terrace past St Nicks church where my mother is church warden. I push my way through hundreds of McGann brothers (in leisure slacks),and the cast of Eastenders as I make my way to the Brighton Natural Health Centre in Regent Street. Once there before I settle down to writing I submit to a torture session of gyrotonics with my 'trainer' Laurie Booth (famous dancer and capoeira expert). Emerge cursing but about 4 foot taller and say to the people lining up to do yoga or 5 rhythms or bellydancing, "Just popping to Infinity." Which is an hilarious joke in anybody's language. Infinity and Neals Yard just opposite are where I spend my happiest hours buying healthy snacks and remedies. Neals Yard is brilliant because you can moan on about your symptoms for centuries and they are still nice. On Fridays I do love to go to the Regency Fish bar on the seafront. Sometimes Red Ken goes as well and we chat about old times when he and I ran London. (Well, we both wrote for the Evening Standard. And I admire his safari jackets..er... and ultimate power over people).

Louise Rennison, *writer and performer*

05.1

● AFRICAN

The Nile House
17 Preston Street,
Central Brighton
01273 326003

Sudan may not be well known for its culinary excellence - and The Nile House doesn't even attempt to take you there - but the aroma of cardamom is almost enough to give you a whiff of Africa.

● AMERICAN

Brighton Rock@Beach House
6 Rock Place,
Kemp Town
01273 601139

Distressed and battered beach house walls, faded canvas and decking make this a new addition to increasingly trendy Kemp Town. The idea is based on a New England Beach House, with Manhattans and Martinis joining the Boston Meatloaf (with mash and cranberry marmalade at £6.50) and Maine Crab cakes (in warm lime marmalade and chilli dipping sauce for £6.50) to add to the American mix. In reality, anything less American would be harder to find; this is true Kemp Town

hospitality with Barbie and Ken, legs akimbo, hovering over the loos and Rory, Neil and Richard fussing over their punters like a Jewish mother. Lisa sings a capello on Sunday nights and Sunday brunch is likely to become a Kemp Town institution

Momma Cherri's Soul Food Shack
11 Little East Street,
The Lanes
01273 774545

Plates are big in the Deep South. The Soul Food Breakfast (£7.50 including two slices of fried ham and onions, hot buttered grits, eggs, fried apple with bacon, biscuits, juice and coffee topped off with pound cake or sweet potato pie). Mains cost from £6.50 - £7.50 ranging from Aunt Mae's Southern style meatloaf, Aunt Delia's special soulburger and cornmeal coated fish all of which come with "soulful trimmings' such as candied yams, black-eyed peas, and sweet potatoes. For those new to soul food, Momma Cherri offers a funky translation of all the dishes and dares you to try Aunt Delia's Special Jambalaya, a New Orleans style stir fry of prawns, chicken, spicy sausage, rice and vegetables (£9.50).

● ASIAN

Bali Brasserie
Kingsway Court, First Avenue, Hove
01273 323810
Maximum kitsch. A bizarre eating experience in the ground floor of a block of flats in Hove with a Saturday night clientele stuck in the Seventies and foreign exchange students posing in Balinese saris. The Tropical Bar - all bamboo, mirrored mosaic tiles and pool table, is worth a visit in, but the food, while authentically Indonesian, lets the side down and is no better than OK. The three-course rice table at £15.95 is the most popular with a buffet main course, but a mee goreng and Tiger beer will still give you change from £10.

The Coach House
59 Middle Street, The Lanes
01273 719000
Popular with cybertypes from the nearby media centre, this is where they munch tortilla wraps and chunky chips with aoili at lunch and schmooze their London clients by night with lamb steaks with thyme, rosemary and apricot sauce. There's a heavy international influence with Thai curries, Lebanese falafels and Indian chowders to make everyone happy. £20 per head.

The Fish Bowl
74 East Street, The Lanes
01273 777505
Nice little find at the seafront end of East Street where the fish and the music are mellow by day and hopping at night (see Bars section). A surprisingly easy place to get great fusion food for kids while gorging yourself on tuna, pepper and red onion wrap (£4.50), seafood linguini pasta with squid and mussels (£6.95). The kitchen closes at 7.00pm - that's when the music takes over.

Jim Thompsons
Unit 1, The Terrace, Madeira Drive,
Kemp Town
01273 666920 or freefone 0800 1959333
www.jimthompsons.com
You really do take a trip though Asia without cutting any corners at this bar, restaurant and bazaar. The food is irritatingly erratic though; some days the Malay curry can be sublime, on others a vegetarian spring roll can squirt you in the eye and the tofu would be better used as a mattress. The menu is probably to blame - too much to choose from and not enough love in the kitchen. Prices from £15.95 per person for the vegetarian feast to £24.95 for hungry meat lovers.

Krakatoa
7 Pool Valley, The Lanes
01273 719009
Tucked next to the bus station, but near enough the seafront to feed a more chilled-out club crowd, Krakatoa's not an Indonesian restaurant, more Asian fusion of Japanese, Thai and Indonesian. And maybe Balinese. Upstairs the low tables with floor cushions encourage you to take your

shoes off, assume your best lotus position and idle the night away over a nasi goreng and a Tiger beer. The menu takes the best from the Orient with sushi preceding Gado Gado and sake an alternative to Tsing Tao. Sotong Goreng (Singaporean style deep fried squid in a herbed crispy batter served with chilli sambal) £4.50. Sake Yaki (Japanese style grilled salmon with a Japanese sauce on a bed of fresh spinach leaves) £7.95. A breath of Eastern goodness in the heart of Brighton. Averages £15 per head.

Wok Wok

34 Duke Street, The Lanes
01273 735712
Indonesian noodles (specially sweetened on the kids menu) and delicious Asian dishes at reasonable prices - around £6. Wok Wok used to pitch itself as the place for a family lunch with face painting on Sundays, but the service has soured recently. Avoid the buffet and save up for the nasi goreng for the outrageous price of £7.75 (it's only rice for God's sake), have a mango champagne cocktail and forget the bill for a while.

● CARIBBEAN

The Tamarind Tree

48 Queens Road, Central Brighton
01273 298816
Gentle vibe and Jamaican fare from brothers Mike and Kush who came to Brighton University from south London and stayed to build a little slice of Jamaica in Queens Road. Fish roun de road, jerk chicken, akee, rice and peas (£6-£8), the ingredients come fresh from Brixton market to Kush's kitchen where he paints his plates with mangoes and avocados, flau flau and roti to the low throb of dub reggae. By the weekend, the music cranks up and the birthday parties turn it into another country, but try it on a rainy Wednesday evening to get a taste of a West Indian summer. The lack of good wine (it's BYO although they do have a wine list) and the refusal to take credit cards means that you have to plan a little in advance; the off licence is towards the station and the cashpoint is on the station concourse.

● CHINESE

China China

74 Preston Street, Central Brighton
01273 328028
Straight out of the back streets of Kowloon, this is about as earthy (but authentic) as Chinese food gets. £4.50 for a set meal.

China Garden

88-91 Preston Street, Central Brighton
01273 325124
The most opulent Chinese restaurant in town. A piano player playing smoochy jazz accompanies your meal adding to the sophisticated ambience that permeates the atmosphere. The food is superb but pricey: set dinners range from £16.50 per person to £32 per

person. The drunken fish fillets (£7.95) are sublime and their crispy duck Cantonese style (£6.95) is unbeatable. The staff are efficient but not over-friendly and the wine list is extensive.

Gar's

19 Prince Albert Street, The Lanes
01273 321321

Popular Chinese restaurant that bustles at night with post-cinema and theatre diners. The food is standard Chinese fare but the atmosphere buzzes. Lemon chicken (£5.50) fresh asparagus, mange tout and beanshoots in garlic (£4.50). Half price food for the theatre goers and early eaters if you're in before 7.30, but you can stay all night.

Gourmet Palace

48 St James Street, Kemp Town
01273 604060

The Gourmet Palace has expanded recently and now it's a huge enterprise, complete with resting area and architectural fish tank that separates the restaurant and café/bar areas giving it a romantic feel. Try the Emperor's Special Mixed Hot Hors D'oeuvres (£13) to share for starters. Most of the clientele are fortnightly regulars which makes the atmosphere on a Friday night a noisy, friendly affair.

The Pagoda Pontoon

5 North Wall, Brighton Marina
01273 819053

Floating Pagoda in the Marina where the tiles come all the way from China

and the food doesn't - that the Pagoda is stuck in a time before we knew what Chinese food without the MSG tastes like, won't put its clientele off. It's smart and courteous, it rocks with the waves - but not enough to put you off your food - and serves the requisite duck and pancake deal. Steer clear of the blander veggie and chicken dishes and you could even enjoy the food too. Averages £20-£25 per head.

Sunbo Seng

70 East Street, The Lanes
01273 323108/722655

The elegant interiors of this Chinese restaurant might look lovely, but it doesn't really compensate. The sea bass with ginger and spring onions (£12 per lb) and four heavenly vegetables is gorgeous, but the place lacks atmosphere on most nights, and the MSG and soggy noodles let it down badly. When Zen finally realises that most of north London has moved to Brighton and sets up some serious competition, it might encourage Sunbo Seng to pull up its socks.

Yum Yum

22 Sydney Street, North Laine
01273 606777

Authentically sparse noodle bar above a fine Chinese supermarket in the heart of the North Laine. A team of Chinese women toss their nasi gorengs in a line of woks next to the counter, but this is far from the stylish noodle bars of Soho. More Penang night market meets

Camden on a Saturday afternoon, it's a great place to grab a plate of mee before heading back into the buzz of Brighton's best shopping area. Cheap, cheap, cheap.

ENGLISH

Bankers

116 Western Road, Montpelier
01273 328267

One of the best fish and chips shops in town. As much a restaurant as a takeaway, and you've also got the option to have your fish cooked in matzo meal (a light, non-greasy Jewish alternative to batter) which makes all the difference. Under £10 per head.

Bardsley

22-23a Baker Street, off London Road
01273 681256

Repeatedly in the top 50 UK seafood restaurants. The tables are Formica, but the fish is line-caught (so no bruises) and fried in palm oil. Roy and the Bardsley family have been doing it for 30 years and don't seem in the least bit tired of their trade. In fact, they've just opened on Saturday evenings because they love it and people love them so much. They close early (8.30pm) and do takeaways. Bring your own wine and enjoy. Under a £10 per head.

The Beach

Kings Road Arches, Brighton seafront
01273 722272

With a sun terrace and the only food on the beach after El Taco Way has packed its bags at 8pm, how could it fail? But fail it does, if you're looking for something to write home about. The pizzas are all right, and the lager is suitably cold, but this is simply somewhere to fill your boots when you can't be bothered to cross the road. Service is friendly, with students doing the honours. Pizzas are around £5.

Bennetts

32 Egremont Place, Queen's Park
01273 674456

Cheerful, unpretentious, wine bar that serves an extensive and eclectic menu: peppered swordfish (£8.95), deep-fried brie (£3.95), vegetarian lasagne (£5.95), Thai-style mussels (£6.95) deep fried onion rings (£2.65), Cajun vegetables en croute (£7.85) and traditional English breakfast (£3.95). The staff are lovely and the cocktails are fab - Bennetts specialise in Brighton's favourite drink, Sea Breeze, a double vodka, cranberry and grapefruit (£3.90).

The Boardwalk

250a Kings Road Arches,
Brighton seafront
01273 746067

If location was everything, we'd all be living at The Boardwalk. This much needed wholefood café sits just to the west of Brighton Pier and has a decked terrace leading out on to the beach. Inside, the two tiers are always packed on a sunny day, although the service is typical of Brighton's beachside fooderies.

They're getting better and they try hard, but what is it with service and the beach? Still, if the weather's good and you're not in a rush? Try the sardines, sip a hot chocolate, hang out and relax with the sun.

Brighton Pier Fish & Chip Shop

Brighton Pier

The one eaterie in this guide that - odds-on - everyone will go to. Come down for the weekend as a tourist and you'll end up there. Live here? Then have your friends visit and take them there - it's worth it. Expect change from a tenner.

Browns

3-4 Duke Street, The Lanes
01273 323501

Part of the Oxford/Bristol/Cambridge/London/Edinburgh chain, this is the seaside sister where you know you'll get good latte, pine-nutty pesto and trendy service. Always busy for lunch, but not so hot on dinner. Don't bank on Browns bar next door for a sandwich; a bar is a bar, and bless, they can't do everything well. Average per head for lunch is £10.

Bushby's Brasserie

24 Ship Street, The Lanes
01273 321233

Modern English cuisine served in a warm and cosy environment by relaxed and friendly staff. Bushby's is a showcase for English cooking and each beautifully presented dish has been created using a delicate fusion of flavours. Salmon fishcakes on a bed of mixed leaves with a fresh Thai dressing (£4.65), pan roasted breast of duck, served pink dressed with a plum sauce, garnished with game chips (£10.95). But if just want to snack, try one of their baguettes: goat's cheese and char-grilled vegetables (£3.85).

The Curve Bar @ Komedia

45 Gardner Street, North Laine
01273 603031

Since opening a couple of years ago, The Curve has developed an ambivalent relationship with the North Laine crowd. Attached to the Komedia Theatre, the bright spacious bistro is the obvious place to have a coffee or a meal after a show, but the mosaic entrance, stainless steel bar, soft moving light show and mezzanine internet cafe is almost too glitzy for its own good. The food is so-so but pretends to be posh Modern European (pan fried duck breast on orange scented sweet potato mash with fresh raspberry vinaigrette (£12.95); the coffee tries to be sophisticated, but what is that business with the latte in a glass that's too hot to hold and a spoon wedged in the handle that's bound to burn your fingers? The service is perfunctory when all around is so much friendlier. £18 per head is the average for dinner. (see Restaurant section).

The First Floor Restaurant

25-26 New Road, Central Brighton
01273 682401

Upstairs at Mrs Fitzherbert's, The First Floor has only been open since August 2001 but is already into its stride. Setting itself apart from the rabble beneath, the food is fab modern British and the fish/seafood menu, put together by Leighton Jones (a refugee from the Atlantic Bar in Covent Garden) and is as good as you'd hope. Mains (Slow Roasted Monkfish wrapped in Pancetta, served with Risotto and Tomato Sauce) come in at around £12. If you're really hungry, the house speciality is the Seafood Platter for two at £59.95.

Food For Friends

17-18 Prince Albert Street,
The Lanes
01273 202310

Solid old-fashioned type of veggie food with its emphasis on raw and crunch. Staff are as kind and reconstructed as you would expect, and the pinboards are stuffed with ways to help you to similar enlightenment. Newspapers, water and empathy are free. Under £10 per head.

The Golden Girl

10 Manchester Street,
Kemp Town
01273 603147

Lurking behind the pastiche name is traditional English cafe food at its best, served in cosy, homely surroundings. One of the oldest buildings in Brighton, it boasts charming waitresses who will go out of their way to accommodate children, but be warned, it can get smoky. The chips are perfectly cooked:

cod and chips (£4.75), plaice and chips (£4.50), egg, sausage chips and peas (£3.90), Roast beef (or lamb or pork), Yorkshire pudding, 2 vegetables and potatoes (£5.25 or go large for an extra £1.60). Or go for a blow out and have a three-course meal for (£8.95). If you want comfort food, they specialise in steam puddings drowned in custard (£2.25).

Ha! Ha!

2-3 Pavilion Buildings,
Central Brighton
01273 737080

First things first. If you've got a child with you, don't bother. If you like being surrounded by children, don't bother. Probably, if you're pregnant or thinking of having a baby, don't bother. They don't like children here. (Which, in a curious way, reminds you of the Jerry Sadowitz gag about old people: Old people? They should be shot at birth). Anyway. It's actually a good place. Perfect location (bang opposite The Pavilion), plenty of space, different areas for drinking, for doing café type stuff and eating. The stripped pine minimalism and spacious, canteen-style area, the hot chilli onion rings or bruschetta (£3.50) and char-grilled tuna (£9) look good, and the kitchen delivers. The Warhol-type glass wall cabinets displaying Ha! Ha!'s own products, and the waiters' brown leather aprons and matching upholstery are dead chic. But it's a shame about the kids. There isn't even a shed outside.

Hanrahan's

Village Square, The Marina

01273 819800

Brighton's answer to the Sistine Chapel, Hanrahan's is worth a visit for the ceiling alone. Frescos and Arabian silks billowing over your Tex Mex is a weird enough experience, but the camel and swordfish on the balcony? Still on a beautiful summer evening, you can join them and watch what happens on those posh yachts after the sun has set. Good solid fodder from steaks and ribs to pies and lasagnes and all around the £8 mark.

Indigo Café

52 Lansdowne Place, Hove

01273 775565

Indigo buzzes at lunchtime, but by the evening it has lost its fizz with George Michael's greatest hits droning incessantly against a backdrop of its modern interior. But it is a treat for children. Go for the tasty lunch menu offering gourmet sausage and mash smothered with gravy (£6.95), or garlic-baked red pepper served with tomato, anchovy, onion, and garlic (5.95). Puddings include creme brulee served with mixed berries (£3.50), sticky toffee pudding (£3.25) and tart au citron (£2.95).

Jackson's Wharf

The Marina

01273 675365

The church pews and monastic thrones lend a solid theme to this Scottish and Newcastle hostelry where you can grab a bite before or after a film at the UGC if a Big Mac isn't your thing. The bar food is something you'd expect from an M&S chiller cabinet, but there's nothing wrong with that unless they boast otherwise. And they don't. The restaurant upstairs looks like it might offer more (wild boar sausages with mash and rosemary and redcurrant sauce - £7.45) but doesn't. The kids' food includes real vegetables though, which is a rarity around here. Get a good chef in and this place, with its lunchtime views over the harbour, could be rocking.

Lucy's

26 Kings Road Arches, Hove seafront

01273 220222

If you've got sunshine and kids, this is perfect for a late breakfast or long lunch. Cast in the shadow of the West Pier, just below the hideous Alfresco, it's next to the children's playground and you can sit there and eat and chat and drink while your little angels throw themselves around the climbing frames, safe and in view, but still out of the way. At weekends from Easter till autumn they'll stay open to 8 or 9pm if the demand is there. The posh calves liver has been replaced by home made burgers and sizzling platters because the playground was putting off the serious diners. Nothing is over a tenner.

The Regency

131 Kings Road, Brighton seafront

01273 325014

Once upon a time, The Regency was a typical seaside restaurant. The fish was atypically fabulous for a seaside restaurant, but the décor and the service was, shall we say, unreconstructed. When the mighty Loch Fyne moved in around the corner with its chain of fish restaurants around the country serving organic this and sustainable that, we thought they'd eat The Regency for breakfast. And, bless, what did it do? It got itself a facelift. The banquettes and enormous windows, posh graphics and a palatial extension haven't changed its spirit, there's not a Soil Association label to be seen and they haven't a clue about sustainable farming, but by using local fishermen and their little nets, they're less likely to decapitate or mutilate the millions of fish ejected from the vast nets of the trawlers simply because their faces don't fit. Expect to pay anything between a fiver and £20 per head for the best fish in town.

Richards

106 Western Road, Hove
01273 720058

Spacious wine bar with a good menu, but too many people have reported the poor delivery and sketchy service, so forget dinner; there's plenty more fish on the seafront. A great breakfast bar to enjoy one of the best cups of coffee in town over the (free) newspapers before heading out on to the Western Road, it's also big enough to accommodate the evening crowd.

Room 101

101 Trafalgar Street, North Laine
01273 704000

Trafalgar Street, the northernmost fringe of the North Laine, has been enjoying a bit of a renaissance over the last year or two, and Room 101 provides some much-needed trendy drinking and eating space. Lamentably, as with so many refurbished spaces in Brighton, attention has been lavished on the aesthetics and interior fittings to the detriment of service and quality of what's on offer. The food is 100% vegetarian and although well prepared and put together, was pricey given the location and service. Cold too; a Post-it note stuck over the designer radiators read "Please do not remove the radiator covers" suggesting that previous occupants of our table had taken decisive action against the chill.

Saucy

8 Church Road, Hove
01273 324080

Get past the terrible name and the garish interior and you'll start to realise that first impressions can be misleading. The dishes are more traditional than you might expect; liver and bacon (£11.25), fillet of beef (£14.25) and beer battered cod (£9.50), except here the beef fillet is stuffed with oysters, sealed in fresh prawns and served with tempura onion rings. Oven roasted chicken (£11.80) comes with a mango glaze and served with wild mushroom rice topped with Parmesan and pine nuts. There's a wide selection of vegetarian dishes, which (unusually) live up to expectations. Saucy kids (£4.50-£5.50) can choose from classics such as bangers and mash, bubble and squeak (topped with a poached egg with a vine tomato and baby spinach sauce) which does seem like a bit of waste when all they really want is a bag of sugar and some MSG. Desserts (£4.50-6.25 with a glass of dessert wine) range from the nostalgic Bakewell tart with custard to the contemporary raspberry and chocolate torte.

The Station

100 Goldstone Villas, Hove
01273 733660

Looking like Ha! Ha! but with little of the culinary charm, this is the pub which gets up more Hoveites noses than any other we heard about. It may be good looking but remember that beauty is only skin deep. The food is a shocker, the welcome is lacking and most locals prefer the smoky old gin palace which it replaced. At least the old pub had Sky and allowed children in during the day. Still, bang next to Hove Station, it's somewhere for travellers to wait while someone clears the rain off the track and at weekends, there are enough gorgeous young things to distract you from its inadequacies.

The Strand

6 Little East Street, The Lanes
01273 747096

Tucked behind Bartholomews away from the traffic of The Lanes' tourists, The Strand is one of Brighton's more interesting restaurants. The waiters are trendy, friendly and as the head chef is a vegetarian, particularly accommodating to the more sensitive food fan. The three-courser is great value and doesn't skimp on the quality for the price; mackerel salad with lime and dill dressing followed by chicken burritos and chocolate muffins to finish and all for £13.95, the same price as one helping of the a la carte Spanish Chicken with Chorizo sausage.

Tiger Bar

98 Trafalgar Street, North Laine
01273 693377

What it doesn't quite deliver after dark when the North Laine traffic has gone home, the Tiger does surprisingly well at lunchtime. The service is still a little dazed and confused, but the Jamaican Jerk Chicken (£7.95) is actually quite good. It's also one of the few places where you can take a carnivorous mate who likes a drink in the North Laine. Beware the house red; it's powerful stuff.

Tootsies

15/18 Meeting House Lane, The Lanes
01273 726777
www.tootsiesrestaurants.co.uk

Not traditionally the place for a good big weekend breakfast, this char grill restaurant stands out a mile. It's always quiet first thing, perfect when you want to relax with a paper and a big breakfast. For £6.50 you get sausage, bacon and tomato (all char grilled), eggs, mushrooms, plenty of toast, freshly squeezed orange juice, and a pot of tea or coffee with a free refill. You can add hash browns and baked beans if you want to. Taking into account that drinks are included, it's great value. They're also particularly kiddy friendly and there's enough space inside (up and down) and outside to get away from the little monsters if you're not that way inclined. Booking at the weekend is advisable as it gets very busy and they won't cater for a party over 20. It is also very wheelchair friendly.

Troggs Café Bar

124 Kings Road, Brighton seafront
01273 204655

If you've ever considered veggie food to be dull, visit Troggs for a serious eye opener, thanks to the imaginative and beautifully presented vegetarian and vegan cuisine. There is a relaxed and friendly atmosphere with informative waiters happy to discuss the menu - none of that "why ask me" attitude. We took an out of town vegan friend there for dinner, who was adamant that it was one of the best vegan restaurants experiences she'd ever had. Equally telling (from the point of view of a confirmed carnivore) Troggs is a number choice for eating out simply because the food is always so reliably delicious. The food in the café next door isn't quite so hot, but the cool blue is a treat on a baking summer lunchtime, and the basement courtyard is a suntrap for those looking for something to eat near the beach.

● FRENCH

Café de Paris/ La Parisienne

40 St James Street, Kemp Town
01273 603740

During the week, this bistro looks more like a tribute to Toulouse Lautrech or a bottle of Perrier Jouet. Come the weekend though, the place hops with the kind of hedonism the French haven't seen since the days of Lautrech himself with local raconteurs such as Victor Spinetti sending the invited crowds into a whooping, table top frenzy. The set menu means that you'll still have to pay at least £10.95 even if you can't find room for the moules, pork Dijonnais and tiramisu (tiramisu??) The two names refer to the weekday split in focus from the downstairs venue to the street level bistro.

Café Rouge

24 Prince Albert Street, The Lanes
01273 774422

One of the good things about being a chain is that it gives you time to sort yourself out and, like Pizza Express, Cafe Rouge has sorted itself out just fine. Consistent quality and service is the key to success - and that's what they provide. Newspapers for non-rush hour types, areas for the smokers and a great stress-free attitude towards kids. Average for lunch is £10.

Crepe Dentelle

65 Preston Street, Central Brighton
01273 323224

A warm little bistro with reasonably-priced galettes and crepes. The atmosphere is a little clichéd - piped Piaf, an exhibition of Breton Marionettes, Philippe's cocked chef's hat - but the welcome is genuine and the food good. Average per head is £10-£15.

La Fourchette

101 Western Road, Montpelier
01273 722556

Haute cuisine with a personality chef, this nationally acclaimed little corner of France in Western Road offers a range of delicacies from locally caught fish to maigret of duck and foie gras. There's a two course menu for £18.50, £22.50 for three. At lunchtime, you can get a fabulous two courser for £8. For pudding, try the assiette de gourmet, the chef's selection of the best in the house. The service is erratic but truly gallic.

Fruit De Mer

42 Waterloo Street, Hove
01273 733733

Intimate dining experience at this small fresh fish restaurant lit by fairy lights with only half a dozen or so wrought iron tables,. The food is Modern British with a twist of the Far East (Thai fish kebabs grilled on lemon grass sticks with cucumber and chilli dipping sauce, coconut chicken with basil and coriander with jasmine, spiced beef with houmous). There are two two-course menu to choose from, the first for £15 and the second for £22.50

Le Gastronome

3 Hampton Place, Montpelier
01273 777399

Surprisingly unpretentious French restaurant just off the main drag of the Western Road with a sumptuous, but inexpensive menu, considering the quality of the fare. Of the five menu options, try the menu gastronomique for three courses of the chef's favourites at £17.95, or £19.95 for four courses. The breast of duck with green peppercorns, cognac and cream is sublime, but the fish, fresh from the market, is to die for. The menu has stayed much the same since the first edition of the Juicy Guide which suits its solid clientele perfectly.

The Greys

105 Southover Street, Hanover
01273 680734
www.greyspub.com

Hearts of palm, mushrooms à la Grecque, olives, sun-dried tomatoes, egg Choron and a guest peppadew for £4.00 is not what you might expect from a dark little pub in the heart of Hanover, but this is where you'll find quality food, quality music and the kind of barmen who know their beer. Now they're doing Sunday breakfasts - only for an hour between 11am and 12pm but it's BIG - bacon, egg, lamb cutlet, beautiful sausage, fried mushrooms, salad and new potatoes all for £6.

Mangerie

164 Church Road, Hove
01273 327329

One of Hove's best kept secrets. The walls are adorned with paintings by local artists which adds to its cosy but aesthetic interiors. Three courses for £14.95 would include King Prawns in Garlic Butter followed by Duck Breast in Mango Sauce and a selection of puddings Delia would beg for. Booking is essential as the space is small but intimate. BYO and credit cards are not accepted.

La Marinade

77 St George's Road, Kemp Town
01273 600992

Extraordinarily good French cuisine tucked away in the residential end of Kemp Town. More like a front room than a restaurant, the three tables on ground level give the impression that you've been invited to some posh dinner party which the hosts have left you to enjoy by yourselves, while the maitre'd/chef silently oversees your night's feasting. Three sumptuous courses for £22 (£18.50 without dessert) might include poached sea bass with a lemon and saffron butter sauce and tarte tatin flamed with Calvados.

La Petite Fourchette

8 East Street, The Lanes
01273 711001

Nominated for this year's Juicy Award for best restaurant in the first round of voting, the is the little sister of the highly rated La Fourchette. The Mediterranean style rotisserie with cold marble tables and a hanging rug makes it homely and warm while the food (salad nicoise with fresh tuna and anchovies or maybe sauté king prawns with leek, garlic and parsley) is quality but inexpensive at around £4.50. Mains (roast chicken with herbs, wild mushrooms, parsley and olive oil mash or grilled smoked haddock with dauphinoise potatoes and spinach) are around £7.00. Or you can choose two fish courses from the blackboard for £15.

One Paston Place

1 Paston Place,
Kemp Town
01273 606933

Formerly Langans when Michael Caine owned the keys, the owners now pride themselves on buying the best ingredients money can buy. The food is fabulous and changes two or three times a week: expect light langoustine soup with sorrell and caviar (£9.50), Dover sole with baby squid, mussels, jus mariniere, potatoes with spring onion and olive oil (£21), pan-fried frois gras, rhubarb, sichuan pepper and crispy beetroot (£12.50) to start, and roast fillet of seabass with asparagus and salsify, blood orange and watercress salad (£22.00) The wines match to perfection, but the atmosphere is stifling, the music and ambience dull, and questioning the bill had us banned. Make sure you know your poulet de Bresse from your Hoads Farm.

● GREEK

Ipanema

121 Western Road, Hove

01273 779474

Warm and friendly Greek where, if you time it right, you can join in with the karaoke, dancing on the tables, plate smashing and all that malarkey. Foodwise, it's a bit of a mix here: tapas, Italian and Greek mezze but you can also get pasta. The rest of the menu is varied: paella, moussaka, plenty of fish and seafood - lobster, sea bass, red mullet.

● INDIAN

Ashoka

95-97 Church Road,

Hove

01273 734193/202112

It's got a reputation as the best Indian in town and after a night there, it's hard to disagree. In 1995 it was The Daily Mirror's Indian restaurant of the year. That's big. Maybe the staff were a little too attentive, but it's difficult to find fault. The food was just right. Nothing fancy, just right. It doesn't try to be flash or fashionable or cool or anything really other than what it is. Prices are also what you might expect (Tandoori chicken masala £7.45), there's also a large vegetarian menu and the food matches its reputation. Listen, if it's good enough for Cliff Richard, whose pictures shaking hands with the ecstatic manager adorn the walls, it's good enough for us.

Bayleaf

104 Western Road, Hove

01273 722280/773804.

Modern British Indian food without the flock wallpaper and sitar muzak. No one's going to persuade us that cheddar and mozzarella can be used in Indian cuisine, but their more traditional food is better, and the Habitat crockery shows that at least they're trying to pitch a groovier crowd. All the food is cooked to order, so allow a good lump of time for your meal. The menu changes regularly and vegetables and side dishes vary daily according to the mood of the chef. Even the raita and chutney served with the complimentary pappadoms were home-made. Try the takeaway too; if everyone else is too busy, chances are that your korma will be delivered by the boss in his Mercedes and Indian livery. Averages £15-£18 per head.

Goa

4-5 Richmond Parade,

Old Steine

01273 818149

Hidden around the back of the Pressure Point off the Old Steine, it's worth a visit - if only for the fantastic animated waterfall painting, the likes of which are rarely seen outside New Delhi. Even if apparently the nearest they get to Goa is the fact that the (Bangladeshi) chef was trained by a bloke from Candolin, the food is good. Specials include Dosas - stuffed pancakes filled with various vegetable fillings like lentils, spinach or potato (£3.20), Xacuti roasted in aromatic spices and coconut milk and Balchao cooked in shrimp preserve and steeped with rum and Goan spices. It's BYO, but you can get your booze from the Pressure Point. Students can eat as much as they like for £6.50 every Tuesday between 6pm and 11pm as long as they bring their ID.

Indiana Tandoori

4 Church Road,

Hove

01273 731354

Smart blue interiors and halogen lights give Indiana a sophisticated feel. This is a quality Indian and the tandoori dishes, barbecued in a clay oven and marinated with mustard oil and yoghurt are superb. Try the tandoori shaslik, grilled with onion, tomato and pepper (£6.95), or the succulent king prawn Kashmir (£7.25).

Kemp Spices

51 St George's Road,

Kemp Town

01273 623331

An unusually modern local Indian with Brasserie-style cane furniture, starched uniformed and courteous service and tablecloths which set it apart from the local takeaway. The menu is what you'd expect, but the spices are well marinated and the meat and fish is freshly cooked. Wooden floors and dark blue ceiling creates a soothing atmosphere. Kingfisher lager is on tap and takeaway is available. Averages slightly over £10 per head.

● ITALIAN

Al Duomo

7 Pavilion Buildings, Central Brighton

01273 326741

Favourite among families with young kids, and a perfect lunch break after a visit to the Pavilion. The pizzas are delicious and big enough for two, and the choices of pasta, carne and pesce are good enough to come back for more. The service is friendly, the welcome generous, and the atmosphere cosy. Set menus for lunch and dinner are around £10, including a glass of wine which makes it one of the best value Italians in town.

Al Forno

36 East Street, The Lanes

01273 324905

Nice, kid friendly Italian in the centre of town. There's all the usual pizza/pastas with some nice additions like Sardine Fritte that were just right. A two-course menu with a choice of five pizzas and four pastas plus dessert, £5.95.

Alfresco

The Milkmaid Pavilion Under the West Pier, Kings Road Arches, Hove seafront

01273 206523

The dearth of places to eat on the beach is a strange and bizarre thing and until Lucy's opened, life began and ended with Alfresco's. And that made Al a fat and lazy boy with rubbish service, passable food and an attitude that was distinctly lacking. But they got away with it because the position was perfect.

Now, maybe because of Lucy's, they seemed to have pulled up their socks. OK, it's still not the place to go if you're in a hurry, but although the food is still uninspired, the portions are generous - which is - useful with kids - and, unlike the old days, the waiters get the order right. It's still a place to go because it's easy rather than great but, what Al knows is what all estate agents know: the three most important things in life are location, location and location.

Ask

58 Ship Street, The Lanes
01273 710030
Tasty if unadventurous Italian food served in modish blue and white surroundings. Popular with business folk and ladies who lunch. A convivial atmosphere and excellent service adds to its charm. The thin crust pizzas compare nicely to Pizza Express, but don't expect anything outstanding. Try their Di capra (£6.95) or the penne con pomodoro secchi - sundried tomatoes, artichokes with green chillies and a light tomato sauce (£5.90). There are two new options: Pizza Genovese - pesto, sauteed courgettes, roasted aubergine, olives and mozzarella (£6.10), and Crostini al Tonno - Tuna mixed with celery, onion and mayonnaise on grilled cibatta (£3.30). Other merits include a garden and a separate non-smoking room.

Bella Napoli

2-4 Village Square, The Marina
01273 818577

Packed with Italian families at the weekend, this Neapolitan family run business will twirl its pizzas, kiss your babies and entertain your little ones all day while you quaff your way through their wine list. Excellent (and genuine) Italian ice-cream - and the coffee is straight out of Naples.

The Brasserie

15d The Village Square, The Marina
01273 818026
So huge are the portions that you could almost forgive them for charging so much for your dinner. If anyone is ever that hungry, it could be a good deal, but as the only posh Italian in the Marina (the only posh anything in the Marina - apart from the yachts) it does a roaring trade. On a beautiful day, the tables are shuffled out onto the waterfront and if you half close your eyes, you could almost imagine that you were in the Bay of Sorrento. £25 per head for three courses.

Donatello

1-3 Brighton Place, The Lanes
01273 775477
Bright and breezy family of pizzerias with Italian largesse and small bills. The food and the waiters are unreconstructed Italian, so the service is friendly, children are welcome, and the pizzas are damn fine. The biggest of the brothers commands an impressive presence in the heart of the Lanes, with nooks, crannies, conservatories, lounge bars and enough space to seat a Sicilian

extended family. They do a two-course menu for £7.95 and three course for £9.95 (£10.95 on Saturday night). Under 12's can have smaller portions of any pizza or pasta for £3.00. They do Gluten free pasta.

Latin in the Lane
10-11 Kings Road, The Lanes
01273 328672

The weight of expectation rests lightly on Latin in the Lane's shoulders. Widely felt to be Brighton's best Italian, it was lauded in the last edition of The Juicy Guide as "Brighton's favourite restaurant". Happily, it doesn't let you down, and from the counter of fresh oysters that greets you as you walk in to the Sardine al succo d'arancia (sardines cooked in orange juice) (£4.95) to the locally caught fresh fish. The menu is enormous, everywhere you look there's a "Mmmm. Maybe I'll have that". And if you don't want fish, well, that's OK too. Ostrich in port wine with spinach in cream (£14.95)? Chicken in brandy, cream and pink peppercorns (£9.95)? There are private rooms, and booking is advised.

Leonardo
55 Church Road, Hove
01273 328888

A big favourite among Hoveites, this is a top Italian which uses a touch of Modern British presentation to mark it out from the other Italians along this stretch. Unlike most good looking Italians, beauty here is more than skin deep and the Risotto alla Risacca di

Mare (£7.50) is possibly the best in the city. The special set menu of £7.95 for two courses is astonishingly good value and the service has been hauled up since the last review. The only problem is the lack of no-smoking areas; it doesn't matter how good the food is, when someone's puffing away behind you, it'll always taste foul.

Mama Lemon's
8 Neville Road, Rottingdean
01273 390998
www.bluescompany.co.uk

Down in deepest, darkest Rottingdean is this offshoot of Blind Lemon Alley in Middle Street. Mama Lemon's has the same laid back atmosphere and taste in music but with pizzas not burgers. Thin crust and proper. A bit out of the way, but if you're in the area, a nice option.

Mamma Mia
68-71 Preston Street, Central Brighton
01273 326823

One of the best Italians in town but, like its ex-partner, Alfresco, it falls down on the service. But the food is gorgeous. The risotto Italia (£5.95) was rich with parmesan and sweet with red pepper and sun-dried tomato, the mussels were New Zealand (although not green-lipped) and the prawns (also £5.95) paddled delicately in their garlic butter. There's also Salmone Verde - poached salmon in lime, butter, dill and white wine sauce (£9.10) or Pizza Mamma Mia - tomatoes, mozzarella, salami, ham, fresh egg and peppers (£5.50).

NTI

The Marina, just outside
David Lloyd centre
01273 681200

It doesn't look much from the outside, just a pre-fab type building where Fatty Arbuckle's used to be. But behind the façade and the terrible name - NTI stands for Now That's Italian – lurks a bit of a find. Good solid food – pizzas, pasta… the usual – and friendly staff who really don't mind that your kids are dismantling the restaurant.

Orsino

141 Church Road, Hove
01273 770999

Big spacious Italian pizzeria where the waiters tickle cute kids and sing to beautiful women and where the risotto marinara reminds you of every other risotto marinara you've ever had in a big spacious Italian pizzeria where the waiters tickle cute kids and sing to beautiful women. Which is why it's always packed to the gills from midday to midnight. Average £20 per head.

Picasso

24 Ship Street, The Lanes
01273 321233

Another posh pizza place in The Lanes, this time from the people behind Waikika Moo Kau. Like its cousins in The Lanes and Kensington Garden, the plates are brimming with nice enough fare, but despite the added extras like Italian lessons piped into the loos, it hasn't got their character etched onto the walls or their smiley service. £10-£15 per head.

Piccolos

56 Ship Street, The Lanes
01273 203701

Extremely popular Italian for a Pizza restaurant which doesn't boast an Italian family ownership. Particularly child friendly with two floors for them to run around in. The pizzas are good too and they do take away.

Pieros

30 Spring Street,
Montpelier
01273 329426

Just off the Western Road, this authentic family run Italian has been serving up its traditional take on what Brits want from their pasta for 15 years or more. Lots of insalata tricolore, Chianti and good old fashioned Italian fussing.

Pinocchio's

22 New Road,
Central Brighton
01273 677676

Part of the Donnatello chain (see above), Pinocchio's specialises in classic Italian fare. The atmosphere is both lively and welcoming, and appeals to a good cross section. Pinocchio's excels at making children feel extra special; go for a birthday treat and you'll receive the standard Pinocchio treatment of a cake lit with a sparkler and a silver plate dropped on the floor in an ear-shattering clatter.

Pizza Express

22 Price Albert Street, North Laine
01273 323205
107 Church Road, Hove
01273 770093

By now, an institution. In the last few years, Pizza Express has repositioned itself and now sits head and shoulders above the other pizza chains. The staff are endlessly patient with children, and it's the place to take young kids if you know they're going to throw their food at the wall. If you don't want to be surrounded by young families, don't go on a Saturday or Sunday lunchtime. By night, the lights dim, and the atmosphere is more chilled.

Sole Mio

64 Western Road, Hove
01273 729898

Posh nosh set in the airy surroundings of the lovely old Nat West bank opposite the floral clock. The Italian chef has a bit of a penchant for all things Spanish, hence the patatas bravas (£3.95) next to the anti-pasti and pizzas on the menu. Other options are deep fried calamari (£4.95) or Filletto al Pepe (fillet steak with brandy, peppercorns and cream) £14.95. The food is excellent and the service is what you'd expect from a more expensive restaurant.

Terracotta

28 Church Road, Hove
01273 328837

Friendly little Italian serving extremely good value lunches (country sausages with mashed sweet potato at £4.50) and not such a bad value dinner (fillet steak with thyme and oregano butter; grilled tiger prawns with lime and chilli sauce, both £8.50). The service is genuinely Italian and, stuck in the middle of Hove's eating quarter, it's one of the best.

● JAPANESE

Moshi Moshi

The Optican Building,
Bartholomew Square, The Lanes
01273 719195

Conveyor belt sushi blazing a trail of Asian food from London Town, Moshi has stamped its chopsticks in the heart of Brighton, rebuilding its original shell into the glowing lanternesque Octagon in Bartholomews. Cool (sake cocktails?) stylish and the best fast (and healthy) food in town with sushi from £1.20 - £3.50 from the conveyor belt and hot dishes from the menu. Bento Boxes (starter and main course on two decks) cost £14.50. The Kaiseki 12 courser at £22 is an interesting introduction to Japanese Haute Cuisine but can't beat the array of delicacies flirtatiously circling your table.

Oki Nami

208 Church Road, Hove
01273 773777

Stylish little Japanese which sits quietly at the Hove end of Western Road, doing very nicely thank you for the best part of six years. Rather too stark for a two-hour evening, with absolutely nothing to look at other than your food, your partner and the straight lines of the benches and tables, it could do with the fascinating focus of the sushi bar generally found in such places. They even provide a little origami to help pass the hours, but the food is fab: try the Tsunami set meal (£21.95 per head) to have your tongue tickled as the five courses of sushi and teriyaki build like the tidal wave it's named after.

Sapporo

38-40 Preston Street, Central Brighton
01273 777880

Not so long ago, this was a tame Japanese with so-so food in the street of so-so food, and apart from the extraordinarily over-the-top central sushi bar where you'll be entertained by the juggling of pepper pots and tossing of prawns, it still is. Taking tips from The Mongolian Brasserie and chefs from The "let-me-entertain-you" Philippines, the owners have made sure that chicken teriyaki will never seem the same again. As the flames shoot and the crowd whoops, the diners in the cheap seats vow to book the hot spot next time or go to Oki Nami for the real thing. Averages £15-£20 per head and try the teppanyaki Goma-Yaki (Chicken breast coated with sesame seed) £10.90

● LEBANESE

Kambi's

107 Western Road, Montpelier
01273 327934

Authentic Lebanese in the heart of Western Road which, to a less discerning eye, looks like the kind of kebab takeaway which might serve an inebriated clubbing crowd. Peek inside to find a genuinely Middle Eastern atmosphere with gentle and unassuming service and vegetarian and meat mezzes to make your mouth water. The fare is what you'd expect in towns where there's more of an Arabic connection than Brighton; even the signs on the loos are in Arabic. After dinner, ask to partake of the shiha, a kind of elegant version of a bong, and you're in for a truly Alice in Wonderland experience. Averages £15 per head.

● MEXICAN

Los Amigos

60 Church Road, Hove
01273 778777

A bit of wild Mexico in genteel Hove. On Thursday nights, things can get a bit excited with guitarist and music. But you can avoid all that and it's worth the effort for this excellent Mexican (with a hint of Italian) food. There's all the usual Nachos and Fajitas and tortillas, but try the Sin Cronizadas - a kind of Mexican style toasted sandwich.

Blind Lemon Alley

41 Middle Street, The Lanes
01273 205151

Boasting a funky location tucked away at the end of an alley in The Lanes and an upstairs room with lounging facilities perfect for birthday celebrations, this is a hit with students. The vibe is cool, with Phil Mills, the celebrated slide guitarist, playing every Sunday night, but the Cajun/Southern influenced food is not cheap and isn't as tasty as the menu promises. A 4oz beefburger with fries is £6.50 (6oz for £7.25), and tortilla served with salad, sour cream and guacamole is £7.95, burritos filled with feta cheese and mushroom, £8.25. The charming staff and warm ambience makes up for the food's shortcomings. Booking is essential.

The Cactus Canteen

5-20 Brighton Square, The Lanes
01273 725700

Big servings and kicking music have the weekend crowd thronging their way into these Tex Mex banquettes in the heart of the Lanes. 12oz steaks go for around £13.95 and there are plenty of veggie fajitas (£10.95), Quesadillas (£9.95), enchiladas (£9.95), Pollo a la Creole - char-grilled chicken breast in home-made tangy Creole sauce (£9.95) to make the Brighton crowd happy. It's also a top choice for a kiddy friendly lunch.

The Grapevine

29-30 North Road, North Laine
01273 703985
www.grapevinewebsite.co.uk

There's an impressive range of traditional Mexican fare on offer at this cool cafe/bistro and they apparently import 11 different types of chilli direct from Mexico. All starters are £3.95 and are quite traditional such as nachos. Most mains are £8.50, try the fried tortillas filled with chicken, pork or veggies, or butternut squash and goats cheese served with spicy potatoes, Mexican rice and salsa fresca. Try the flautus tortilla flute filled with maple roasted parsnip and plantain, served with rice, beans and fruit salsa (£8.95) or maybe the quesadilla grande with vegetable filling (£6.25). They also have a hotel upstairs (£10 if you don't mind squashing in a dorm or £15 for a double - this is negotiable in the week) so they can put you up for the night if you have a little too much tequila. But if you do, it's your own fault: The Grapevine is BYO.

El Mexicano

7 New Road, Central Brighton
01273 727766

www.elmexicano.co.uk.

One of the handful of genuine Mexican restaurants in the UK, El Mexicano doesn't do the Tex Mex thing with its chimichangas. In fact it doesn't even do chimichangas. Instead, you'll get a bitter green tomato salsa which we think is delicious but which is probably an acquired taste, and a hot chilli salsa to spice up your own enchiladas (£7.95). Some of the dishes you may never have come across before: Mole (£9.95) is a chicken bathed in over 100 ingredients, including chillies, nuts and chocolate, Crema de frijoles (black bean soup, with cheese and strips of crispy fried tortillas

£3.25), Picadillo (authentic Mexican chilli con carne with almonds, potato and raisins £7.75). The Margaritas and the Sols, the big party bookings and the Latino music are more of what you might expect. Top service makes the night a friendly one.

● MODERN EUROPEAN

Arundel Restaurant

The Metropole Hotel, Brighton seafront
01273 775432

Posh nosh in faded grandeur, but probably only for those with dowager aunts willing to foot the bill. The food is excellent (artichoke hearts with mushrooms and truffle essence (£6), corn-fed chicken stuffed with mozzarella (£16), pan-fried sea-bass with fennel and shallots (£17), lemon and passion-fruit torte with raspberry coulis (£4.90), all served old-style on silver platters with complementary sorbets between courses. Yet despite the magnificence of the high-ceilinged Georgian banqueting hall, the atmosphere is dismal: piped muzak, "Wines of the World" posters and the unpleasant salmon-pink decor all detract from what could be a grand eating experience.

Barry at the Tureen

31 Upper North Street, Montpelier
01273 328939

There are a few really intimate dining rooms in Brighton, but none as genuinely welcoming as Barry's. Queen of The Tureen, he's a self taught chef who cribs his dishes from The Evening Standard and buys his roast potatoes in a pre-prepared pack from Tescos ("well, why bother with all that par-boiling when Aunt Bessy's are just as good?"). Somehow he manages to bake the perfect cheese soufflé while settling his giggling table of eight, advising on wines and sizing up just how much chat his customers are up for. Three courses for £19.50 (£17 for two) is great value ; try the caramelised red onion and sun dried tomato tart followed by chicken breast, boned and wrapped in bacon with an apple and thyme stuffing, roasted and served with a red wine gravy and a frozen blackberry liqueur soufflé.

Blanch House Restaurant

17 Atlingworth Street, Kemp Town
01273 645755
www.blanchhouse.co.uk

Si Gwynne is now wearing the apron as hotel owners, Chris and Amanda claim the restaurant formerly known as C, and spread their trendy but casual attitude through to the stunning white leather dining room and into the kitchen. The food is about as good as modern British gets in Brighton, but although he's being touted as Gordon Ramsay's protégé after working in his kitchens in the early days of Aubergine, it's Paul Clarkson of the very fine Menzies Hotel in Oldham to whom Si doffs his cap. After five weeks over the stove and Blanch House, the food is looking good with the ceviche of monkfish and tuna (£7.50) perched perkily on its cucumber spaghetti, and the corn fed chicken stuffed with prosciutto, asparagus and sun blush tomatoes (£14) daring the desserts to be any better. And the banana and toffee crumble tart with brown bread Morgan spice and raisin ice cream (£6) really really is. And because there's no 2 or 3 course menu, you can pop in for a drink and a pud after the cinema and hang with Brighton's coolest clientele.

The Eagle Bar and Bakery

125 Gloucester Road, North Laine
01273 607765

With the Jubilee Street development about to reinvent the North Laine, the arrival of a chic, arty, vegan bakery is a smart move by the boys behind the Hop Poles. The menu is mouth-wateringly fusion (Thai Chicken Breast on a wild mushroom risotto (£7.50), Goats Cheese and Red Onion Tartlett (£6.95) with a side order of honey roast squash on a bed of roquette (£2.95), while the interiors are earthy metals and solid wood. The goats cheese was more of a slab than a slice and the roquette salad would have overwhelmed a rabbit, but we'll put it down to teething problems. £15 per head.

English's

29/30/31 East Street,
The Lanes
01273 327980

Brighton's oldest fish restaurant celebrates its antiquity with the walls of its Red Room almost whispering stories from the Edwardian gay days. A favourite with Charlie Chaplin and Lawrence Olivier, it is housed in three fishermen's cottages dating back 400 years on the edge of the Lanes, and creaks with authenticity. Inside for a posh dinner, it delivers, but don't try the cheaper weekend lunch menu if you want to sit outside and watch the jazz band in the square. It's consistently poor and lets the whole place down badly.

Fish *(Opening June 2002)*

165 North Street,
Central Brighton
0845 100 4555
on-line booking:
www.fishdiner.co.uk

With around 20 restaurants around the country – mostly in London - Fish has caught on big time with its policy of serving the freshest fish and allowing you to choose your own style of cooking it. Our reviewer went to the Borough restaurant in south London and reported a busy, bustling atmosphere with attentive and knowledgeable staff who were more than willing to talk through the menu and suggest the best cooking method for your choice of bream, seabass, salmon or any one of 23 different fish on offer. Although he swears he was with a delightful companion himself, he mentioned that the open kitchen/serving area and American style-diner bar means that if you're dining solo you don't have to make out you're waiting for a tiresomely late date.

Gingerman

21a Norfolk Square, Hove
01273 326688

Tucked away between Western Road and the sea is the Gingerman, one of Brighton's gourmet treats - particularly for meat fans. A simple yet elegant decor creates an atmosphere of calm, enhanced by efficient and helpful waitresses with nice little extras like the delicious olive oil and home baked bread and post dinner home-made chocolates. The menu includes seared peppered salmon with herb creme fraiche, feuillete of snails and chorizo with grilled baby peppers for starters. A main course might include fricassee of artichokes with air-dried ham and roasted foie gras, corn-fed chicken breasts with roasted garlic mash, garlic and thyme sauce. Menus cost between £9.95 for one course at lunch and £23.50 for three courses at dinner, but take our advice and book well in advance.

Havana

32 Duke Street, The Lanes
01273 773388

Havana is turning into one of Brighton's consistently good restaurants from what was once a parochial pretender. The food is fancy; warm salad of wood pigeon with cep and foie gras at £12.50 followed by crisp Scottish salmon on spinach with honey and cumin dressing at £14.95. There are cheaper options of course, but it's hard to leave Havana with enough cash for a cigar.

Hotel du Vin

Ship Street, The Lanes

Not due to open until the autumn, Hotel du Vin should be more than just a great place to stay if its hotels in Bristol, Birmingham, Winchester and Tunbridge Wells are anything to go by. With four different dining rooms including the bistro, the deeply gothic cellar and a vine covered pergola in the courtyard, there will be plenty of room to feast on the Modern European food such as roasted buffalo mozzarella wrapped in bacon with plum chutney and toasted sesame seeds (£5.25) followed by honey roast confit of duck with rocket and mango, chilli and coriander salsa (£12.50)

Loch Fyne Restaurant and Oyster Bar

95-99 Western Road, Central Brighton
01273 716160

One of a stable of 25 restaurants spawned from the Scottish Loch. A card on the table exhorts you to join the Loch Fyne "club", with the menu presentation and sepia-toned pictures continuing the ersatz Scots-ness. The sea bass with lime and coriander sauce (£12.95) was full of promise, but sadly lacking in execution. The smoked haddock chowder (£4.55) was superb as a starter with just the right blend of winter heartiness and sophistication. But it felt like the wallet was being pumped just a little too much, though when vegetables and fries have to be ordered separately to a £13 main course.

And it's a smoke-free zone, though you can retire to the bar area and squash in with the other refugees.

No Name Bar

82 St James Street,
Kemp Town
01273 693216

A small but perfectly formed menu (although the 'choice' of one vegetarian dish slightly marred that perfection) with one or two specials on the blackboard) waits for you once you get past the nameless fascia and drinking-only tables. It's not cheap, but the food's good and the service sweet. A nice place to go for a low-key unpretentious evening out.

Quentin's

42 Western Road, Hove
01273 822734

One of the least pretentious of Brighton's fine eateries, the atmosphere is understated but convivial with large wooden tables (no tablecloths) and smiley waitresses. At £19 for three courses or £17 for two, the choice of dishes looks good, but beware the hidden costs. The house champagne is £55, and a bottle of West Chiltington's finest impersonation is £49. Our roast sea bass was undercooked while the breast of duck was done to more than its turn, and we were seriously put off when we realised that the appetisers we'd been tucking into turned out to be skewers of kangaroo. If you want to party you can book the downstairs room.

Quod

160-161 North Street, Central Brighton
www.quod.co.uk

Opening this summer, Quod's new restaurant and bar brings its Tuscan interiors and dramatic artwork by the UK's most interesting new artists from its successful bars in Oxford and Haymarket. Using natural materials such as stone, leather, oak and zinc, Quod is into earthy quality. The food is Modern European; Duck Confit, with mashed celeriac, pan fried caramalised prunes and bacon lardons (£9.95) and Monkfish and Speck Brochette, roasted monkfish, wrapped in smoked ham, served on Tuscan cannellini beans, cherry tomatoes and rocket (£10.95) are typical examples of their menu. The pastas and risottos are what they're famous for.

The Saint

St James Street, Kemp Town
01273 607835

It's difficult to move for new drinking and eating venues on Kemp Town's Main Street and while The Saint bills itself as a bar/café, it's the food that has really got the plaudits flowing. The cocktail list is excellent (£4.50 each), and the round of one classic and one house special that we ordered was a distinct success. Food is mostly "high carnivore" - generous cuts of meat with rich sauces and various scrumptious accompaniments (Mediterranean sausages served on a mixed pepper and nutmeg mash, £7.50) but there's some fish (seared monkfish, £11.95) and some vegetarian fare. Service always came with a genuine smile, but the bill was substantial - £25 a head.

Seven Dials

1-3 Buckingham Place, Seven Dials
01273 885555
A genuine five star London experience in Brighton. Super-chef Sam Metcalfe's pedigree is proper job (Chez Nico, The Terrace, Pied a Terre) and his menu looks like Seven Dials should ease effortlessly into the gap in Brighton's Gastroland. There's an interesting menu combining some unusual combinations (exquisite goats cheese on lentil base followed by beautifully cooked steak), some lovely touches (delicious free appetiser in the form of a mini carrot soup with roasted pumpkin seeds. There was an unusual wine list, but the waiter was knowledgeable and made some excellent choices. If we had to make a criticism, the acoustics make it a bit noisy and they don't segregate smokers and non-smokers. But that aside, a treat.

Terre á Terre

71 East Street, The Lanes
01273 72905
Last year's Juicy Restaurant of the Year, Terre a Terre has grown up since the days when it crouched in Pool Valley making up its bizarre but beautiful veggie feasts. These days the Himmel Und Erde latkes, Congee Shiso Yuzu Puff Clusters and Ash Crotin and Parsley Shooters are still distracting the

carnivores from the fact that there's no meat on the menu, but they're also attracting the attention of the national newspapers and a worldwide fan base. A new fairy lit decked patio has opened up the once dark interiors, and the enlightened service, although sometimes too slow, is still the best in the city. Expect to pay between £20 and £30 per head with wine.

Whytes Restaurant

33 Western Street, Central Brighton
01273 776618
www.whytesrestaurant.com
Just off the seafront, Whytes has two small rooms on different levels for smokers and non-smokers. Music is not too loud for easy conversation, comfortable decor and a very imaginative menu. The dishes are described in detail but not pretentiously so, and a vegetarian option is always included. 'roast mushrooms with cashel crumble and cannelloni of Jerusalem artichoke', desserts to die for, but leave room for the homemade truffles with the coffee. Starters and desserts around £5, mains £14. Open for dinner Tues to Sat.

● MOROCCAN

Coriander

5 Hove Manor, Hove Street, Hove
01273 730850
Located in a bit of a cultural desert, Coriander is a relatively expensive North African/Middle Eastern restaurant, an organic fusion. Check out the baked

aubergine, Moroccan lamb and date tagine or maybe guinea fowl or ostrich steak. Other choices include the chicken briouate (£5), a filo parcel with a spicy tamarind relish, or the king scallop and crab claw stuffed baby squid (£7). If it sounds a bit meaty, it is. But there are plenty of get-out options. The staff are friendly and sweet though and committed to using the best (and if possible, organic) produce in their Moroccan influenced dishes.

● SPANISH

Casa Don Carlos
5 Union Street, The Lanes
01273 327177
Every day is a holiday at Carlos's house with Carlos and Ramon taking turns to provide the unrelentingly authentic Spanish service to a backbeat of Ricky Martin and (natch) the Gypsy Kings. The food is fab and inexpensive - marinated anchovies and prawns with garlic mayonnaise (both £3.95), patatas bravas (£2.95), calamares (£4.25) - which means the place is always packed. Book if only to check that there's no Sangria-swigging birthday party in that night.

El Porron
14 Ship Street, The Lanes
01273 737322
Still empty after a year next to the Sussex Arts Club, it promises much and because of the hideous acoustics and lack of ambience, delivers little. The food's fine; the gambitas a la sarten (£4.50) are suitably garlicky and lemony, but with Casa Don Carlos down the road packed to the gills with folk who come for its Ricky Martin vibe, such a cool competitor might find it has a short run.

● THAI

Aumthong Thai
60 Western Road, Hove
01273 773922
Always packed and one of the most popular Thai restaurants in town, but the staff exude a Zen-like tranquillity even when faced by large numbers in the party mood. Expect authentic Thai food served with great style. The staff dress in beautiful traditional outfits and the cutlery is gorgeous. Memorable dishes include spicy prawn cakes served with sweet and sour sauce (£4.50), crispy fish served with dry curry sauce (£6. 95), and duck marinated in special Thai sauce (£6.50).

Grape
45 Trafalgar Street, North Laine
01273 601894
The grey paint on the fascia may look like undercoat, but don't be fooled - the grape noodle bar and Thai restaurant is now open for business. From the same stable as the interiors shop further down Trafalgar Street - and just as coolly modern in its décor and quirky chairs - grape is another feather in Trafalgar Street's cap. A wide range of dishes, our

choice from which arrived carefully and minimally presented to match the interior design. Though not cheap, quality of food and service was high. But it's not just the food that's up for grabs at Grape; everything, including the Italian tiled walls is for sale.

Muang Thai

77 St James Street,
Kemp Town
01273 605223

Takeaway or sit down in the heart of Kemp Town. All the favourites are here from green and red curries to Phad Thai and Tom Yum, and the service is typically humble, courteous and attentive. The average price for a main course is £4, but the (huge) set menus are between £28 and £33 for two with the vegetarian version at £25. More of a last minute idea than a birthday treats for no reason other than its position in the heart of a quiet residential area.

Sawadee

87 St James Street,
Kemp Town
01273 624233

Trendy new Thai restaurant decked out with an enormous mirror (from Silver down the road), big windows and open spaces. The service is quietly Thai and the food imaginative and authentic (mussels steamed in lemon grass, sweet basil and chilli at £7.50; sea bass with lime, garlic, coriander and chilli dressing at £9.50). Average per head is £15 including wine. Not open Monday.

Shada Thai

4 Lewes Road,
Hanover
01273 677608

Unassuming little Thai on the outskirts of Hanover where the soups are hot and the prices are good. Its location means that it feeds a local or passing crowd and tends not to buzz with the birthday parties you'll find at Aumthong Thai. But the food is consistently fine, the service is what we've come to expect from the gentle Thais and that's more than you'd get at most restaurants in any town. Averages £10 per head.

Silk Thai

High Street,
Shoreham
01273 441500

Unpretentious Thai with good service and good prices.

Thai at the Pond

49 Gloucester Road,
North Laine
01273 621400

While it's not really the place to go to for a quiet romantic night a deux, don't let that put you off. It's good quality Thai food in a little room over the Pond Pub, and if the ambience (and noise) carries up from the pub, well, that's just the way it is. But it does what it does well (red and green curries, sweet chilli sauces, noodles) and it all come with good vegetarian options. Under a £10 per head. They also do Thai bar snacks if you're fed up with chips and cheese.

● WORLD

Black Chapati

12 Circus Parade, Preston Circus
01273 699011

Oh how we'd love to love this place. The food is fabulous, the chef is said to be the "father of fusion" - in this country at least - but despite it all, eating at the Chapati is a sour experience. The waitresses seem terrified of chef Steve Funnell which means that any questions about the food or wine has them quaking at the prospect of asking him on your behalf. Service can take an age, and the spraying of Mr Muscle on the next table is as off-putting as the bullying from the kitchen. Unless you just have to taste the genuinely exquisite food, save your money; there are so many nicer places in town.

Rendezvous Casino

Brighton Marina Village
01273 605602

The great and the good were out partying at the launch of London Club International's only London style casino out of the Big City itself last month. The food was fab and the champagne flowing, but it'll probably be a while before Juicy readers will call it their own. In the meantime, Hove's Flash Harrys steer their tottering trophy wives around the gaming tables after a spot of lamb shank on saffron risotto (£15) and peppered tuna on wasabi and pak choi (£13) in the restaurant and have the last laugh; this is a free members bar and the

perfect spot for a post cinema drink. And the food is a delight, with Chinese and Indian options to a Modern European gastro feast - even if the service is straight out of Debrett's.

● SNACKS, TAKE AWAYS

Like pubs, everyone's got their favourite takeaway. So what that it's usually only in your heart because it's round the corner or on the way home from the pub? It's your and that's all that counts. Anyway, here are a few of ours.

Agra Tandoori

263 Ditchling Road, Fiveways
01273 503676

Recommended by Rosario who used to run Victor's restaurant (gone but not forgotten), so it must be good.

The Cheeky Chip

147 Eastern Road, Kemp Town

Pukka pies (including chicken Balti curry pies), great chips with extra friendly service and probably the only deep fried Mars bars outside Glasgow.

Delhi Darbar

40 St George's Road, Kemp Town
01273 606677

William G is the only proper job Indian chef in the whole of Sussex and is keen to let everyone know that although he was the architect of the now famous Nishat, he's since left and gone to set up his own empire in Kemp Town. Nishat still his uses his menu but not his culinary prowess and the best of Goa is now in Kemp Town.

The Market Diner

19-21 Circus Street, Carlton Hill
01273 608273

A Brighton institution. The all-nighter café for clubbers and cabbies (and who can tell the difference?) for those tipping out of the Ocean Rooms

Jethros Organic Chicken

35 Queens Road, Brighton
01273 325888

Surprisingly successful for such an ambitious project with its promise of home delivery (within reason) of freshly cooked organic chicken in five styles from Thai (coriander, chilli and lemon) to Provence (lemon, rosemary and bay). The whole thing (or leg or breast) is grilled to order right before your eyes, so allow 15-20 minutes drooling time before you get to eat. There's also salads, couscous, halloumi and roast potatoes to go with it. Book early if you do want the delivery, or pop in and watch to see just how fresh it is. Delivery is free if you spend over £15.

Nishat Tandoori

58 Preston Street, Brighton
01273 321701

Once upon a time Julie Burchill mentioned in *The Guardian* that Nishat was the Goa of the South East - and the queues started queueing. That galled ex-chef, William G who then set up and left the Delhi Darbar in Kemp Town.

The menu's the same, so it's worth ringing a couple of hours ahead to make sure that you get your curries before midnight.

Sea Breeze

Southover Street, Hanover

No phone number that we can find, but it's worth taking a trip to Hassan and Melika's on the right as you go down Southover Street for the best fish and chips this side of town. They also do North African take away, although you might have to twist their arm a little to do you a special.

Spice Nutriment

66 Queens Road, Central Brighton
01273 777746

Midfield General's favourite Indian if that colours your judgement.

Woodingdean Fish Bar

6 Warren Way, Woodingdean
01273 303 061

The sign outside proclaims it "The best fish and chip shop in town". Is there another chippie in Woodingdean? Whatever, the fish is fried in fresh oil and the chips are excellent. Mr Papadopoulos will also fry the fish of your choice while you wait.

CAFÉS

05.2

Alice's

113 St George's Road, Kemp Town
01273 691790

Homely, clean and friendly cafe, that serves a good range of lunch time grub in a non-smoking environment. Roast chicken and mayonnaise baguette, jacket potatoes with cheese and onion. The American breakfast is particularly scrummy: two grilled bacon, two hash browns, griddled egg, toast, tea or coffee.

The Bagelman

7 Bond Street, North Laine
01273 387171
www.bagelman.co.uk

The Bagelman does exactly what you want done with your bagels with the freshest ingredients - and he doesn't charge a fortune. There's no need to stray from smoked salmon and cream cheese (the lox deluxe) and many people don't, but if you do two popular choices are the ATM (avocado, tomato and mozzarella with basil) and the Funkly Tuna (tuna, avocado, lemon juice, olives). With a new bigger, better bakery behind the shop, world domination awaits. For Bagelman obsessives there is a reward card system - buy 10 get 1 free. Also at Sussex University.

Bamboo Bar

10 Kensington Gardens, North Laine
01273 684426

It used to be known as Grinders and while the name might have changed, it's basically the same story. Go here to escape the bustle of Kensington Gardens, then watch the shoppers bustling without you as you sit high above on the balcony, sipping a coffee and feeling ever so slightly smug. A cool smoothie or freshly squeezed orange juice? In the mornings they serve one of the biggest breakfasts in town and DJ's play in the evenings.

Becky's Cafe

Warren Road, Elm Grove
01273 628184

You can't miss Becky's London Underground sign and splendid racing mural right opposite the race course. The place to go for quality fry-ups. If you want to pig out try their Gut Buster: two eggs, two rashers, two sausages, bubble and squeak, black pudding, mushrooms, chips, beans, tomatoes, toast, and tea.

The Boardwalk

250 Kings Road Arches,
Brighton seafront

01273 746067
New, and much needed wholefood café just to the west of Brighton Pier with a decked terrace leading out on to the beach. Perfect location and if the sun's shining and you've got nowhere to go, you really couldn't ask for more. (See Restaurant section).

Bona Foodie
21 St James's Street, Kemp Town
01273 698007
Upmarket deli and café with a patio for summer lounging. Organic goods, locally sourced foods and New York pastrami are just some of the delights.

Billies
34 Hampton Place, Montpelier
01273 774386
The place for all-day breakfast. There's no chance that a normal person will ever finish one of the enormous hashes - but the effort is worth it. They come in a variety from farmhouse (eggs, bacon - the works on top of a hash) to Ranchero (salsa, guacamole and sour cream on top of your hash). At the weekend, you'll be lucky to get in, and space is tight: if you've got a buggy or a wheelchair, forget it.

Capers
27 Gardner Street, North Laine
01273 675550
Sitting in the middle of the North Laine... sometimes you feel a place would have to try hard not to work - and then you wonder why so many places don't work. Capers serves good, old-fashioned food properly. Sausage and mash made from locally produced pork and sage, smothered with thick onion gravy. Baguette full of chicken and things. Toptastic banofee pie. They do a good breakfast and do it with a smile too.

Centre Ville
34 Church Road, Hove
01273 202744
www.cafe_centreville.co.uk
Until recently, Centre Ville was happy just being a café. Then it had the bright idea of becoming a food kind of place. Rather than simply buy a new oven, they gave themselves a complete ambience update, with clever use of mirrors, candles and soft, cascading fairy lights. Most of the main courses (comprehensive but straight forward) come in at around a fiver and at the weeekend there's live music. A nice option.

Costa Café
42 Market Street, The Lanes
01273 329575
2 Dyke Road, Seven Dials
01273 725124
32 Bond Street, North Laine
01273 772024
Spacious cafes offering a blinding array of coffees to an increasingly bean-and-steam-literate clientele. As the sun moves round, so the mood changes as bustling workers grab their takeaways, lazy shoppers watch the world go by,

before a buzzy afterwork crowd cranks up the energy. Too much of a chain to be truly cool in Brighton, but more coffee in town can be no bad thing.

The Curve Bar @ Komedia

45 Gardner Street, North Laine
01273 603031

Since opening a couple of years ago, The Curve has developed an ambivalent relationship with the North Laine crowd. Attached to the Komedia Theatre, the bright spacious bistro is the obvious place to have a coffee or a meal after a show, but the mosaic entrance, stainless steel bar, soft moving light show and mezzanine internet cafe is almost too glitzy for its own good. The food is so-so but pretends to be posh Modern European (pan fried duck breast on orange scented sweet potato mash with fresh raspberry vinaigrette (£12.95); the coffee tries to be sophisticated, but what is that business with the latte in a glass that's too hot to hold and a spoon wedged in the handle that's bound to burn your fingers? The service is perfunctory when all around is so much friendlier. £18 per head is the average for dinner.

The Dorset

28 North Road (corner of Gardner
Street), North Laine
01273 605423
www.thedorset.co.uk

A bustling Brighton institution which stands out in the mix of chic and scruffy cafes around Gardner Street. On Sundays it's packed with families who come for a post Kids@Komedia lunch because they do good food for kids and throw the crayons in for free. By night the vibe is more Herbaliser than Gruffalo, and the food's getting better all the time. Friday night is DJ night.

The Dumb Waiter

Sydney Street, North Laine
01273 602526
Monday-Saturday 9.00-6.00
Sunday 10.30-3.30

What was originally a regular bacon and eggs cafe, The Dumb Waiter has moved with the times and is now a top notch vegetarian based café where the food is properly home made. Vegan pastry, vegan bread and vegan soups are all made on the premises, but there's always the odd cow knocking around if that's your fancy.

Feedwells

325 Kingsway, Hove
01273 417705

Basic, cheap but ever so tasty, fry ups, roast dinners and steam puddings. gammon steak, egg, chips, and tomatoes, scampi and chips, steamed toffee pudding. Only open for breakfast and lunch. Mon-Thurs 6am-2.30pm, Fri 6am-2pm and Sat 6-11pm.

Coffee Republic

39-40 Bond Street, North Laine
01273 723912
16 Prince Albert Street, The Lanes
01273 727726

41 Trafalgar Street, North Laine
01273 674608

Brighton born and bred, The Good Bean family have recently sold out to Coffee Republic, but the range of coffees is the same as it was. The list of coffees is endless, if slightly ridiculous, but try the hazelnut latte (£1.75 - £2.30 depending on size), a sublime mix of hazelnut syrup, espresso and steaming milk. The vivid Rothkos, cool clean interiors at Bond Street look a little like a Habitat showroom, but the papers are free, you can take the kids and you know you'll get a good cup of coffee.

Frank in Steine

Old Steine
01273 674742

With English language students, Media Centre workers and all those new business start ups doing their courses at the Enterprise Agency spilling onto the gardens the sun shines, someone just had to open a cafe on the Old Steine. But in the toilets? Well, where necessity is the mother of invention, it was only fitting that a glittering cafe was grooved out of conveniences. The coffee's good too.

Hove Tea Bar

Station Approach, Hove Station

Loved by taxi drivers - always the sign of a good café - Hove Tea Bar serves the best hot, chunky, sarnies and rolls in town. The fried egg and sausage rolls, (£1.30) served on thick white bread are unbeatable. On a cold day, sit outside, sip your steaming cappuccino, and savour the succulent flavours of fried egg, sausage and soft bread.

Infinity Café

50 Gardner Street,
North Laine
01273 670743
www.infinityfoods.co.uk

Small but popular café, a workers co-op that offers fans of the organic foodstore (around the corner in North Road) somewhere to go. The food is, as you'd expect, organic, the salads crunchy and wholesome. The coffee is delicious (and, of course, fair trade) but it is small and at lunchtime you'd probably do well to get a takeaway.

Kai Organic Café

52 Gardner Street,
North Laine
01273 684921

Kai, it seems, is Maori for 'real food' and, fittingly, absolutely everything here is organic. Everything. All that's fine and laudable, it's just a shame they didn't know the Maori for 'pleasant environment' because although there's plenty of seating space upstairs and it's in a great location, the décor is appalling. There's such potential and they've obviously put a lot of energy into the food but the environment they've created is simply not very appealing. Still, the chocolate cake was a treat. The sandwiches are packed for take-away, so maybe they're as aware of the problem as we are.

Kensington's Café

1 Kensington Gardens, North Laine
01273 570963

Possibly the best thing about this gaff is the small balcony where you can watch the bustle of the street from a safe distance whilst tucking into a steaming jacket. They sell booze, but only with food and for those who love their caffeine there is a coffee loyalty card.

Lunar Bar and Café

5a Castle Square, The Lanes
01273 220014
www.zelnet.com

One of the few places in Brighton to have a whole menu dedicated to Tuaca, the perfect winter warmer. There are a variety of cocktails (prices ranging from £2.25 to £4.50) and new crazes like vodka which tastes like your favourite sweets: Skittles vodka is ingenious. Drinks and food are all brought to your table. Trust us - this place is not just for coffee. Open 11am-11pm.

Mac's Cafe

30 Arundel Road, Kemp Town
01273 692621

You know how you can always tell the best caffs because they're the ones the cabbies go to, well Mac's is a bit like that. The best fry-up breakfast shop in town, it opens at some ungodly hour and is always but always busy. A proper institution.

The Mad Hatter

Western Road, Hove (corner of Montpelier Road)

Newish café with an attitude as good as the coffee. They provide papers to read (an obvious thing to do but still not so common) and do proper croissants and light food. Sweetly, when the sun came out they put an Indian rug on the pavement outside foor the more laid back clientele.

The Meeting Place

Hove Sea Wall, Hove seafront
01273 738391

Right on the seafront (opposite Brunswick Square) and open all year, this is a top place to meet friends because you can't the bright yellow wind barriers. There's an outside heater lamp and great toasted sandwiches, so you can eat out in midwinter - though why you'd want to...

The Mock Turtle

4 Pool Valley, The Lanes
01273 327380

Tea, egg and cress sandwiches and the best cakes in Brighton. Very traditional with table cloths and the works, but the cakes are fab. Take away if you haven't got time to watch the world go by.

Nia Café

87/88 Trafalgar Street, North Laine
01273 671371

One of the nicest café's in the North Laine, but because of that it's often difficult to get into. The décor is wooden and solid and straightforward and the service friendly. The menu is varied with drinks, cakes, light meals, main meals and breakfasts (like Oak Smoked Kippers with Rye Bread and Lemon at £4.95). They also do sarnies - baguette, bagel, ciabatta or panini - with fillings including salami, smoked salmon and feta. Try the Welsh rarebit for £4.50 or the Fish Cakes with caper and coriander salsa for £6.50. The specials tend to be more vegetarian but Sausage and Mash is always on at £6.50. By the time you read this they should have a drinks licence ("It'll only be a few weeks now" they said as we went to press), and if they do they'll open till 11pm on Thursdays, Fridays and Saturdays.

Parisa Café Bar

4/5 George Street,
Hove
01273 733359

As much a restaurant than as a café (let's define the difference as whether you go to eat or to lounge) and renowned for it's wine. The menu lists 250, but don't be perturbed: the staff know what they're talking about. They also brew their own beer here. The food varies from breakfasts to posh salads and burgers and it ticks the right boxes.

Peters

Ship Street Gardens,
The Lanes

Very cheap and cheerful cafe in a twitten. The service is friendly. A nice little hidey-hole. Only open during the daytime.

Philippe De France

69 East Street, The Lanes
01273 220691

The decor is minimal, the ambience urban and the menu mouth watering. There's a huge range of tantalising delicacies - patisseries, coffees, home-made chocolates, ice-cream and savoury snacks. Try the croute Provencal (French bread, tomatoes, garlic, olive oil, black olive tapenade, anchovies and melted goat's cheese, £5.95), the Saucisse de Toulouse grillee au jus (Grilled Toulouse sausage with onion jus and mashed potatoes, £7.00) or the Tarte Nicoise (tuna, onion, black olives and tomato tart, £4.95).

Puccinos

1 Bartholomews, The Lanes
01273 204656

Comfortable, friendly café in the Lanes which teems with breast feeding mothers and young children in the upstairs lounge by day, and chills into a feet up, sofa seated bar by night. In the summer the windows disappear (as long as the rain stays away), lending a laid back, watch-the-world kind of feel as you scoff their fine cakes. The comfy sofas by the window make you almost feel as though you are in an episode of Friends: this is Brighton café life at its chummiest.

Redroaster

1d St James Street, Kemp Town
01273 686668

Can it really be the only café in town to

roast their own coffee beans? Last year we gave this spacious Euro style café a bit of stick over its slow service. Happily, now under new management, that's all changed. Try the panini with honey roasted aubergine and courgettes and black olive tapenade (£3.70) with a sweet banana smoothie (£2.75). Grilled ciabattas and sandwiches all freshly made to order. Very gay friendly.

RedVeg

21 Gardner Street, North Laine
01273 679910

Veggie fast food with no frills. The posh sofas and cardboard Big Mac style boxes seems an odd set of priorities, but hey, if it works in Soho, it'll probably keep the students happy here too.

The Rock Street Café

7 Rock Street, Kemp Town

Affectionately known as Sally's, The Rock Street Café is the sort of place that's less a café than a lounge for regulars. The cakes and comfy sofa offer refuge to the area's writers and actors who idle away an afternoon, playing Solitaire or Backgammon. Mediterranean Sardines and creamy cheese toast are the best in town. One of the most kiddie friendly cafes, with children's books nestling among the stacks of the magazines.

Room 101

Trafalgar Street, North Laine
01273 687064

Trafalgar Street no longer feels like it's on the fringe of the North Laine, and Room 101 was an early gentrifying influence on the street. As a place to eat it has now found its niche after a period where the owner's parking disputes brought the place more fame than its food. 100% vegetarian with vegan options, the menu is pared-down and all the better for it. Service comes with a genuine smile, and gripes of old were all but forgotten. Leave the crowds at Nia and head here instead for a more relaxing drink and a bite to eat that's wholesome without being too worthy.

The Saint

22 St. James's Street, Kemp Town
01273 607835
www.thesaint-brighton.co.uk

Café restaurant bar serving the likes of pan fried zander (£14.50), artichoke, goats cheese and sage ravioli (13.95) or Tofu Laksa with Udon Noodles (£12.95). There's also a good selection for meat eaters. (see Restaurant section).

The Sanctuary Café

51 Brunswick Street East, Hove
01273 770002

The winner of the "Best Café" gong at the last Juicy Awards, The Sanctuary is a refuge from the madness of the high street. Last time we called it a "funky but friendly Vegetarian café." And that's still essentially the case. Late night coffee and cake on the ground and upper floors with poetry readings, cult films and Brighton Underground network meetings in the Beatnik basement, and sunny lunches out of windowless windows. The look is sculpted Boho, the vibe predominantly gay. They've opened the upstairs and you can get proper food (salmon fillet with a lemon grass, chilli and dill sauce £6.75, tagliatelle with porcini, aubergine, roasted courgette and tomato sauce, £5.25) and all is well with the world.

Scene 22

129 St James's Street, Kemp Town

01273 626682

www.scene22.com

Just off the Old Steine, Scene 22 is Brighton's only gay shop and coffee bar. It's fully stocked with club wear, safe sex aids and toys for both men and women. Those looking for accommodation in gay friendly households should make Freddie's noticeboard first port of call.

Starbuck

210 Western Road (next to M&S),
Central Brighton

01273 324097

18/19 Market Street, The Lanes

01273 328157

www.starbucks.com

Corporate coffee at its most corporate, Starbucks is what America does best. And you can take that how you will. It's there and functional, but the execution is lacking: luke warm lattes, cold croissants and pains aux chocolats were off when we went to the one in the Lanes. But the "have a nice day" style service is suitably Brightonised by its Ozzie waitresses, and really, who can complain about yet more coffee to try?

The Street Café

101 St. James's Street, Kemp Town

01273-673891

Good food with a bit of culture. There's a gallery upstairs and a large bright patio garden. All day breakfasts from £3.95, sandwiches from £2.65 plus all the usual café fare.

Strength Coffee Bar

111 St. James's Street, Kemp Town

01273-624632

Bright and clean, cool jazz sounds and prompt service are why you might choose to take your latte and toasted panini here while reading one of the many newspapers on offer for customers.

Waikika Moo Kau

11a Kensington Gardens, North Laine

01273 671117

Meeting House Lane, The Lanes

A Juicy favourite in the North Laine with a welcome to complement the size of the meals. Order a mezze for the entire family and you'll be pushing it to finish the plate. Despite its popularity, the laid back staff don't try to move you on once you've finished your coffee, and the smiles are genuine. Could be the influence of all those buddhas and gods on the walls. The Kensington Gardens branch is now open all week 9am-6pm. Meeting House Lane is open till 11pm.

05.3

● Pubs and bars, bars and pubs; the city is heaving with both. And in Brighton, at least, there's enough of a crossover to send a small minority screaming about the sanctity of the Great British Tradition. In particular, Zel and C-side, the architects of a new genre of pub-bar, offer a welcome blend of the best of bar and pub culture, making Brighton and Hove the distinctive place it is. If it's pub walks you're after, that lunchtime meal thing, check out the Sunday Lunches & Days Out chapter.

Barley Mow

92 St George's Road, Kemp Town
01273 682259

Very mixed and probably the most 'gay friendly' pub in kemp Town. At a first glance it may look like a traditional pub with the velvet covered pews, but it has a lovely friendly atmosphere. The food is home made and plentiful and is served well into the night (about 10pm). The fish is fresh from Shoreham. The Mexican-style chilli con carne with rice and fired potato skins (£6.25) is one to try if you're hungry. The menu changes weekly and is different at the weekend.

The Basketmakers

12 Gloucester Road, North Laine
01273 689006

Not a virgin wall in sight. Cigarette cases, Victorian toffee boxes, photographs and old posters compete for space in one of Brighton's best loved pubs. Popular with art students, lecturers and the sort of clientele who appreciate its intimate atmosphere and cask-conditioned ales.

The Bath Arms

4-5 Meeting House Lane, The Lanes
01273 329437

With guest ales which change every week, if you like to sample beer this is the place for you. The Full of old Brighton memorabilia, The Bath Arms is a good refuge after a shopping trip around The Lanes. Attracts a young crowd who somehow manage to chat above the deafening background music.

The Blue Parrot

6 New Road, Central Brighton
01273 889675

More a cocktail bar than pub (though you can get a big glass of wine for £2), this is where you'll want to sip your Long Island Tea and gaze at the gorgeous Pavilion by night. Right next door to the Theatre Royal, it's a late night option to The Colonnade Bar after sitting through the evening performance.

Brighton Rock Beach House
6 Rock Place, Kemp Town
01273 601139
Distressed and battered beach house walls, faded canvas and decking in this New England Beach House, with Manhattans and Martinis joining Boston Meatloaf and crab cakes on the menu.

The Bristol Bar
Paston Place,
Kemp Town
01273 605687
The Bristol's punters range from the cool and collected, to Kemp Town dignitaries and singleton women. Set just across the road from the sea, The Bristol has wonderful views and they serve proper coffee all day long and the usual standard pub grub between 12 and 2.30pm (but not curiously at weekends), so why doesn't the landlord turn the largely unused car park into a garden?

The Bulldog
St James's Street,
Kemp Town
01273 684097
Established gay pub in the heart of St James's which has sat back and watched the area develop into a classy quarter while still retaining its position.

The Charles Napier
57 Southover Street, Hanover
01273 601413
Longstanding local community pub with great beer that makes it very popular with the forty-something social worker and teacher crowd. Check out the upstairs sofas - once you're there...

Chequers Inn
45 Preston Street, Central Brighton
01273 329922
A hard-bitten pub worth a visit on a Sunday night just to see the oldest DJ in town in action. Rocking Bill has been spinning his discs for more than 30 years. It's said that the Fatboy learnt everything he knows from this man.

The Colonnade
10 New Road, Central Brighton
01273 328728
Gloriously luvvie and packed to the gills with actors in residence at the Theatre Royal next door. Expect to see famous faces and wannabes alike merging with the many portraits adorning the walls.

The Constant Service
96 Islingword Road, Hanover
01273 607058
www.cside.co.uk
A favourite among Brightonians, The Constant Service is more of an evening experience than a daytime haunt. The warm, welcoming atmosphere attracts a mixed crowd and the ultra-efficient, but courteous staff will put you at your ease, whoever you may be.

Coopers Cask

3 Farm Road, Hove

01273 737026/736945

This is a real locals' place, but don't let that put you off because the locals here come in all flavours - gay, straight, young and old. It's tiny but that just adds to the warm, friendly atmosphere with some top tunes kicking out of the speakers. The exotic menu with daily specials is great value. The range of old fashioned sweets like strawberry bon-bons are just for big kids though, children aren't allowed.

The Cricketers

15 Black Lion Street, The Lanes

01273 329472

www.goldenliongroup.co.uk

Graham Greene's favourite is the oldest pub in Brighton, and the olde interiors are gorgeous. Popular with tourists and office parties, but cooler Brighton heads tend to ignore it.

The Dragon

58 St George's Road, Kemp Town

01273 690144

Bordering on the Gothic, expect a mixed-age grungy crowd, tables lit by dripping candles. Sadly, they don't have weekly backgammon anymore. There is live music on a Monday, and you'll get the likes of The Kinks and The Who and maybe a bit of Blues if you're lucky. DJ Jamie Rainbow pulls in the youngsters on Friday. All Sunday lunches are £5.95.

Dr Brighton's

16 Kings Road, Brighton seafront

01273 328765

It looks like a run-of-the-mill, traditional seaside pub, but it's quickly obvious that looks can be deceiving. Dr Brighton's is a legendary welcoming local without the cliqueyness of other gay pubs. Official host of the pre-Wild Fruit shenanigans, there's no room for mundane traditions here. Last year we wrote that they've got 12 different flavoured Schnapps on offer. Well, now they've increased that to 21.

The Druid's Head

9 Brighton Place, Central Brighton

01273 325490

Close to the Open Market, The Druid's Head used to cater solely for market workers but that's all changed now. The clientele spreads right across the spectrum from 18-year-old student to the old locals nursing their half a Guinness. Music mags are scattered over the tables and it likes to play its music, loud, loud, loud. Popular with students, the staff will not only wait on your table, but also give you a free lolly-pop when you leave!

Earth and Stars

46 Windsor Street, Central Brighton

01273 772282

www.zelnet.com

Zel's been busy in the centre of Brighton with two new announcements. Earth and Stars is its eco, fully environmentally-balanced pub, and is now offering a full organic menu. Everything here is organic: from the food to the cigarettes to the beer to the hemp t-shirts the bar staff wear. Waste is recycled, they've applied for permission to put up solar panels and just ask them about the carbon footprints.

The Evening Star

55-56 Surrey Street, Seven Dials

01273 328931

For proper real ale, you can't beat The Evening Star. The landlord changes the barrels every two days. A must for those who crave the real beer-drinkers experience.

Freemasons

39 Western Road, Hove

01273 732043

One of the best pubs in central Brighton and a haven from shopping hell. It's recently been revamped and it's all very nice - grown up rather than disco dolly and stylish in a simple but stylish way. Food is served from midday until 8pm and has a good selection, from bacon and brie baguette with chips and salad (£4.50) to chicken tikka masala, mushroom and spinach lasagne and Thai crab cakes with nothing priced over £5.50. Food served: Mon-Fri 12-8pm, Sat & Sun 12-6pm.

The Fiddlers Elbow

11 Boyces Street, Brighton

01273 325850

www.zelnet.com

Authentically Irish as opposed to some

of those themed pubs, The Fiddler's Elbow is more chilled than its hectic neighbour The Full Moon, but it's still decidedly happening. Punters are a mix of students, trendies and lovers of all things Irish. It also has live Gaelic music.

Fishbowl

74 East Street, The Lanes

01273 777505

www.zelnet.com

An official pre-club bar for The Escape, this is a great place to kick the night off to a good start. It's packed every night with a young and stylish crowd enjoying the laid back atmosphere, cheap cocktails and regular DJ's. (See also restaurant section).

The Fortunes Of War

157 Kings Road Arches,

Brighton seafront

01273 205065

Maybe it's because this pub is so reliant on passing tourist trade that it lacks atmosphere, but seafront places often do. Never mind, you can't have everything. The Fortunes is always popular as a meeting place in the summer to sit outside and bask in the Brighton seaside atmosphere.

The Full Moon

8 Boyces Street, The Lanes

01273 328797

A Brighton institution, the Full Moon is the hangout for Brighton's young and beautiful who go for its relaxed vibe and gorgeous organic Sunday roasts. The bar is mostly a chemical-free zone with organic beer, wine and cider on offer.

The George

5 Trafalgar Street, North Laine
01273 681055

Even the staff admit the beer is expensive here, but that doesn't put off the North Laine crowds. It's one of the best places in the North Laine for lunch. The food is vegetarian and vegan (separate cooking pans are used for each), but there's enough meat if that's your thing. Burgers, nachos, sausage and mash, ploughman's, Thai fishless cakes and Japanese salad. Something for everyone. Food is served all day and kids are allowed in until 8.30pm. They'll do anything for kids for £2.25. The roaring fires make it the cosiest pub in the North Laine. Though frequented by a cool crowd, the no smoking policy until 8.30pm every night means that kids are welcomed so it is a must on the family pub list. You can barely move for buggies at the weekend, as families take advantage of the large no smoking section and substantial kids menu.

The Great Eastern

103 Trafalgar Street,
North Laine
01273 685681

One of the most popular pubs in Brighton frequented by trendy young things and old regulars alike. The bar-staff are friendly and efficient, food is served between 12 and 4pm and they make the best Bloody Marys in town.

The Grey's

105 Southover Street, Hanover
01273 680734
mike@greyspub.com for the live music
newsletter www.greyspub.com

The culinary delights of the Greys kitchen are not quite so thrilling since the departure of Jean-Paul Salpetier, but move on we must. Spats Picken has replaced the once famous mussels and Thai curries with the likes of Gressingham Duck and smoked fillets of eel with lemon and horseradish. Good honest French and English grub. Now they're doing Sunday breakfasts - if only for an hour between 11am and 12pm, but it's BIG - bacon, egg, lamb cutlet, beautiful sausage, fried mushrooms, salad and new potatoes all for £6. The legend of live music lives on, and Mike Lance still books the bands more out of a love for greatness than a dollar sign in his eyes. The Belgian beer menu is comprehensive enough to confound the CAMRA crowd, and with the kind of bar staff who know about music and an old-fashioned welcome, it's no wonder that this dark little hostelry in the heart of Hanover is still one of the best pubs in town.

The Hanbury Arms and Ballroom

83 St George's Street, Kemp Town
01273 605789
www.zelnet.com

A cracking new comedy night has rejuvenated the Hanbury Arms. Shaped like an Indian temple, the drinking space is minimal but does great party nights, including Stick It On every second Saturday where you can choose your top five tunes. It can be a wild party. The Ballroom next door the pub specialises in the weird and wonderful, and hosts nights like jazz, diy DJing, manga screenings...

The Hand In Hand

33 Upper St James Street, Kemp Town
01273 602521

The weeniest, teeniest pub in Brighton known for brewing their own beer and having a diverse range of drinkers in such a small place. Oozing with character, the Victorian ceilings are splendid, as is its incredible collection of ties hanging from every available space. Popular with ageing Thespians and sea captains, it is worth a visit if you can find a place to squeeze in at the bar.

Hangleton Manor

Hangleton Valley Drive, Hangleton
01273 413266

One of the oldest buildings in Hove, this 16th century pub has a garden with plenty of room. The food is typical pub grub. Usually easy parking too.

The Heart In Hand

North Street, North Laine
01273 624799

A stone's throw from all the action in the busy North Laine this is a quiet pub to hide away from the crowds. It's popular with the market-traders of Upper Gardener Street so there's always the

chance of securing a bargain over a pint. The Heart In Hand is a small but comfortable pub with a superior selection of beers and nibbles and a jukebox stacked with classics from Marvin Gaye to Tim Buckley.

Hectors House

51-52 Grand Parade, Old Steine
01273 688869

Lively starting point for a night at the Ocean Rooms and jumping with students and late teens most nights of the week.

Hop Poles

13 Middle Street, The Lanes
01273 710444

Small, lively and trendy pub, popular with students and media types from the Brighton Media Centre. The friendly bar staff serve excellent value food all day. In the evening, things get a bit more intimate with tables lit by dripping candles. Very fine music and there's a small 'Secret Garden' at the back.

The Leek and Winkle

39 Ditchling Road, London Road.
01273 624434

Right next to The Level it is hard to miss the turquoise façade of this lively pub. This funky style is continued inside with a mix match of décor and colours. This doesn't, however, take anything away from the cosy, friendly atmosphere created by the sociable crowd and the candlelit tables. Attracts a generally young clientele but is also welcoming to others, especially during the day. A popular pre-club venue offering drinks promotions and in-house DJs.

The Lion And Lobster
24 Sillwood Street, Montpelier
01273 776961
Cosy, traditional pub extremely popular with a thirty-something crowd, so get there early if you want a seat. The lager is organic (Bittburger and Warsteiner), and the live Irish music on Sundays helps the two-course roast lunch (£5.50) go down a treat.

The London Unity
Islingword Road, Hanover
01273 888319
www.thelondonunity.com
Beloved by locals who come for the warm atmosphere, roaring fire, original stripped floors and the sounds of hippy hits from times gone by. The free newspapers on a Sunday with a Bloody Mary for only £1.50 is a great hangover cure - allegedly. During Happy Hour (4.30-6pm) pints are £1.70. Surprisingly it is not studenty - yet.

The Marlborough
4 Princes Street, Kemp Town
01273 570028
Tucked away behind the bustle of Pavilion Parade, The Marlborough has been known as the lesbian's local in the past but although more female dominated than the other gay pubs is now much more mixed. A film screen is opening in the theatre upstairs so when

there are no shows on, you can pay £2 to watch anything from Carry On classics to art house obscurities.

Mash Tun
1 Church Street, Central Brighton
01273 684951
www.zelnet.com
Funky pub with two floors depending on your mood: slouching sofas upstairs and more prim pew-like chairs below. Deliberately employing the best-looking bar staff helps to give the place a bit of a buzz. 'Friendly food, tasty staff' boasts the blurb outside, pretty much summing it up really. During the day there are newspapers on tap and coffee served. Just the way it should be.

Mrs Fitzherbert's
25 New Road, Central Brighton
01273 682401
A cosy and intimate atmosphere, you can eat tapas, canoodle in the cubby holes, or just enjoy drinking in central Brighton.

The Nelson
36 Trafalgar Street, North Laine
01273 695872
A proper, old-fashioned local. The beer is excellent and the staff well trained.

No Man Is An Island
106 Lewes Road, Bevendean
01273 622310
www.zelnet.com
Slapbang in the centre of the Lewes Road junction, the large and eclectic

collection of slightly dodgy looking sofas, coupled with the occasional tie-dye drape, gives this pub the atmosphere of a student bedroom. Albeit one that serves food, screens films every night and has live DJ's on Fridays and Saturdays.

The Office

8 Sydney Street, North Laine
01273 609134

A young and trendy crowd flock to this pub in the heart of the North Laine. The décor is light and airy, the music chilled and unobtrusive and the food delicious authentic Thai. They're renowned for their extensive selection of exotic spirits such as cachaca, a Brazilian sugar cane drink, and if there's a new product out they'll probably have it. But if it all gets a bit too calm and sophisticated they also do jelly vodkas.

The Open House

146 Springfield Road,
by London Road station
01273 880102
www.zelnet.com

One of the most community spirited pubs in Brighton. Not just a place for the locals to enjoy a drink, the mosaics, paintings and sculptures and art on the walls are by local Fiveways artists and the pub is planning street parties for the summer, which should bring the cosy community even closer together. Even if you're not a local it's still a great place to while away a few hours, relaxing in the lounge on cold midwinter days or

sunning yourself in the garden during summer. A child friendly place to enjoy a spot of lunch by day, at night it turns into a lively place for a night out, with DJ's playing at the weekend. The decked garden is splendid for a spot of lunch in the summer (plate of humus, olives and ciabatta for around a fiver) and the lounge bar is cosy and child-friendly in the coldest days of midwinter with its Chesterfields and low-slung tables.

Park Crescent Pub

39 Park Crescent Terrace, Elm Grove
01273 604993

High on our list, it sits in the middle of a Regency estate, has a lively, friendly atmosphere and a sweet garden.

Pressure Point

33 Richmond Place, North Laine
01273 235082

A relaxed place to have a few beers and a chat, and a popular alternative to the nearby Student Union. But the Pressure Point is mainly known as a music venue and upstairs is one of the best indie type places around (all black walls, fading posters and sticky floor - just the way it should be).

The Prince Albert

48 Trafalgar Street, North Laine
01273 730499

Unassuming little pub just down the road from the station, it's the preferred watering-hole of Brighton's clubbing giants. The Prince Albert shares its owner with Concorde 2, so anyone wanting tickets for whatever the Next Big Thing is can ask for Chris.

Prince Regent

29 Regency Square, Brighton seafront
01273 329962

Step through the door and enter a time warp. It is as though this pub has been frozen in the era of Prince Regent. Probably then, as now, this is a relaxed haunt for a mix of gay and straight drinkers. The no-frill's style of most of Brighton's pubs hasn't touched The Regent, where recreating the grandeur of a royal hangout is more the theme. Ornate brassware and cheeky cherubs adorn the walls and not a DJ in sight.

The Prodigal

80 East Street, Brighton seafront
01273 748103

Under new management and trying to find its feet. Still pretty much the same but are having a quiz and open mic night on alternate Tuesdays. Sunday roasts from £4.95 with the sea view thrown in for free

The Pub With No Name

58 Southover Street,
Hanover
01273 601419

Juicy Award winning pub in the heart of Hanover. There's no sign outside but you'll know it when you find it. The wooden tables, guest DJs and cool ambience attract the young and hip crowd, as well as large sections of the Hanover community. It's a stripped-pine kind of joint but nicely rough around the edges. Upstairs there is an exhibition space for local artists which is also used as a function room for private parties. You'll find a seat mid-week, but at the weekend the place heaves with pre-clubbers. At the weekends families move in, attracted by the covered deck for kids at the back. The menu is pub grub, Brighton style. A fine choice of meals, half of them vegetarian, most for around a fiver. From pasta to seared tuna (marinated in lime and coriander served with vegetable chow mein) to asparagus and fetta puffs with a chive sauce, sauté potatoes and salad (£5.95). They also serve chips, sandwiches and staple children's meals.

Queen's Head

3 Steine Street,
Old Steine
01273 602939
www.zelnet.com

If the Freddie Mercury picture hanging outside isn't enough to tempt you inside this gay local then the home-cooked food will. There are DJs two or three times a week. Student night on Tuesday with drink offers. £5 for any baguette or jacket and a pint/glass of wine/soft drink is a popular offer. Sunday Roast (£5.95) is 'ab fab' and 'well endowed' says the chef, Mrs Mark. Not intimidating as some gay bars can be. The upstairs lounge bar is available for private hire for free. At the weekends it's a lively place to drink before cruising round the corner to Pool or Revenge.

The Regency Tavern

32 Russell Square, Brighton seafront
01273 325652

Wonderfully camp pub tucked behind
Regency Square where landlord Chris
Ryan is more Bet Lynch than Alex
Gilroy and serves his pints under the
watchful eye of a bunch of gold cherubs.
At last orders, a glitterball replaces the
standard lighting as the PA croons a
midnight tune to its largely gay
clientele. Sunday lunch is exquisite,
although Chris compares it to the first
day at the Harrods sale. No booking so
get there early! The vegetarian menu is
one of the big pulls and the loos are
possibly Brighton's most glamorous.

The Rock

7 Rock Street, Kemp Town
01273 697054

Rather quaint pub in a quiet street with
a small patio. Even though the floors are
fashionably bare it exudes an old-
fashioned atmosphere and boasts two
roaring fires, one of which is in the
rather gentrified lounge bar. Perfect if
you want a quiet drink and a chat. They
have an open mic acoustic night twice a
month in the basement bar (which is
only open in the evening) where anyone
can get up there and have a go.

Royal Pavilion Tavern

7-8 Castle Square, Central Brighton
01273 827641

A Regular Joe kind of pub which
harbours a well kept secret upstairs in
the form of the Tavern club. Once the

bar shuts it's time to shimmy up the
stairs for a Sixties showdown on
Saturday nights, or the rock/indie nights
on Wednesdays and Thursdays. Fresh
on Friday caters for a mixed gay and TV
crowd, while MFI (Mad For It)
celebrates everything Mancunian mid-
week.

The Shakespeare's Head

1 Chatham Place, Seven Dials
01273 329444
www.zelnet.com

Only in Brighton would you find a pub
with a tiled bar, giant Elizabethan-clad
dummies, purple walls and
backgammon tables lit by night-lights in
glass jars. The perfect place to hang out
with friends, while instrumental jazz
plays in the background.

The Sidewinder

65 Upper St James Street Mews,
Kemp Town
01273 679927
www.zelnet.com

Hip yet unpretentious, The Sidewinder
is popular with students, media types
and all those who crave an urban
atmosphere. The fabulous large garden
is perfect to spend hot summer evenings
in or afternoons with the family.
Refectory tables and comfy sofas that
meet most needs, it also supplies a large
range of mags and newspapers. One of
the best places for a quiet lunch in
Kemp Town, the mezze of olives,
roasted peppers and humus goes down
particularly well. Sausage and mash with

a difference (£4.95) or choose from a selection such as leek, cheddar, mushroom and sundried tomato sausages with sour cream and chive mash.

St James's

16 Madeira Place,
Kemp Town
01273 626696

Huge choice of spirits including rare stuff not found elsewhere in Brighton. DJs play seven nights a week for a mixed bag of drinkers. St James's has same chef as The Office and will unveil a new Thai menu - soon. The newly designed menu promises is organic with a wide range of veggie options.

The Station

Goldstone Villas,
Hove
01273 733660

Cool drinking den next to Hove Station for youngsters who don't care about the chilly atmosphere. It's open late Thursday to Saturday and if you're going for food, try the oven-baked pizzas.

The Star of Brunswick

32 Brunswick Street West,
Hove
01273 771355

The Star of Brunswick is something of a Brighton-drinker's institution. For those who want a late night, there's the option to pay £2 and you can booze till 1am. Check out the downstairs.

The Sutherland Arms

14/15 Sutherland Road, Queen's Park
01273 603059
www.zelnet.com

It was once the rockers hangout, but The Sutherland has recently had a change of management, so is no longer catering for the few rock chicks and aging musicians in the area. Now there's even has a disco on a Saturday night.

Three Jolly Butchers

59 North Road, North Laine
01273 239259
www.zelnet.com

Part of the Zel chain of pubs, the newly refurbished Three Jolly Butchers is smart and relaxing and has started to get itself as a bit of a reputation for somewhere to hang out. You can get a a selection of sandwiches, panini's, homemade lasagne, frittata's and bakes all for between £3-5.

The Wagon and Horses

109 Church Road, Central Brighton
01273 602752

With all the alternative trendy places in the North Laine, there are few places left where you can get a decent ploughmans (£3.75). The traditional name means they do traditional pub grub as well. Catering for a younger crowd, although not particularly students.

Walmer Castle

95 Queen's Park Road, Queens Park
01273 682466

The Walmer Castle is an increasingly

groovy environment to drink in with the young and the gorgeous. Expect it to be lively whatever night you go. They do a lovely jerk chicken Sunday lunch and complete the mood with a soundtrack of lovers rock reggae.

The Western Front

11 Cranbourne Street, Central Brighton
01273 725656
www.zelnet.com

It's impossible to miss this canary-yellow pub right next door to Churchill Square shopping centre. One of the best of the Zel pubs, it's conveniently located for chic shoppers in need of liquid refreshment or a light snack. It's kind of sparse inside with a tatty Mediterranean feel, a mixed bag of daytime punters,

rusty tables and laid-back jazz. The staff, the food and the building itself seem relaxed and cool without really trying. It would be nice to hide out in here all afternoon and never quite get around to going back to work. At lunchtime it's still quite relaxed, at night it gets heaving. There's no food after 8pm, only alcohol, including Absinthe.

The White Horse

30 Camelford Street, Kemp Town
01273 603726

A gay pub for all ages that still has the warm atmosphere of the local it once was. One of the few gay pubs to still have a pool table, you will be enticed by the fabulous drink offers and no cabaret policy.

● *I am a real Brightonian; I moved here. I'd done London and it was time to move on. Brighton is a very small place, a bit like Chelsea but with a beach, and I can cycle everywhere. Montpelier Villas, where I live, is a bit like living on the set of Mary Poppins with the cast from Coronation Street, and only a stone's throw from Waitrose and Oddbins. My favourite places are the open market in London Road, the Italian shop at Seven Dials and Archers butchers in Islingword Road. My job means that we eat out all over but we always return to Latin In The Lane and Tsing Tao. I hide out at the Sussex Arts Club and the Regency Tavern, but we stay home a lot, or visit friends. People just pop by in Brighton and I love that. It wouldn't happen in Chelsea.*

Andrew Kay, *art director, food writer and restaurant critic for* The Latest Homes *and lives in Montpelier*

BARS

05.4

05.4

Alfresco

The Milkmaid Pavilion

Kings Road Arches, Hove seafront

01273 206523

More restaurant than bar, but given that it's got Brighton's best sunset viewpoint overlooking the West Pier, it's the perfect place to hang out and sip a vodka or three. The staff have got a bit of an attitude, but let's not concern ourselves about that: that's their problem.

Ali Cats

80 East Street, The Lanes (behind The Prodigal pub)

01273 220902

If louche lounging is what's in your heart, this is the place for you. Ali Cats is, in every senses, an underground dive. Where are the windows? There are no windows. Where's the air? No air. There's regular DJ spots, cult movies every night and reasonably priced booze. Different nights have different themes so it might be an idea to check what's what.

Amsterdam

11/12 Marine Parade,

Kemp Town

01273 688825

One of the biggest, best-established gay bars on the seafront. Based on the tried-and-tested bar and sauna formula, the Amsterdam has managed to create a relaxed atmosphere for its mixed gay locals. With a predominantly wooden décor, this bar has an uncluttered vibe while still feeling fairly intimate. The seafront location makes the Amsterdam a convenient pre-club detour as well as a real suntrap, ideal for those summer drinking sessions.

Babalabar

7 Albion Street,

Old Steine

01273 699840

In a quiet residential street behind the Pressure Point sits the Honey Club's pre-club bar. Popular with a mostly student crowd taking advantage of the 5-8pm happy hour, reasonable food and big screen entertainment. Saturday to Monday it's sports on TV, then films and live music during the week. providing cheap drinks, love spuds (with salsa and soured cream) and fizzy vibe before a free mini bus transports you to the club. The bus leaves between 10.30 and 11.30pm - ask for a hand stamp to jump the queue down the road at the Honey Club.

Candy Bar

33 St James Street, Kemp Town
01273 622424

Sister of the legendary lesbian Londoner, The Candy Bar is what Kemp Town kittens have been waiting for. The UV lit main bar is an art exhibition every month where the walls are adorned with erotic photography and pop art. Downstairs is decorated in brown and has a more retro feel to it. Different nights have different themes; quiz night (Wed), Open Mic night (Sunday), live DJs (Friday) and a theme night once a month. The menu varies daily but the range is always satisfying. And if you can't decide what to eat, the Bailey's latte is always a treat. Blokes are allowed in as long as they're a guest of a suitably oriented female.

Casa

155 North Street, Brighton
01273 738763

Strange mix of style and girls out on the town that spreads across two floors with a swanky mezzanine for diners. Their innovative idea of ordering your food over the Net before you arrive has failed, but who's really that busy anyway? Well at least they have tapas now to compensate. Tends to attract the central town post work crowd, and heats up to a pre-clubber as the night goes on.

Charles Street

8-9 Marine Parade, Kemp Town
01273 624091

A slice of metro-chic finally hit Brighton's gay scene last year with this two-level bar (Charles Street) and club (Pool) on the seafront. The swish downstairs bar, Charles Street, offers daytime table service and food, sofas, strategically lit standing room (you'll see) and a glam walkway for that all-important entrance. Positively teeming at the weekend with pre-clubbers, this bar's success seemed almost guaranteed - if only they wouldn't announce last orders and promote the club over the tannoy in such a tacky fashion. The upstairs club, Pool, although clearly the poorer sibling, still exudes bags of style. Having found its feet after an initial identity crisis, it's now the perfect intimate venue for one-nighters to suit all tastes. And when nanny knocks on Charles Street's door at 11, it seems rude not to sashay upstairs and hit the dance floor.

Circus Circus

2 Preston Road, Preston Circus
01273 620026

Standing loud and proud on the Preston Circus junction where The Stanford Arms used to be, this is the closest thing to a style bar in the area. All the key ingredients are there: large spacious bar, brash and bold walls and the odd settee. They've made an effort with the food - simple things like the chunky paprika fries are great - which is good and all, but people aren't going to go here to eat. The location dictates that this will probably remain a nice place for a few pints before nipping over the road to the Duke Of York's cinema.

Cord

Queens Road,
Central Brighton
01273 737770

Cord is where CTs used to be and is an intimate, groovier option to Polar Central next door. A pre-club bar with cocktails and local art inspiring the clientele upstairs while the DJ downstairs broadcasts on a monitor above the bar, the sounds are deeply cool even if the décor looks like a discarded backdrop for BBC Choice's "60 Seconds" news.

Easy

10 Cranbourne Street,
Central Brighton
01273 710928
www.cside.co.uk

Bang in the centre of town next to Churchill Square, this is a bit of a refuge from the madness of the shops and the beer monsters in West Street. Stylistically similar to the Polar bars - didn't we spot the same stools?

The Fish Bowl

74 East Street,
The Lanes
01273 777505

An official pre-club bar for The Escape, this is a great place to kick the night off to a good start.

It's packed every night with a young and stylish crowd enjoying the laid back atmosphere, cheap cocktails and regular DJ's. (See Restaurant section).

The Fringe Bar

10 Kensington Gardens, North Laine
01273 623683

Downstairs from the Bamboo Bar, The Fringe is a mad eye-fest, what Dali might have come up with after a night out with Gaudi. Mosaics, prints and curled-up, metal light fittings. The food doesn't match - how could it? - but it's a place to lounge, to escape the crowds, and to be seen rather than a fine feast.

Gemini Beach Bar

127 Kings Road Arches,
Brighton sea front
01273 327888

The largest and liveliest of the bars on the seaside strip, Gemini's epitomises summer in Brighton. Chrome seats spill out onto the promenade where carefree drinkers get an unrivalled view of the sea. Impromptu skate boarding stunts and live jazz bands help give the atmosphere a Brighton twist. By dusk the party's moved inside the cosy bar where securing a seat is as important as being noticed. The small capacity makes Gemini's fairly exclusive at weekends when the rich and famous come to mingle in the mellow ambience.

Greens

62 West Street, Central Brighton
01273 778579
www.cside.co.uk

Coffee bar by day and a lounge bar by night but still looks smart enough to get a cocktail. The window seating is great for watching the world go buy.

Guarana Co. Bar

36 Sydney Street, North Laine
01273 621406
www.goguarana.com

Not so much as café as an all purpose Guarana shop, but while you're there stocking up on your energy bars and natural stimulants you might as well have a coffee or (maybe better) a 'Guarana tea'.

Kai's Bar

(under the Star Of Brunswick pub)
Brunswick Street Hove
01273 771355

What used to be the Vats bar is now Kai's bar - but the late night story remains the same. Monday to Saturday it's open till 1am with snacks available until 12.30am. There's DJs, cabaret, cheap drinks...

Koba

135 Western Road, Montpelier
01273 720059

As you might expect from somewhere set up by the man who owns The Oriental Hotel, Koba is chic and stylish, small but cool. A discrete spot in one of the busiest parts of town, it's set above Waitrose, the kind of place where you'd only go if you knew it was there, or if a friend had recommended it. Go through the door and up the stairs and you're in an environment out of Wallpaper magazine; from the purple velvet panels lining the walls to the deep, dark wood tables and matching stools. It sounds a bit melodramatic, but it works. And if you like cocktails, you'll be a happy bunny.

Kruze

8 Madeira Drive, Kemp Town
01273 608133

A trendy gay bar, perfect for those who love to drink in style. By day, it's got a quiet American Piano Bar atmosphere with lounge singers, but by night things change when the serious clubbers move in. Cocktails are available (£2.95) from 5pm every day, while upstairs in the Lizard Lounge the bunny boys will serve them to your table - and with an offer like that you are guaranteed to be back next day. It's very busy on Fridays and Saturdays with the boys preparing themselves for Pool or Revenge.

Leo's Lounge

54-55 Meeting House Lane, The Lanes
01273 207040

Formerly The Lanes End, Leo's is (according to www.peoplenews.co.uk) where the celebs hang out in Brighton. Well, we've been there a few times, so maybe... EastEnders filmed here and you don't get much hipper than that. Maybe it was the omnipresent leopard skin print that attracted them... Still, it's cool with the after work crowd and at weekends does a good trade for the pre-club gang.

Legends

31 Marine Parade, Kemp Town
01273 624462
www.legendsbar.co.uk

Actually the bar for the seafront New Europe Hotel, but don't let that put you off. Its vibrant and funky, though its being refurbished at the moment to create more space. Is planning to have a complete new range of products such as shooters and cocktails and a new food menu. They promise there'll be no loud music so you can have a comfortable social experience. In the evening there's cabaret acts (although the bar staff are known to break into song at all other times) and on Wednesdays it's a full house for bingo. Sunday night is cabaret night. Legends is the official warm-up bar for Revenge and there's usually some free tickets up for grabs if you ask behind the bar.

Medusa

20 Preston Street, Central Brighton
01273 326408

What was once Skid Row is now... Medusa. A new name, a new management. It's too early to give an opinion really – everywhere needs some time to settle in – but if it's half as successful as Skid Row was, it'll be alright.

No Name Bar

82 St James Street, Kemp Town
01273 693216

A lack of a name could be this bar/restaurant's first mistake - a simple recommendation requires a convoluted 'that place with the green front and the red circle painting in the window' description. Still, it never did its sister

pub any harm. There's a small bar with a few drinking-only tables as you come in, but it's as a restaurant that it excels (see Restaurant section). A welcome addition to the burgeoning inner Kemp Town scene.

Penthouse

1 Phoenix Place, Old Steine
01273 603974

Hiding away upstairs at The Freebutt, The Penthouse is a sofa filled bar ideal to while away some time. Drinks, pizzas and music – nice little secret bar.

Polar West

114 Western Road, Montpelier
01273 733245

The first Polar Bar and it's starting to show. A relaxed place to hang out during the afternoon or a steaming madhouse by night, it's the business with its friendly service, architectural flower arrangements and cool Chesterfields. It gets very crowded here at weekends - in the summer I wouldn't even think about it. But if you're young and in a small-ish crowd, it's a good pre-club option.

Polar East

8 St George's Road, Kemp Town
01273 683334

The usual leather sofas and vodka shots, but there's an American pool table (I think that's a reference to the off-putting red cloth) and out back a honeytrap sun terrace for those long summer evenings. There's food, but the menu is straightforward - food isn't why you're here - chicken nachos, chicken breast and coriander, breakfasts and roasts on a Sunday.

Polar Central

11-12 Queen's Road, Central Brighton
01273 325793
Central opened in December 2001 (three years after the first Polar) just up from the Clock Tower. The downstairs is done up in the (by now) standard Polar style (newspapers, table football, sofas), while upstairs there's another bar, more sofas and two American pool tables.

Rendezvous Casino

Brighton Marina Village
01273 605602
www.lciclubs.com
American and Electronic Roulette, Blackjack, Casino Stud Poker as well as Dice and Slots and Punto Banco. There's a private high stakes room and separate card room with beginners Poker classes and even Ladies Poker games! Membership is free but compulsory and allows you to drink late after a night at the UGC (the bar is open from 2pm to 2am every day except Sunday when it closes at 12.30am). No jeans or trainers.

Reservoir

I Howard Road, Hanover
01273 269728
From the family that brought you The Pub With No Name and The No Name Bar, this is the grown up version with no food, no kids and beautiful water features in the garden. They will be

doing food, but right now they're basking in the courtyard, sipping their cocktails and taking life very easy as the Barons of Brighton.

Riki-Tik

18a Bond Street, North Laine
01273 683844
Primarily a pre-club bar where glamour and lager are dished out in equal measure. Playstation junkies, Internetters and dressed up clubbers adorn this stylish den. DJs get the young and hip clientele going around six nights a week. On Fridays fight through the crowded ground floor and relax with a cocktail in the more salubrious upstairs lounge bar. Those who find it all too much can ask at the bar for a Playstation and pretend that they are actually alone in their front room.

Shark Bar

57 West Street, Central Brighton
01273 822555
www.cside.co.uk
Inside, the purple exterior, it's minimal chic, and is a swanky space to stand and sip in style or slouching in the sofas. Often used as a pre-club bar and there's a sound system that could blow the cobwebs off places you didn't even know you had cobwebs.

Squid

78 Middle Street, The Lanes
01273 727114
www.cside.co.uk
Squid claims to be Brighton's original

pre-club bar and... maybe. Doesn't matter. It's a stylishly designed - all retro-kitsch and funky lights, vibrant orange walls and Mexican style mosaic bar. Popular with a funky, laid back crowd who happily hang around while enjoying bargain priced shooters and chilled tunes on the stereo, its central location makes it a natural choice for clubbers heading down to the beach. It's the official pre-club bar to Superstars and Chopper Choons at The Zap and you can get your free entry on Mondays and Wednesdays here and queue-jump. But if clubbing's not your thing, you can hang out in the large bay window ideal and check out the crowds.

Sumo

9-12 Middle Street, The Lanes
01273 749465 www.cside.co.uk

On a mission to be first in the style bar stakes, Sumo's doing rather well. By day Sumo's an internet café with 12 ISDN lines, fax and printer and all that for £2 an hour. If work gets too much, there are two Playstation consoles so you can take out your frustrations and kill some Space Invaders or whatever. Downstairs there's space to dance to the DJs, although elegant toe tapping on your classy yet uncomfortable stool is more Sumo etiquette. This is where the fashion conscious converge, kick back and look cool. Sumo also benefits from having an extended licence, leaving plenty of time for another G&T, darling. Open till 1am on Thursday, Friday and Saturday.

Tiger Bar

98 Trafalgar Street, North Laine
01273693377

Struggling to decide if it's a restaurant or bar - as it can't seem to do both. A more restrained warm-up for the clubber who wants to start the evening in a more laid back style and one of the few bars to visit if you fancy a few quiet beers. Listen, you can always meet here and go on to somewhere wilder if you want. (see Restaurant section)

The Tin Drum

95-97 Dyke Road, Seven Dials
01273 777575
43 St James Street, Kemp Town
01273 624777
www.tindrum.co.uk

Winner of the Juicy Best Bar award in May 2000 and deservedly so (despite taking the mushroom risotto off the menu). The Tin Drum is more than a bar/restaurant. Spacious and chilled during the day, parents flock in with their toddlers after it opens its doors at midday and workers pop in. By night, it's a hopping venue where Seven Dialers and Kemp Towners end their day with poetry readings, live DJs and a good dinner. In Kemp Town there's usually jazz on Sunday lunchtimes. The menu has a Polish twist, try the Zakushki, traditional Polish bar snacks served on blinis (£2.75-£3.50), or the more substantial Salmon Gravadlax at £5.50. They've just set up an on-line food ordering service. (See Restaurant section).

● *New York was out of the question, so in September '99, I moved to Brighton, spurred on by London property prices and a disinclination to live in a flat the size of a bus shelter. I had a "woman-by-the-sea observing dramatic sunsets, hair billowing in the breeze" kind of vision of myself, but sadly this came with deeply neurotic undertones; what if I make no friends, never go out, become sad and lonely and start harassing naked men on the beach? I shouldn't have worried. My house is a seven minute walk to the beach - on a good day, i.e. not a day following a night of several vodka and Redbulls too many, nor a day that started with a champagne brunch. This louche existence means that I've haven't seen much of the sea or the Downs, but that I have met some absolutely gorgeous people. Brighton's size allows for the sort of spontaneity Londoners can only dream of. It's just not the sort of place where you have to synchronise diaries at 20 paces. Three months in and not only do I feel totally at home, I'm having a complete ball. And I've even started baking.*

Anna Arthur, *42, has a PR company (Anna Arthur PR) in London and lives in Kemp Town.*

05.5

Arc

159 Kings Road Arches, Brighton
01273 770505

It used to be Cuba, now it's Arc. Plus ça change. Jump (UK garage and funky house) Wednesday, Step It Up (Steve Hillier from Dubstar plays 90s dance and pop) Thursday, Love Train (disco, soul and funk) Friday, Decoy (Wild Fruit's techno) Saturday.

The Beach

Kings Road Arches, Brighton
01273 722272

Open door beach bar/cafe by day, closed throbbing heart of the seafront by night, everyone goes to The Beach at least once. Partly due to its name but mostly due to its location, The Beach is a favourite haunt of weekend trippers and anyone looking for that authentic Brighton clubbing experience. To locals, it's more the baby brother of the legendary Concorde Club, it was the temporary home of Friday night favourite Big Beat Boutique until it was claimed back. Still, it's always a good night out - just be prepared to queue.

Brighton Gloucester

27 Gloucester Place, North Laine
01273 688011

The Gloucester's been going since the game began and deserves its place in history. But now, re-made and re-modelled it's up for the cup. Mama G's Soul Kitchen (Wednesday), Back To School (school disco classics) Saturday.

Casablanca

3 Middle Street, The Lanes
01273 321817

Not the most cutting edge clubs, nothing much seems to change here, but when you've got a formula that works why change it? It's always popular with a crowd that ranges from students to older clubbers, who come for two floors of jazz and funk delights with the odd bit of salsa and 70's disco thrown in too. Upstairs the front half of a purple Beetle fits two turntables and one DJ quite nicely, while downstairs real live bands play every weekend. I once saw a whole crowd of clubbers entertained by a troupe of drummers during a powercut here, now how many clubs can offer you that?

Club New York

11 Dyke Road,
Central Brighton
01273 208678

Monday night is salsa night.

Concorde 2

Madeira Drive, Kemp Town

01273 606460

Arguably the best music venue in town and a legendary club, the Concorde re-opened January 2000, and not before time. Down at the Black Rock end of the beach in a building which was originally a bus shelter, then a Victorian reading room and latterly a biker's cafe, and has a Victorian lift which is the oldest in the country linking the lower Madeira Drive to the road above. But does it work? Home to the fabled Big Beat Boutique night on Fridays. For tickets, ring or pop in to The Prince Albert in Trafalgar Street (01273 730499) to find out who's selling them this week. One thing: if Mr Scruff's in town, get there early. Very early.

Creation

West Street, Central Brighton

And a £5million refit later... Due to open late May on the site of what was once Paradox/Club Barcelona, Creation will be a bar by day, a club by night. Three different rooms, three different types of music with everything changing through the week. Wild Fruit has ear-marked Creation as its new home. The look is all drapes and burgundy and there'll apparently be "dramatic-historic themes". So nice and understated, then.

Enigma

10 Ship Street, The Lanes

01273 328439

Not the chicest club in town, but for those whose priority is great music, not trendy toilets, this is the place to be on a Saturday night. Ninja Tune's Phonic Hoop is a beautiful mish mash of old-school hip-hop, jazzy breaks, drum and bass... anything goes as long as the emphasis is firmly on funk and every tunes a floor filler. Imprint (hip hop) Thursday.

Escape

Marine Parade, Kemp Town

01273 606906

Away from the seafront, The Escape is probably Brighton's most successful club. Set in a perfect Art Deco building just the Kemp Town side of the Brighton Pier, it is young but not too young, hip but not too hip and dangerous but not too dangerous. Beware though, there's always a queue. An Evening With The Vegas Lounge with Steve Hillier on Friday, Mezzanine with Norman Jay are the top nights.

Funky Buddha Lounge

169 Kings Road Arches, Brighton

01273 725541

The winner of the last Juicy Award, the Funky Buddha is small but perfectly formed. From the funky dance floor to the chilled out lounge, it's just there and feels just right. Created with an eye on design - it's one of the few clubs to take its shape into consideration - it boasts state of the art light and sound equipment. Supercharged (breaks and beats) Thursday, The Last days Of Disco (what do you think?) Thursday,

Stompaphunk (electro funk) Friday, Soul Weekender (classic soul) Saturday, Sweet Like Chocolate (soul and garage) Monday, Move (progressive) Tuesday.

Hanbury Ballroom
83 St George's Street, Kemp Town
01273 605798
All sorts of things go on at the Hanbury, but Clubs-wise check out Stick It On, the legendary DIY night on Saturday. Visit www.stickiton.co.uk

Honey Club
214 King's Road Arches
07000 446939
Remade and remodelled, the Honey Club is a sophisticated and stylish haven for dance types, and until Cream opens (whenever, if ever...) this is the closest in Brighton to a 'super club' with three gleaming bars, Tardis-like toilets and a spacious chill out room in the back arch. There's a new balcony bar to watch the revellers while for the more adventurous there's enough podium space for those eager to strut their funky stuff.

The Jazz Rooms
10 Ship Street, The Lanes
01273 321692
If modern jazz is your thang - jazz funk, Afro-jazz, Latin jazz, whatever - this will be your Nirvana. Down in this small, dark basement DJ Russ Dewbury - the man behind the Brighton Festival Jazz Bop - spins a sweat-soaked array of discs that, thanks to a conversation-killing sound system, sound fab. It's the sort of place where people go to dance and be friendly, not show off and be seen.

The Joint
West Street, Brighton
01273 321692
Smoky basement club with kitsch, cosy seating and an intimate feel (it's that red lighting that does it) that aims to emulate that boho beatnik vibe. If you're into lounge and all that easy listening thang, then this is the place for you. Dynamite Boogaloo (disco trash) is the top night on Thursday.

The Ocean Rooms
Morley Street, Kemp Town
01273 699069
bar: Mon-Fri 10pm-2am, Sat 8pm-2am
restaurant: Mon-Fri 8pm-2am, Closed Sundays
Had one of my best nights recently here with Felix Da Housecat. Said to have the best sound system in town, there's a cushioned-walled restaurant on the middle floor and a basement bar spruced up by glowing UV tabletops. Dollywood (house, soul, jazz) Wednesday, Gossip (cabaret and disco) Thursday, the very lovely Ninja Tunes have a night on Friday, Space (house) Saturday, Minimelt (dum'n'bass) Tuesday.

Pool
8-9 Marine Parade, Kemp Town
01273 624091
www.cocolatte.net
Does not offer cabaret like the more

traditional boozers. With music from the last three decades, Monday night has become very popular with everyone on the scene. Weekends have a welcoming atmosphere and with resident DJs from London's Atelier and Heaven, Revenge finally has some proper competition. Coco Latte, again a London influence, is every Sunday night for those who don't want to leave the weekend behind. Bent Resurrection on Thursday is another top night.

The Pussycat (at the Zap)
Kings Road Arches, Brighton
01273 202407

Five years and going strong, this is a one-nighter that's been going so long it's an institution. The Pussycat operates every Friday night at the Zap and kicks out a disco friendly mix of hard house and kicking glam.

Revenge
32, Old Steine, Brighton
01273 606064

The largest gay club in the south of England, Revenge has a faithful following of gay men and women and their straight guests. There are two floors to check out with two different styles depending on your taste. The atmosphere is happy and hedonistic - the ideal start to the weekend. Less room to move on Saturdays when it's hands in the air dance anthems 'til 2am. If all that's not enough, the second floor has panoramic views out to sea and over the floodlit pier.

The Tavern Club
Castle Square, Central Brighton
01273 827641

Every Friday at The Tavern Club is a night for the girls at Refresh and they are still packing them in five years down the line. The music is trashy and again, although welcome, men are few and far between. When the dance floor gets to full to strut your stuff, it is pretty easy to get someone to budge over on the huge sofas.

Volks Tavern
Madeira Drive, Kemp Town
01273 682828

Volks always was the perfect antidote to both the big, showy nightclubs and the bigger name beachfront places. It was the place you would go if you wanted a good night free of poseurs and tourists. Happily, it still is. Despite opening the basement and expanding, it's still groovy and slightly down-at-heel. Bargain beer prices and cheap entry have long attracted a loyal following of friendly up-for-it clubbers. Stash (hip hop) on Wednesday, Lunarcy (techno and breakbeat) Friday, Our Thing (Catskills Records night) Saturday.

Zap
Kings Road Arches, Brighton
01273 202407

The oldest and the first. With two main rooms and a maze of arch shaped corridors to explore, the Zap is the original raver's playground. Sin (Wild Fruit night) on Thursday, Superstars (old hits and party anthems) Monday.

● CLUBBING GUIDE FOR THE MID-20s

BY BELINDA & SAL @ MIDNIGHT

Dynamite Boogaloo @ The Joint

The Joint, West Street, Central Brighton
01273 321692

every Thursday, £4/£3

If you are after fabulous fun on the dancefloor and are happy to jump around to everything from Abba's Dancing Queen and We Will Rock You by Queen to Kids by Kylie & Robbie then Dynamite Boogaloo is definitely the night for you! The happy, albeit sweaty atmosphere that greets party-goers every Thursday night promises not to disappoint the eye or the ear. Boogaloo Stu works his magic on the decks and dazzles in his flamboyant suits while Dolly Rocket entertains during the dancefloor interval with naughty tunes and the best cleavage in Brighton! If mad dancing, larger than life personalities and chocolate willies is what you want from a night out, Dynamite Boogaloo is the perfect destination.

Big Beat Boutique

Concorde 2, Madeira Drive, Kemp Town
01273 606460

second and fourth Friday of the month,
£8/ £6-50 concs

This bi-weekly Friday nighter at the Concorde 2 has become one of clubland's institutions. Not only is the mighty Fat Boy Slim resident, but the Boutique proudly showcases some of the world's best DJ's spinning beats, house and cut-up breaks to a faithful following of sweaty backed clubbers. From its humble beginnings four years ago at the Concorde, the relocated Concorde - now Concorde 2 is more school hall than state of the art club haven, but the vibe remains killer. Believe the hype!

BoyGirl

The Ocean Rooms, Morley Street,
Old Steine
01273 699069

every Saturday, £8/£7 concs

With its combination of funky house in the dingy basement, classic house in the middle floor and relaxed beats cushioning the ears in the velvet covered VIP room upstairs, BoyGirl is an extravaganza that promises to please everyone. With a variety of DJs every week including residents and very special guests this night mixes up a storm that is best not to be missed.

Mezzanine

The Escape, Marine Parade,
Kemp Town seafront
01273 606906

every Saturday , £8/£7 concs

Aimed at the more discerning clubber, Mezzanine offers people the opportunity to warm up slowly and then let it all hang out with two floors of killer tunes including a mix of hip hop, funk, new jazz, breaks and house. Located in the Escape, one of the more popular venues in Brighton, Mezzanine keeps all the punters happy by offering loud music mixed by the resident Blackgrass DJs alongside secluded spots where the speakers are turned down low for more chilled out chatting zones. Perfect for those of us with not quite enough energy to keep going all night!

Phonic Hoop @ The Enigma
10 Ship Street, the Lanes
01273 328439
every Saturday, £6/£5 concs

Robert Louis is something of a breakbeat luminaries around town. He's got his own radio show Unfold, he's got his own record label Tru Thoughts and if that's not enough, he's the figurehead behind Brighton's most reliable weekly beat fest Phonic Hoop. Well into it's third year in residency at the Enigma and the Phonic Hoop Express shows no sign of slowing. The loosely formed musical foundation of hip-hop, drum and bass and everything in-between has kept the crowds queuing, as well as attracting a constant flow of top tier DJ talent. Weekly residents include Rob himself, Al Stylus, Bonobo, Amalgamation of Soundz and Rodney P and Skitz with the decks being recently blessed by special guests Richard Dorfmiester, LTJ Bukem and DJ Bizniz. The Enigma might not be the most glamorous club in Brighton, but for a beat fuelled Saturday shakedown Phonic Hoop is one of life's few certainties.

Steady Rockin'
The Beach, Kings Road Arches,
Brighton seafront
01273 722272
monthly, £8-10

One of Brighton's newer nights, Steady Rockin' has already gathered a staunch following of hip hoppers and funk-soul brothers and sisters. The Beach has always hosted the seafront's more credible club nights and Steady Rockin' is no exception. The list of talented turntablists has included Norman Jay, 4Hero and Cash Money. The massive circular bar inside the club means queuing for drinks needn't rule the night, but be warned the queue to enter can be a big one. So get there early!

Supercharged
Funky Buddha Lounge, 169 Kings Road Arches, Brighton seafront
01273 725541
Wednesday's weekly, £4/£3 concs

Wednesday night at this cosy and stylish venue is considered to be one of Brighton's best clubbing experiences. Founding talents Krafty Kuts and Skool of Thought are dedicated to bringing Brighton the hottest in hip hop, funk and breaks and with basslines to make your jaw rattle this night is a guaranteed winner. 2001 saw Supercharged grow from breakbeat mecca to a fully-fledged record label with storming releases from the founders as well as fresh beats favourites. The sheer quality of Supercharged ensures this respected night will run and run.

● CLUBBING GUIDE FOR THE OVER-30s

TOP TEN CLUBS BY LOUISE ACFORD, CLUBBING EDITOR OF *THE INSIGHT*

Etch @ Concorde 2

Madeira Drive,
Kemp Town seafront
01273 606460
first Friday of the month,
9pm-3am, £8/£6

Resident Mr Scruff keeps it unreal playing his own blend of beats and breaks at this very, very popular night.

Stompaphunk @ The Funky Buddha Lounge

169 Kings Road Arches,
Brighton seafront
01273 725541
every Friday night,
10pm, £6/£5

Local boys Stompaphunk mix jackin' house, tech funk and electro on sea.

Positive Sound System @ Concorde 2

Madeira Drive,
Kemp Town seafront
01273 606460
third Saturday of every month,
10pm, £7/£7.50

Positive at the Concorde 2 is a true Brighton legend- always a guaranteed winner!

Class @ The Pressure Point

Richmond Place, Old Steine
first Friday of the month, 10pm, £6

Old skool boys and girls get messy to acid house and breaks/techno. Live sets from Liquid Laugh, if you eat all your dinner up.

Bedrock @ The Beach

Kings Road Arches, Brighton seafront
01273 722272
1st Friday of the month, 10pm, £10/£8

Hard house and techno courtesy of John Digweed and Phil Thompson.

Soul Weekender @ Funky Buddha Lounge

169 Kings Road Arches,
Brighton seafront
01273 725541
every Saturday, 10pm, £10/£9

Classic soul, raw funk and good grooves from back in the day- pure class, no cheese!

Phonic Hoop @ The Enigma

10 Ship Street, The Lanes
01273 328439
Every Saturday, 10pm, £6/£5/£4

Residents (Robert Luis chief spinner) plus special guests play the finest break beat and drum n bass.

Roots Garden @ The Jazz Place

10 Ship Street, The Lanes
01273 328439
every Tuesday night, 10pm,
£3/£4 after 11pm

Mid week reggae and roots at one of Brighton's most chilled, intimate venues.

The Boutique @ Concorde 2

Madeira Drive,
Kemp Town seafront
01273 606460
2nd and 4th Friday of the month, 10pm,
£10/£9
No club listing is complete without the Boutique, this splendid night continues,

deservedly so, to be one of Brighton's favourites.

Vavavavoom! @ The Brighton Gloucester

Gloucester Place, North Laine
01273 688011
3rd Thursday of the month, 10pm,
£7.50/£7
Decadence and deviance directed by Stella Starr - dress according to the theme and leave inhibitions at the door.

TEEN LIFE (& TWEENAGE) 05.6

05.6

● **WRITTEN BY
LIZ FLETCHER,
DANIELLE HAYWARD,
HANNAH POTTER AND
DAVID IMMS AT
PATCHAM HIGH SCHOOL**

● Brighton and Hove City is definitely the place to be for today's teenagers, offering a wide range of entertainment and activities to suit all interests. Weave your way through its numerous streets and discover some of the most individual places you'll ever see.

Two organisations that might be useful are the Brighton Youth Theatre (01273 673211) and Brighton Youth Orchestra (01273 643350).

The Animal House
12 Bond Street, North Laine
01273 206836
Like walking into Noah's Ark! Soft toys, ornaments, mobiles and more than just moggies.

The Arches Between the Piers
The artists' quarters. Consume fish and chips, gamble in the many arcades or simply soak up the sun.

The Beach
This fun filled place can keep you occupied for hours, with beach volleyball, basketball courts or people watching. And it's free!

The Bead Shop
21 Sydney Street, North Laine
01273 675077
This amazing and unique shop contains a cascade of pendants, threads, fasteners and, not surprisingly...beads!

Brighton Pier
Packed with amusements this has to be a teen paradise as well as a national landmark. Rides and games for everyone and the novelty shops and food stalls should sweeten your palate.

Caramella
29a Kensington Gardens, North Laine
01273 570118
If you love sweets then this is the shop for you. Everything you desire and more!

Cissy Mo
25 Church Street, North Laine
01273 205060
38 Sydney Street, North Laine
01273 607777

Kitsch paradise! With a cool selection of the funkiest bits and bobs in Brighton.

The Concorde 2

Madeira Drive, Kemp Town

01273 606460

Rock on at this top music venue and bar. Many famous acts have appeared here including The White Stripes, The Lost Prophets and Hundred Reasons. Most nights over 18s only.

The Duke of York's Cinema

Preston Circus

01273 602503/626261

Not just your everyday cinema. Re-screenings of classics and minority interest films are shown on this screen. Film festivals held at times. Cosy.

The Dumb Waiter

28 Sydney Street, North Laine

01273 602526

Funky, friendly atmosphere with a vast vegetarian range of grub!

Fat Mamas

15 Sydney Street, North Laine

01273 685110

Fun and friendly atmosphere stocking clothing, accessories, boards and more.

Ju-Ju

24 Gloucester Road,

North Laine

01273 673161

New and second hand clothing. Excellent value if you're short of cash and needing the greatest fashions.

Kensington's

1 Kensington Garden, North Laine

01273 570963

Yummy food, friendly staff and cool balcony seating where you can watch the world below.

The Level

Without a doubt, the top skating attraction locally with competitions from time to time.

Oddballs

24 Kensington Gardens, North Laine

01273 696068

The place to go if you're into a playground craze. Selling diablos, yo yo's, juggling accessories, skating equipment, clothing etc.

The Pavilion Gardens

Relaxing area with beautiful views. Chilling, chatting or just wandering through, these gardens are the place for you.

Planet Gadget

39 Gardner Street, North Laine

01273-603800

19 Meeting House Lane, The Lanes

01273-227778

73 George Street, Hove

01273 772636

Everything from the latest gizmos to the fun fashions. A world of choice.

Rag Freak

15 Cranbourne Street, The Lanes

01273 775117

A Gothic haven brimming with clothing and accessories for your darker side.

Rounder Records

19 Brighton Square, The Lanes
01273 325440
Independent music store stocking everything from steps to slipknot, plus tickets for gigs around the city.

The T-Chest

13 Gardener Street, North Laine
01273 620950
Fun and funky T-shirts for everyone. Snappy slogans or pretty patterns, you're bound to find something to "Oooh, suit you sir".

To Be Worn Again

51 Providence Place, London Road
01273 624500
24a Sydney Street, North Laine
01273 680296
Relive past fashions with this fab collection of retro clothing.

● TWEENAGE BY HAYLEY SENSICLE (AGE 10)

Brighton is a fun and lively city, where you can do nearly everything that a tweenager wants to do, like shop, eat out and have fun!!

These are my six fave places:

1. Bella Pasta, *the Lanes*

My fave restaurant, it has excellent spag bol and the puddings are great.

2. The Pier

Great rides, especially the waltzers, they are my fave.

3. Churchill Square

The best shopping mall there is. I like H+M and O'Neill, the clothes there are *the business*.

4. The Bead Shop, *North Laine*

You can make really cool jewellery and you choose everything yourself.

5. Quadland, *at Washbrooks Farm Centre, Hurstpierpoint (01273 834403)*

I went quadbiking there for my b'day, it was so cool, and we got really muddy.

6. Turner Dumbrell Workshops, *North End, Ditchling*

Loads of craft workshops, including painting on pottery. I have decorated flowerpots, biscuit jars and plates. They have so many colours you can paint anything on anything.

● *Well I was born on one side of Hove Park and now I live on the other, so how handy was that to move? I am one of few Brighton folk to be born here and having lived in Ireland, Scotland and the USA, the lure of mussel and the odd cockle was just too much. Favourite pub (this week anyway) has to be The Colonnade, right next door to the Theatre Royal. It was probably quite fashionable about 50 years ago, but it's still fascinating looking at the faded signed photos of various E-list celebs who've been on stage at the Theatre (check out the sexy picture of Playaway's Brian Cant). It's the best place to chill out after a long day's work (but keep that to yourself). Once we've got the engines burning, a trip to The Honey Club is in order. I don't know about you, but there's nothing more off-putting than going to a club where everyone's a complete minger. Well not at The Honey Club. It may have been in the ladies toilet, but I've met male models and the like in there. Gorgeous. Saturday nights are the best because they'll bring the best-looking people to the front of the queue. Hence I normally get in the club about 3:30am.*

John Chittenden *born and bred and still living just off Dyke Road.*

● In the city that only stops for coffee, more and more are being drawn to the glittering lights of the gay scene. Painting the town pink has become one of Brighton's main attractions with Revenge as a temple of worship for the many scene queens. It boasts 'keeping it sweet seven nights a week' with the most recent addition to the club's schedule being MASS on a Sunday night. The obvious place to start our queer tour is Kemp Town, affectionately known as 'Kamptown' and St James's Street as the heart of the gay village. This is the Soho of London and the Canal Street of Manchester in a way which is so typically Brighton, where you'll find the new classy bars but the more traditional leisure activities also available in all corners of this hedonistic sea side location. From saunas to gay ice-skating at the Brighton Centre - there is everything you could possibly need. Many establishments now see themselves as gay friendly, and undoubtedly most are genuine as the rainbow flag continues to appear on every street corner. Bona Foodie should not go unnoticed, a gay run and owned deli which serves eager Kemp Town foodies.

One place which always seems to remain predominantly gay is the nudist beach, probably because it is near to the cruising ground at Dukes Mound known as The Bushes. It's not all in your face though. There are community projects for those who don't just live for Cher and Steps such as the martial arts or the Ourstory project, a gay and lesbian history group who meet once a month. On August 10, Gay Pride will again take the flamboyant floats and 10,000 followers from the sea front to Preston Park. This eight-hour free party gets bigger and brighter every year with dance tents, stalls, rides, cabaret, food, drink and performances on the main stage.

This is by no means a complete guide to gay Brighton. As with all communities, things are constantly changing. For more information and listings look at the web-sites or pick up the local magazines *G-Scene* and *360*.

● ACCOMMODATION

Most hotels listed in our Accommodation section are gay-friendly, but the hotels listed below are more exclusively gay hotels. Most are aimed at gay men, but I guess you'll find out what's what soon enough. Those looking for gay-friendly households should make Freddie's noticeboard in the Scene 22 café (129 St James's Street, Kemp Town **01273 626682 www.scene22.com**) their first port of call.

The Amsterdam

11-12 Marine Parade, Kemp Town
01273 688825
www.amsterdam.co.uk
Bar, sauna and hotel. Hotel prices range from £40 for a single room and £75 for a sea-view double in the winter. Check the web-site for summer prices are they will surely increase. Many of the rooms have a theme at no extra cost. You can choose between being Caesar in the Roman room, Cleo-Patra in the Egyptian room and many others. The sauna is £5 (half price for residents) and is open until 4am in the week and 6am on a Friday and Saturday night.

Court Craven

2 Atlingworth Street, Kemp Town
01273 607710
Gay friendly hotel a hop and a skip from all the major seafront clubs with prices to keep their young(ish) clientele happy. Prices start from £25 per person. Vegetarian breakfasts available.

Cowards Guest House

12 Upper Rock Gardens, Kemp Town
01273 692677
www.surf.to/cowards
Exclusively for gay men but while most come down for the clubbing, there are no age barriers here. Prices start at £30 for a single

Hudsons Guest House

22 Devonshire Place, Central Brighton
01273 683642 Fax: 0870 1275405
info@hudsonshotel.com

www.hudsonshotel.com
An exclusively lesbian & gay guesthouse stylishly converted from an early 19th century townhouse to offer clean, comfortable rooms, some fully en suite but all with televisions, tea & coffee and telephones.

Alpha Lodge

19 New Steine, Central Brighton
01273 609632

Ashley Court Guest House

33 Montpelier Road, Montpelier
01273 739916

New Europe Hotel

31-32 Marine Parade, Kemp Town
01273 624462

Shalimar Hotel

23 Broad Street, Kemp Town
01273 605316

● BARS

Amsterdam

11/12 Marine Parade, Kemp Town
01273 688825
One of the biggest, best-established gay bars on the seafront. Based on the tried-and-tested bar and sauna formula, the Amsterdam has managed to create a relaxed atmosphere for its mixed gay locals. With a predominantly wooden décor, this bar has an uncluttered vibe while still feeling fairly intimate. The seafront location makes the Amsterdam a convenient pre-club detour as well as a

real suntrap, ideal for those summer drinking sessions.

The Aquarium

6 Steine Street, Kemp Town

01273 605525

Old style, it's solid rather than fashionable.

Candy Bar

33 St James Street, Kemp Town

Sister of the legendary lesbian Londoner, The Candy is what Kemp Town kittens have been waiting for.

Charles Street

8-9 Marine Parade, Kemp Town

01273 624091

A slice of metro-chic finally hit Brighton's gay scene last year with this two-level bar (Charles Street) and club (Pool) on the seafront. The swish downstairs bar, Charles Street, offers daytime table service and food, sofas, strategically lit standing room (you'll see) and a glam walkway for that all-important entrance. Positively teeming at the weekend with pre-clubbers, this bar's success seemed almost guaranteed - if only they wouldn't announce last orders and promote the club over the tannoy in such a tacky fashion. The upstairs club, Pool, although clearly the poorer sibling, still exudes bags of style. Having found its feet after an initial identity crisis, it's now the perfect intimate venue for one-nighters to suit all tastes. And when nanny knocks on Charles Street's door at 11, it seems rude

not to sashay upstairs and hit the dance floor.

Kruze

8 Madeira Drive, Kemp Town

01273 608133

A trendy gay bar, perfect for those who love to drink in style. By day, it's got a quiet American Piano Bar atmosphere with lounge singers, but by night things change when the serious clubbers move in. Cocktails are available (£2.95) from 5pm every day, while upstairs in the Lizard Lounge the bunny boys will serve them to your table - and with an offer like that you are guaranteed to be back next day. It's very busy on Fridays and Saturdays with the boys preparing themselves for Pool or Revenge.

● CAFÉS

Redroaster

1d St James Street, Kemp Town

01273 686668

Can it really be the only cafe in town to roast their own coffee beans? Last year we gave this spacious Euro style café a bit of stick over its slow service. Happily, now under new management, that's all changed. Very gay friendly.

The Sanctuary Café

51 Brunswick Street East, Hove

01273 770002

The winner of the "Best Café" gong at the last Juicy Awards, The Sanctuary is a refuge from the madness of the high street. Last time we called it a "funky but friendly Vegetarian café." And that's still essentially the case. Late night coffee and cake on the ground and upper floors with poetry readings, cult films and Brighton Underground network meetings in the Beatnik basement, and sunny lunches out of windowless windows. The look is sculpted Boho, the vibe predominantly gay.

Scene 22

129 St James's Street, Kemp Town
01273 626682
www.scene22.com
Just off the Old Steine, Scene 22 is Brighton's only gay shop and coffee bar. It's fully stocked with club wear, safe sex aids and toys for both men and women. Those looking for accommodation in gay friendly households should make Freddie's noticeboard first port of call.

● CLUBS

Creation

West Street, Central Brighton
01273 321628
And a £5million refit later... Due to open late May on the site of what was once Paradox/Club Barcelona, Creation will be Wild Fruit's new home.

Pool

8-9 Marine Parade, Kemp Town
01273 624091
www.cocolatte.net
Revenge finally has some proper competition. Coco Latte, again a London influence, is every Sunday night

for those who don't want to leave the weekend behind. Bent Resurrection on Thursday is another top night.

Refresh @ The Tavern Club

Castle Square, Central Brighton
01273 827641
Every Friday at The Tavern Club is a night for the girls for Refresh and they are still packing them in five years down the line. When the dance floor gets to full to strut your stuff, it is usually pretty easy to get someone to budge over on the huge sofas.

Revenge

32, Old Steine, Brighton
01273 606064
The largest gay club in the south of England, Revenge has a faithful following of gay men and women and their straight guests. It also has a reputation for consistently wild soirees (and considering it's open 6 nights a week that's some feat!). There are two floors to check out with two different styles depending on your taste. The atmosphere is happy and hedonistic - the ideal start to the weekend. Less room to move on Saturdays when it's hands in the air dance anthems 'til 2am. If all that's not enough, the second floor has panoramic views out to sea and over the floodlit pier.

Wet Pussy @ Pool

8-9 Marine Parade, Kemp Town
01273 624091
Despite the vulgar name, this night

organised by the Candy Bar is where Brighton's babes get their grove on once a month. This busy Friday nighter is soon to go fortnightly because the girls just can't get enough. The glitter covered go-go dancers do make it slightly on the tacky side but altogether it is good light-hearted entertainment. Gay male guests are very welcome, but usually have places they would rather be.

● PUBS

Barley Mow

92 St George's Road, Kemp Town
01273 682259
Very mixed and probably the most 'gay friendly' pub in kemp Town. At a first glance it may look like a traditional pub with the velvet covered pews, but it has a lovely friendly atmosphere. The food is home made and plentiful and is served well into the night (about 10pm). The fish is fresh from Shoreham. The Mexican-style chilli con carne with rice and fired potato skins (£6.25) is one to try if you're hungry. The menu changes weekly and is different at the weekend.

The Bow Street Runner

62 Brunswick Street West, Hove
01273 327688
Well, it's about time we listed something that's not in Kemp Town. A nice, gay-friendly pub. In Hove.

The Bulldog Tavern

31, St James Street, Kemp Town
01273 684097

This is your typical gay man's drinking establishment, apart from maybe the bingo on a Monday night which is more popular with grannies the world over. The black and white photography which covers the walls leaves little to the imagine, the speakers blare the inevitable Kylie and such like at the weekend and happy hour is exactly what is says it is. Whatever floats your boat it's worth going for the experience, even if it is a one off. The staff are charming and if you give it a chance this place could possibly be your second home.

Dr Brighton's

16 Kings Road, Brighton seafront
01273 328765
It looks like a run-of-the-mill, traditional seaside pub, but it's quickly obvious that looks can be deceiving. Dr Brighton's is a legendary welcoming local without the cliqueyness of other gay pubs. Official host of the pre-Wild Fruit shenanigans, there's no room for mundane traditions here. Last year we wrote that they've got 12 different flavoured Schnapps on offer. Well, now they've increased that to 21.

The Hanbury Arms and Ballroom

83 St George's Street,
Kemp Town
01273 605789
www.zelnet.com
rhall@zelnet.com
Has all sorts of alternative nights from comedy to jazz and electronic soul.

The Harlequin

43 Providence Place, Preston Circus

01273 620630

e-mail: harlequin.brighton@talk21.com
One of the few gay bars outside Kemp
Town, this spacious late night venue is
tucked down a dark ally behind
Woolworth's on London Road. Go on a
Monday for karaoke and pretty much
every night if you want the bright lights
of the cabaret and the disco sized dance
floor. It's perfect if you want a few
drinks after a late showing at the Duke
of York's cinema.

The Marlborough

4 Princes Street, Kemp Town

01273 570028

Tucked away behind the bustle of
Pavilion Parade, The Marlborough has
been known as the lesbian's local in the
past but although more female
dominated than the other gay pubs is
now much more mixed. A film screen is
opening in the theatre upstairs so when
there are no shows on, you can pay £2 to
watch anything from Carry On classics
to art house obscurities.

Prince Regent

29 Regency Square,

Brighton seafront

01273 329962

Step through the door and enter a time
warp. It is as though this pub has been
frozen in the era of Prince Regent.
Probably then, as now, this is a relaxed
haunt for a mix of gay and straight
drinkers. The no-frill's style of most of

Brighton's pubs hasn't touched The
Regent, where recreating the grandeur
of a royal hangout is more the theme.
Ornate brassware and cheeky cherubs
adorn the walls and not a DJ in sight.

The Queen's Arms

7, George Street, Kemp Town

01273 696873

www.queensarmsbrighton.co.uk

The rainbow flags blow with pride seven
nights a week at Brighton's premier
cabaret bar. Although male dominated it
is popular with old and young, some
things are truly timeless. At this place
life is undoubtedly a cabaret. Karaoke
competitions are on weekly so you can
have a go yourself if you think you've
got what it takes.

Queen's Head

3 Steine Street, Old Steine

01273 602939

www.zelnet.com

If the Freddie Mercury picture hanging
outside isn't enough to tempt you inside
this gay local then the home-cooked
food will. There are DJs two or three
times a week. Student night on Tuesday
with drink offers. £5 for any baguette or
jacket and a pint/glass of wine/soft drink
is a popular offer. Sunday Roast (£5.95)
is 'ab fab' and 'well endowed' says the
chef, Mrs Mark. Not intimidating as
some gay bars can be. The upstairs
lounge bar is available for private hire
for free. At the weekends it's a lively
place to drink before cruising round the
corner to Pool or Revenge.

The Regency Tavern

32 Russell Square, Brighton seafront
01273 325652

Wonderfully camp pub tucked behind Regency Square where landlord Chris Ryan is more Bet Lynch than Alex Gilroy and serves his pints under the watchful eye of a bunch of gold cherubs. At last orders, a glitterball replaces the standard lighting as the PA croons a midnight tune to its largely gay clientele. Sunday lunch is exquisite, although Chris compares it to the first day at the Harrods sale. No booking so get there early! The vegetarian menu is one of the big pulls and the loos are possibly Brighton's most glamorous.

Royal Pavilion Tavern

7-8 Castle Square, Central Brighton
01273 827641

A Regular Joe kind of pub which harbours a well kept secret upstairs in the Tavern club. Once the bar shuts it's time to shimmy up the stairs for a Sixties showdown on Saturday nights, or the rock/indie nights on Wednesdays and Thursdays. Fresh on Friday caters for a mixed gay and TV crowd, while MFI (Mad For It) celebrates everything Mancunian mid-week.

The White Horse

30 Camelford Street, Kemp Town
01273 603726

A gay pub for all ages that still has the warm atmosphere of the local it once was. One of the few gay pubs to still have a pool table, you will be enticed by the drink offers and no cabaret policy.

● SHOPS

Cardome

47a St James Street, Kemp Town
01273 692916

You know what it's like when you have to get a card at the last minute and the only ones you can find are not suitable in the slightest. Well the answer to all your problems is right here, where you are sure to see something for everyone and for every occasion. If you have time to go downstairs, be warned; don't expect to see more cards.

Clone Zone

32, St James Street,
Kemp Town
01273 626442
www.clonezone.co.uk

One of seven branches, this is the UK's premier gay lifestyle company. They sell everything you need from calendars to clothes, videos, books, magazines and products for those with more specific tastes. Opening hours are GST (gay standard time) which is late (closes at 8pm on a Friday and Saturday).

Out

4 & 7 Dorset Street,
North Laine
01273 623356

Exclusively gay and lesbian bookshop. Along with magazines and videos there's a wide range of gay literature and art on offer.

Penetration

28 Sydney Street, North Laine

01273 623839

Body piercings. Each to their own.

The Pink Pamper

74 St James Street, Kemp Town

01273 608060

Hair, beauty, manicures, massage, tanning, nail extensions, aromatherapy, Reiki and much, much more. Mostly for men.

● USEFUL INFORMATION

Ishigaki Ju-Jitsu Club

Stanley Deason Centre, Wilson Avenue, Whitehawk

www.ishigaki.org.uk

Older Lesbians & Gay Men's Forum

01273 625963

Home visiting and outreach service and support group for over 50's.

GLAM

01273 707963

www.glam-brighton.co.uk

Arts and Media projects and training.

National Lesbian & Gay Switchboard (24 hour)

0207 8377324

Brighton Lesbian & Gay Switchboard (5pm-11pm)

01273 204050

Allsorts Youth Project

01273 721211

www.allsortsyouth.org.uk

Beaumont Society - Transgender Support Group

01582 412220

www.beaumontsociety.org.uk

The Gender Trust

07000 790347

Coming Out

www.comingout.org.uk

Pink Parents

www.deep-blue-design.co.uk/pinkparents/

(Thurs: 7pm-10pm) 0117 3775794

Gay Dads Support Group

www.raintrk.co.uk/gaydads-uk/

Families And Friends Of Lesbians & Gays - parents support group -

01454 852418

www.fflag.org.uk

Mainliners

0207 582 5226

National Aids Helpline

08005 67123

National Drugs Helpline

08007 76600

THT Aids Treatments

08459 470047

THT Helpline

0207 242 1010

06

● Brighton and Hove is a city of opportunity, full to bursting with new people, new ideas and new energy. From the students grafting and sweating at university to the endless stream of removal vans from London and beyond, it's a city which welcomes and thrives on new blood. But if you imagine that it's only in the past ten years that it's been such a honeypot to out-of-towners you misunderstand where Brighton comes from.

Entrepreneurs have been seizing the day since the great storms of 1703 and 1705 when disaster struck and the lower town and most of the shore were destroyed. The population dropped to 2,000 until a gaggle of entrepreneurs spotted a golden opportunity to take advantage of the falling house prices and begin acquiring property. Sound familiar?

By the 1700's, its fortunes were about to be secured as Brighton's two most influential innovators spotted the untapped potential of the good old English Channel. As Dr Richard Russell began to spread the word that Brighton's sea-bathing held miraculous healing properties, the town became London's favourite seaside holiday destination and weekend treat. The court of Prince Regent packed their bathers and set up their seaside home in a new palace fit for a king. Characterised by its flavours of the Orient, it was a brash statement of "Prinny's" flamboyant tastes and the extravagant court life which would soon become the talk of the town. Before long even French aristocrats were fleeing their Revolution to Brighton's new social scene where they found a more accepting home for their ostentatious lifestyles.

Extravagance became Brighton's byword as Regency architects began to showcase their ideas along the now famous seafront from the crescents of Kemp Town to Brunswick Town. Charles Busby, Amon and Henry Wilds were the kingpins in this fertile period of architecture, willing its residents to follow their lead and making a natural home for the future generations of inventors and poets, artists and entrepreneurs.

And the traffic continued to head south, peaking over the last few years as the mass influx of out of towners, mostly from London, burst the city's banks, sent its house prices rocketing and pushed the good folk of Hanover into Saltdean and (God forbid) Peacehaven. But there's nothing that this little city likes more than a challenge and if people still want to live here, then maybe with a bit of ingenuity something could be arranged. Like a good maitre d' anticipating a big tip, Brighton and Hove is prepared to find some room.

The result is an explosion of creativity and style in the most unlikely places. Hove, once known for its blue rinses and zimmer frames, is having a second childhood and flirting outrageously with sexy young architects and suave property developers. Glass facades and loft-style apartments, glass bricks and fantasy gardens leading down to the beach. It's enough to make Brighton blush. Except that Hove's brash big sister is up to the same kind of tricks herself.

Once upon a time (last year, actually) an old fashioned department store called Hanningtons dominated The Lanes, its age and place in Brighton's history giving it an avuncular position in the café society surrounding it. Now, Hanningtons is no more, and what do you think The Lanes has done - even before the dust has settled? Only sneaked a new set of loft-style apartments into Ship Street and their groovy residents. And for more than just a sleepover too. You'd have thought that someone somewhere would take these young upstarts to task, but then you remember that this the way things happen here and that everything is all done in the shadow - and under the silent patronage of - of the most celebrated royal rule breaker, The Prince Regent. We could go on. The North Laine, once a warren of hippy chic and arty cafes, is about to blossom into a sophisticated inner city piazza, with space reclaimed from old warehouses. A state of the art library complex will link the Prince Regent with new office space and (more) loft-style apartments designed by Sir Conran himself.

In previous editions of the Juicy Guide, we've suggested that you're either a Brightonian or a Hoveite. But things aren't quite that simple anymore and the distinctions are slowly beginning to blur. It's all down to the ability of the property developers and architects who are redesigning the image of the city. But they won't change the spirit of a city whose middle name is Evolution.

Wherever you look, from suburban Preston Park to the bohemian quarter of Kemp Town, there are new developments which will bring new neighbours to town. But while the old assumptions might be built on shifting sand, they aren't dead quite yet. Social workers and teachers will still head for the pubs and community feel of Hanover. Expensive cars and big wallets go for the swimming pools of Withdean and Hove Park. And the gay crowd will still feast on the bars and clubs of central Brighton and Hove.

"People spend more time choosing a video recorder than they do a house," Peter Gladwell of Halifax Property Services told us. "On day one, my clients tell me that they want a period character house with garden, garage and seaview. Very often, by the third day of looking, their specification will have changed completely; they realise that a period house near the seafront in Brighton will get them a patio garden and nowhere to park their car so they start thinking about the bigger, newer properties towards the north side of Hove. They think Brighton and end up in Hove. They think seafront and they end up near a park. They think Victorian and end up Thirties. But many haven't got a clue about what a town's really like to live in."

Prices were checked as we went to press at the end of March 2002, but Brighton and Hove is a city moving up in the world, and as more people decide to chill-out by the seaside, the prices will rise and fall and rise again. Until fairly recently, estate agents would tell sellers that a Londoner would pay anything you ask. No longer; while it's true that the proceeds from a small flat in Central London would buy a mansion in Brunswick Town, the average house price is now enough to make you think carefully about where you choose to buy.

● FINDING YOUR TRIBE

The "villages" of Brighton and Hove are as distinct as they are in any city and gather their tribes tightly within their boundaries. This is the key to finding a home rather than a house, and any estate agent who asks how much you want to spend before he asks who you want to live next to should be rapped over the head with your copy of the Juicy Guide. The Greek statues on the front lawns of Withdean's castles might let on that there's money in them there hills, but if you're looking for the local pub or a late-night grocer, this is not your patch. Kemp Town with its bohemian reputation won't seduce many born and bred families with its patio gardens and three-storey houses, but its increasingly Boho feel and Council-funded facades has tempted the likes of Noel Gallagher and Pop Idol svengali Simon Fuller, and both Emma Bunton and Victoria Beckham who, coincidentally, have moved in almost next door.

If it's Londoners you want to live with, chances are you'll buy in London-by-the-Sea, the seafront and streets stretching back to Davigdor, Seven Dials and some roads in Hanover. Increasingly the city centre's groovy loft apartments are attracting the younger end of the Out of London market, while Hove is becoming more and more attractive to the families who've been here a while and are now moving to the bigger properties, wide streets and gardens north and south of New Church Road.

If it's Sussex and Home Counties you feel comfortable with, go for Tongdean and Withdean or Hove Park, where the new development at the old Alliance and Leicester site offering affordable housing is driving the locals to petition signing fury. If your people are the Brighton and Hove families who've lived here forever, you'll find them in most of the above as well as Hanover, Queen's Park, outer Hove, Hangleton, Westdene, Moulsecoomb, Hollingdean, Bevendean, Woodingdean and Patcham.

Take some time out to sit in the cafes, pubs and parks to ponder where exactly you want to buy in Brighton and Hove. More than anywhere, parks are where you will find your particular tribe. Eavesdrop or join in at St Ann's Well or Queen's Park, cheer the football teams at East Brighton and Preston Parks and reminisce about the old days with Hove's born and bred at Hove Park café. People watching is never more fun than when kids are involved, and the parenting skills of St Ann's Well media dads is the stuff of sitcoms. It may seem as if all the best properties are being snapped up, but relax and enjoy the varying vibes of Brighton and Hove before you ring an estate agent.

● PARKING

And now, a word about parking. Once upon a time, parking in Brighton and Hove was easy. Now it's about as easy as finding a space in central London. Traffic is increasing and the wardens are smartening up their act, and worse (or better - you decide) the residential streets in Kemp Town, Queen's Park, Hanover and Hove have recently, or are about to be, allotted residents' parking bays, although non-residents can park here for up to four hours at a time. The standard tariff is £80 a year to park your car. If you want off street parking, your own garage or free street parking, you'll have to go out to the fringes of Kemp Town or Hove.

● SPECULATE TO ACCUMULATE

Where not so long ago houses were tripling in price in a couple of years, things these days are taking a different turn. "Those who thought there's a lot of money to be made out of Brighton & Hove property are now thinking twice" says Paul Bonett. "Sharp price rises and sellers' expectations have made a property 'deal' hard to come by, with as many out-of-towners as local speculators scanning estate agents' and auctioneers' lists for that one-off."

Buying a second flat to let used to be the best investment in the South East, but Bonett says that the game is over. "In the last few months, with studios costing as much as £80,000 and more, and one bedroom flats coming in at well over £100,000 in a good location, the return on investment for would-be landlords is not necessarily the pot of gold they expect" he advises. "Letting agents are reporting a large increase in the amount of property available, much of it due to slightly over-inflated rents needed to cover that 'buy-to-let' mortgage. Would-be tenants are frightened off and go into house-shares rather than single flat life. This might take the edge off the peaking small flat prices and first time buyers, currently looking to buy in Newhaven and Worthing, may come back into the local market."

If you do go for a buy-to-let, a thought; the Council runs a scheme for those who want to stay true to their liberal politics and will guarantee the rent if you agree to house an otherwise homeless family.

If you're driven by the need to have a garden, get yourself an ordnance survey map to see exactly where the gardens are. The roads around New Church Road off Hove seafront and in suburban areas such as Patcham, Westdene, Hangleton and Woodingdean are where most gardens are to be found, as well as Arundel Road in Kemp Town, both with easy access to the sea and City centre. Once in the centre, you'll get little more than a yard or, if you're lucky (and loaded), a roof terrace. But before you dismiss the idea of a backyard, visit the gardens shown off as part of the Open Houses scheme in May's Brighton Festival (see The Season for details). The creativity is inspiring. There are also plenty of allotments available, so ring the Council for details.

Paul Bonett points out that there are still areas in Brighton and Hove where houses with gardens are affordable - even on a limited budget. "To the east is Whitehawk, close to East Brighton Golf Course, the Racecourse and The Downs, while north of Queen's Park is the Queen's Park Estate. Beyond Elm Grove are Bevendean, Moulsecomb and Coldean Estates, handy for the universities, with Hollingdean Estate beyond Hollingbury and near the golf course. Over into Hove, there are estates in Hangleton close to the Downs leading towards Devil's Dyke and the countryside." Prices start at around £110,000.

Bonett suggests that families who want gardens, garages and community could look at Patcham and Westdene, both of which have strong communities linked to the primary and junior schools. "I sold a gorgeous 18th century cottage in Patcham Old Town and a lovely flint-fronted wing of a 17th century mansion house. The family who bought it had moved from Queen's Park to get more of a garden. And they've got access to the best baker in town, Patcham Bakery, which sells the best doughnuts and curry pasties you've ever tasted!" Portslade is also a good place to look for cheaper properties. "A new three-bed semi with a garage and garden will cost you £165,000," he told us. "And it's two minutes away from the A27 and about 15 minutes into the centre of Brighton."

Saltdean, a three-mile hike from Brighton and Hove is becoming increasingly popular, particularly with the Hanover types who want to buy a bigger house, but find themselves trapped by the property boom. As a result, a community of young families seems to be taking over, with the local toddler groups and primary schools the epicentre of social life. Rentals are hard to come by, but a three-bed house with garden is around £900 a month. To buy, two-bedroomed houses - most of them detached bungalows with loft extensions, front and back gardens and plentiful parking, on or off road - begin at £125,000.

Shoreham Beach is the next place to watch if the growth of Brighton-style restaurants and bars is anything to go by. There are three bed, three storey Edwardian houses behind the High Street going for about £170,000 which would cost more like £235,000 in Kemp Town. Fox and Sons tell us of new loft developments in a converted church off the High Street which will probably go from £110,000 for a one bed to £250,000 for the penthouse, a sure sign that the regeneration feather duster is being flicked west of the piers. The rush on the houseboats off Shoreham Beach means that there aren't any up for grabs at the moment, but that the new Bohemians are moving in and that others are sure to follow.

And one for the real property speculators. Hastings. You don't believe us? Have a look into the purse the South East Economic Development Agency is clutching next time it pops on the train east, and don't say we didn't warn you.

● MONTPELIER

Aesthetically, Montpelier is one of Brighton's most appealing areas in a city with so much stunning architecture. Large white houses lurk in streets of pastel hues lending an atmosphere of style rather than wealth, a feel of Mykonos rather than Belgravia. Montpelier is about as close to central Brighton and Hove as you can get. The luvvy of Brighton neighbourhoods, it buzzes all year round, leaving little peace for its chic, funky residents. But that's why they choose to live here: this is where the action is, and most have the money to pay for it.

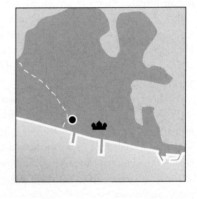

Montpelier is small enough to negotiate and close enough to everything for access. If you live here, you walk. What's the point of the car anyway? Residents pay £80 a year for a parking permit, there are precious few garages or off-road parking, and by the time you get in to your car, drive, find somewhere to park, you could be where you want to be. Montpelier people walk to the shops and the sea. They walk to the schools, to see friends or St Ann's Well Gardens. Soho apart, it's rare to find a community feel in the centre of a city, but Montpelier pulls it off.

Montpelier Villas is one of Brighton's most gorgeous streets with its Mediterranean-style houses and spiky yuccas leading the eye down to the sea. Montpelier Terrace and Montpelier Place leading to Upper North Street has a typically Brighton mix of small, but beautifully decorated houses and large villas. In the Clifton Conservation area, a large four-bedroom house could cost over £850,000, a medium-sized, three-bedroom house will go for between £275,000 and £350,000 or more. You will be lucky to find even a two bedroom for under £225,000. Powis Square, with its elegantly distressed balustrades and peeling white paint, still exudes a Georgian grandeur and attracts a hip but wealthy resident. Set in the heart of the Montpelier/Clifton area, the five-storey houses (some with 30-foot gardens) are worth between £550,000 and £800,000 and the no longer neglected central communal garden is a much-loved play area for the local toddlers. Flats and converted maisonettes are a better buy and go from £125,000 to £200,000.

● SEVEN DIALS

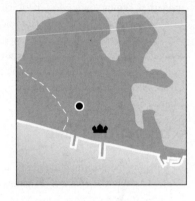

Seven Dials is a self-contained pocket of sophistication, which revels in its autonomous culture. It has become a prime location for commuters being only minutes away from Brighton station, while Hove Station is only a short bus ride away. Estate agents are keen to stress to prospective buyers that you can buy anything you want here. On Dyke Road you'll find a couple of excellent delicatessens, a late-night chemist (Ashtons), a designer florist and an organic greengrocers. The Tin Drum, the coolest bar/restaurant in the neighbourhood, puts its tables on the street pavement when the sun shines, attracting a visible coffee-drinking, paper-reading weekend crowd and enough of an evening buzz to pull the locals in for a Sea Breeze.

Almost all the Regency and Victorian houses have been divided into flats. This year, the wannabe roads are still Vernon Terrace where you'll find a two-bedroom flat for £150,000 and the busy Denmark Terrace where some of the high ceilings and large rooms are magnificent. Beware the shamelessly chopped-up Eighties developments, though. A one-bed in the ever-popular Chatham Place will cost around £95,000 to £110,00. If you want real Regency style with balustrades and balconies, you might just pick up a maisonette in Compton Avenue for around £175,000.

● PORTHALL

Sometimes known as Prestonville, the residential area at the back of Seven Dials is possibly the most popular area among Juicy relocators. The two/three bed terraced houses with gardens big enough for little more than a sandpit and tricycle or two are packed with families who borrow each others' sugar and invite their kids to parties at the

Community Centre in Exeter Street. The kids go to Stanford Infants and Juniors or to BHASVIC while the parents walk to the station and head off to Cape Town on a photographic shoot or cycle down to The Dolphin House Clinic for a shiatsu. Four to five bed houses with big gardens here are not cheap at £350,000 although good value compared to the same size a couple of streets away in St Ann's Well. Jeff Crosier of Fox and Sons says that Hamilton Road is the area to watch. "There are properties going here for between £190,000 and £210,000 with fantastic views over Preston Park" he says, although this only refers to those with east facing gardens if you stand on a ladder on tiptoes. Bless him, but he is an estate agent.

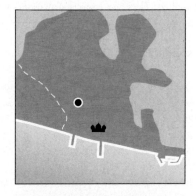

● THE NORTH LAINE

As much as the sea and the piers, The North Laine is the spirit of Brighton. From hippy, dippy, grunge gear, to post-modern garden equipment, you can get it here, and if you want it in pink Day-Glo fake fur, all the better. Sit in any one of the chic cafes or bars and watch the world go by: it's better than anything you'll see on telly.

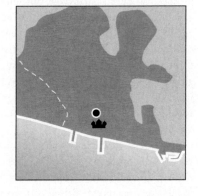

Living here is a buzz - certainly at the weekend and in the summer when the party barely stops. In some of the quieter roads such as Over Street and Queen's Gardens, the residents find their tranquility in their Tardis like homes - a top buy this year with the development of Jubilee Street. The grand plan is to open up the back of the Komedia Theatre to extend their cabaret space and rehearsal rooms, and create a glass fronted box office on Regent Street. If they get permission, Botanica, the garden shop next door, will join The Komedia's extension, creating a winter garden conservatory out the back overlooking the new Jubilee Centre with the children's library attached to the Prince Regent swimming pool. You may not find a garden, but you are right in the centre of town where a small terraced house might cost anything from just under £200,000 to £350,000. A family house In Pelham Square will cost around £300,000+.

● KEMP TOWN

Kemp Town is undergoing a sea-change in its culture and the environment. London media types, the gay crowd, local families and trendy young things of all gender persuasions are the kind of neighbours you'll find in this community. And it's only two minutes from the beach and five from The Downs.

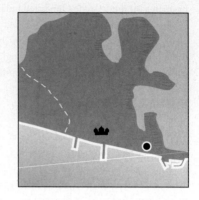

Once a village of beautiful facades where the grimmer reality behind the front doors spilt into the streets around St James's, Kemp Town has been known for its drugs and anti-social behaviour for the last 20 years. But Europe has been generous with its regeneration funding and St James's Street, like many of its residents, has had a facelift. This time, its beauty is more than skin deep and the new shops, cafes and bars have added a new dynamic that has successfully attracted new business and new residents to the area and galvanised the existing community.

The Kemp Town Carnival, a fund raising day with bed races through the streets, Morris dancers, floats and live music, is becoming a yearly event for locals, and the gorgeous lantern festival which leads the community through St James's to The New Steine for the lighting of the Kemp Town Christmas Tree is a real treat.

Further down towards the Marina, the high street of St George's Road is now a bustling thoroughfare with top quality independent retailers from a shoemaker to a quality butcher to a fishmonger to a classy cookware supplier - specialist shops which trade side by side with greengrocers, a bookshop, corner stores, a bank and newsagents.

Stretching east from St James's Street and St George's Road, is some of the most beautiful Georgian architecture in Brighton and Hove. Designed to house the aristocrats who followed the Prince Regent down to Brighton to "take the waters" on the advice of Brighton's most influential alternative therapist, Dr Richard Russell, Kemp Town was built to be grand. Thomas Reid Kemp, a property developer with a vision bigger than his wallet, commissioned the architects Busby and Wilds to build an estate which grew to include one of the most famous examples of Regency architecture, Sussex Square. Its lower lawns which spread down into Lewes Crescent, even hide a secret rose garden with its own tunnel leading to the beach, the spot which, according to local legend, inspired one-time resident, Lewis Carroll to write *Alice Through The Looking Glass*.

Prices in Sussex Square have risen dramatically in recent months, so expect to pay up to £140,000 for a ground-floor, one-bedroom flat, and watch out for maintenance payments on these Grade One-listed buildings. You can add zeros as you add bedrooms, as you can in the Brunswick area. In fact prices are going through the Grade Two-listed Georgian roof - something which won't be helped by The Independent listing it as one the most desirable places to live in England. A five-storey Regency house will set you back anything from £350,000 to £1 million.

● QUEEN'S PARK

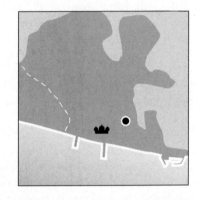

Queen's Park has been called the heart of Brighton - and you can see why. It is a family place; couples move here who have grown out of their flats and want more space for the kids with easy access to both Kemp Town and the centre of town. Queen's Park has to be the most beautiful park in Brighton. It was designed and built as an ornamental garden in 1824, flanked at each end by two formal arches and built in a deep hollow giving the park dramatic views sweeping down to the sea. It is beautifully laid out, with a wild garden, landscaped stream, tennis courts and bowling green, and facilities for the elderly and the disabled. There's also a well-equipped children's playground that heaves in the summer with queues for the swings and the café.

Queen's Park is a strange cross between Kemp Town and Hanover. Some of the biggest gardens and most expensive properties are here, but you can get a three- or four-bed property with seaviews for anything from £220,000. Purpose-built flats such as Carn Court now go for over £140,000 but are unusually spacious. And with views from the top of the hill over the English Channel, you might want to think again about that dive in Montpelier.

East Drive and West Drive, which curve around the park, are the area's best addresses with their large, semi-detached Victorian houses and some of the biggest gardens in Brighton. Expect to pay in the region of £500,000 and more. Freshfield Road runs from Eastern Road and up past the Racecourse towards the Downs. The towering 4/5 bedroom Victorian houses make great family homes and go for around £350,000, although the three-bedroom terraces further up towards the race course are a more modest £225,000 plus. There are still some which need upgrading that you might pick up for under £200,000. Even the more recently built Thirties houses have increased in value as this area becomes ever more popular. Canning Street, home to the band The Levellers, falls in the middle of Queen's Park and Kemp Town area. Popular with families, the Victorian three-bed houses here range from £200,000 to £240,000.

● HANOVER

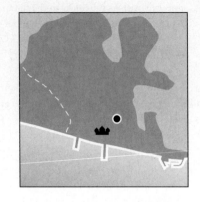

Hanover is a dense spread of Victorian houses that wiggles down from Queen's Park Road to The Level. Originally built to accommodate the train and carriage labourers working at Brighton station, the small terraced houses have historically fostered an intense community spirit. The houses are generally too small to convert into flats - apart from Ewart Street and Albion Hill with their 'older style, purpose-built' flats, some with small gardens. This has built a strong owner/occupier community that still exists, and today Hanover has its own website complete with area pub guide and even its own guidebook.

Hanover Lofts, the beautifully designed flats sculpted from the Old Finsbury School by former It Girl Tara Bernard, and hubby, Manhattan Loft magnate John Hitchcock, cleverly tap into what Hanover may well become. Hitchcock is said to be the man who spots how we want to live before we know ourselves, and if that's the future for Hanover, get saving. They're all sold, of course: £190,000 for a one-bed flat up to £400,000 for a two-bed flat spread over 2100 square feet. But keep an ear out for the patter of tiny feet that will send all those sexy Hanover Loft couples off to Queen's Park in search of a garden and open the communal door to a stream of New Hanoverians.

Hanover is well placed for schools, with access to Queen's Park, Elm Grove, Fairlight and St Lukes which keeps the kids in the community. Life revolves around the plethora of great pubs and the Hanover Community Centre in Southover Street. An eclectic range of events are held here from the annual Hanover Beer Festival in October to yoga, toddler groups and live music. In the middle of August, Hanover celebrates as the streets are closed to cars and a good, old-fashioned street party takes place. For the rest of the year, the party never stops in Southover Street, which boasts an unnatural amount of good pubs.

Hanoverians - characteristically social workers, teachers and first-time Brighton buyers - used to say that you live here until the kids force you to move to Fiveways or Queen's Park. That's changing now as Brighton and Hove become too expensive and locals are beginning to complain about being trapped by the property boom. Not so long ago, Hanover was a haven for first-time buyers, but the prices are moving swiftly upwards and a two-bedroom in Stanley Street will cost upward of £150,000. Hanover Crescent, which is part of the Valley Conservation area, is the smartest road in Hanover with its 24 listed buildings, but it is rare to find a flat or house for sale these days especially with its proximity to the station. Estate agents value flats there from £120,000 depending on room size, and the houses start at around £400,000.

● ELM GROVE

As Hanover's property market reaches saturation point, first-time buyers are looking at Elm Grove, the area on the other side of the hill behind Brighton racecourse. From Elm Grove's lofty peaks you can clamber up on to the South Downs and look out to sea, or take a surprisingly beautiful walk through to one of the cemeteries. Although Elm Grove doesn't zing with community spirit, it's a deceptive area, and within its boundaries

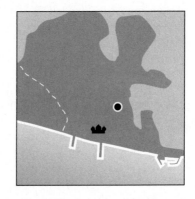

lie some lovely streets. In De Montfort Road the larger houses are worth looking at with substantial gardens. A house here will set you back upwards of £200,000. In Hartington Road you can still find gardens, but they tend to be behind the Victorian houses which cost around £190,000 and some for £235,000. The tree-lined Brading and Bernard Roads are also popular, and a house here will cost around £185,000. Elm Grovers agree that although The Grove has no centre and little ambience of its own, it is close enough take advantage of its more vibey neighbour, Hanover, and that the houses with gardens are substantially bigger here.

A basic one-bedroom flat in Whippingham Road will currently sell for £85,000, while a two-bedroom maisonette in Milner Road, just east of the Lewes Road, will cost £100,000 plus. The Patch - officially The William Clark Park - is one of Elm Grove's best-kept secrets. Directly behind Bonchurch Road and Elm Grove School, it provides Elm Grovers with their own park and children's play area. If you live in Bonchurch Road (£170,000 - £200,000 for a 3 bedroom late Victorian terrace) you can walk straight out of your back garden into the park.

Traditionally, landlords have bought along the Lewes Road and let their properties out to students as the Universities of Brighton and Sussex are both based around here. Parents of students are now getting wise (or their arms twisted) and buying a home for their little darlings who then get to play landord or lady to their student chums, dividing the house into an astonishing number of rooms. The real bargains are in Moulsecoomb and Coldean although estate agent Barrie Alderton warns that students don't stay long in this area and move closer to the city vibe, saddling their parents with an albatross around their necks.

● PRESTON PARK

The well-heeled of Brighton and Hove who care not a jot for a seaview will make their way to the Victoriana of Preston Park. The park itself is a large green space with a clock tower, a scented garden for the blind, two cafés, a playground, a cycle track where kids can learn to throw away the stabilisers and enough squirrels to keep the dogs happy. The two cafes are the Floriana Rotunda with its manicured lawns and perfect

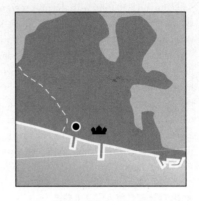

flowerbeds which serves roasts and proper teas from 9am-6pm from March until the nights draw in, and the Chalet where you'll get a cuppa even on a wintry afternoon. The tennis courts, running and cycle track and bowling green are well attended and well maintained, and on a warm summer's evening, the sight of all that activity off the London Road is a tonic to those who've left the rest of the world behind on the M23.

The area tends to attract professional couples and parents-to-be moving down from London (although our 23-year-old club reviewer recently moved out here when the buzz of central Brighton got too much for her. She's still reeling from the shock of living in suburbia, but says her rented flat overlooking the Park is a dream). For most buyers here, the huge pull, apart from the larger Victorian houses and its smart profile, is the local schools. Despite the no-catchment policy, Balfour infants and junior schools and Dorothy Stringer secondary school are said to be the best (academically) in Brighton and they can - and do - pull the net tightly around the local area. See the Schools chapter to see what local parents think of them.

The triangle from Preston Park to Preston Drove and Stanford Avenue are where the biggest houses with gardens are to be found. A two-storey, two-bed house with 25-50 foot garden will go for around £200,000, while a house with loft conversion in Cleveland Road overlooking Blakers Park, might go for about £335,000. But there are some exceptional bargains in the area; some of the smaller-looking properties in the triangle can be deceptive. "They're like the Tardis," a resident of Edburton Avenue who grew up there, told us.

Neighbouring Florence, Rugby and Surrenden Roads with houses ranging from £350,000 minimum to £700,000 or even more, depending on size and garden, can accommodate the bigger families. The prices come down again for the slightly smaller Victorian terraced houses (from £200,000) in the Preston Drove area, and the people tend to be a little less precious. Estate agents will tell you that the Preston Drove divide will cost you £30,000, with the neat rows of well-maintained homes on the Blaker's Park side lending a more genteel air. There really is very little difference to the houses themselves, so if you've got a child who might excel in the academic halls of Balfour, do yourself a favour and go for the north side of Preston Drove which will almost certainly fall inside the ever tightening net. But before you buy one of the tiny two-bed terraced homes with postage stamp gardens which are flooding the market, remember that many of them have been rented out to students with little maintenance over many years, and will need a whack of cash spent on them. Around the Lowther and Hythe Roads, estate agents are also scooping up the few tiny houses here where elderly Preston Parkers spent their last days. With their Sixties gas fires and miniature gardens, the average price of £185,000 means that they are not the best bargains in town despite their access to Balfour.

● PRESTON VILLAGE

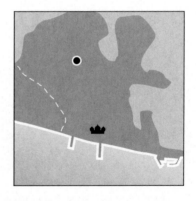

This is not what we expect from a village these days with no shops, village square or real sense of community. In fact, it is no more than six roads off the London Road, stretching from South, Middle and North Roads with their older Victorian cottages and gardens worth between £165,000 and £215,000, to Clermont Road and Terrace at the back of Preston Park station, where substantial houses can set you back anything from £250,000 to as much as £400,000. A hop and a skip from a commuter station, it's beginning to attract more London buyers.

Withdean's Thirties, Forties and Fifties housing, mansions and architectural experiments lead out to Westdene with its Fifties and Sixties estates, bungalows and upside down houses with sitting rooms leading from basements on to sloping gardens. A three bedroomed house in Valley Drive would be between £250,000 and £275,000. If you're mad enough to commute by car, the main routes out, the A23 and A27, are close by. It's also the way to Devil's Dyke with its panoramic views of the South Downs and English Channel.

● FIVEWAYS

Stretching from one end of Ditchling Road to the other, Fiveways refers to the junction of Stanford Avenue, Preston Drove and Hollingbury Road, and is where *the Guardian* readers of Kemp Town and Hanover tend to move to when they have more kids. In the past few years, as the reputations of Downs and Balfour school, Dorothy Stringer and Varndean have grown, *the Guardian* readers have skipped the Kemp Town bit completely and headed straight for the large semis, terraced Victorians and windy roads heading across to Hollingbury to avoid the dearth of secondary schools nearer the sea.

Preston Park and Blaker's Park are within walking distance if you can manage the hills, and Hollingbury Park and golf course stretches out towards the South Downs for the serious walkers. Brighton is one of the few places where the golf courses are public and open to dog walkers. Keep to the edge and watch out for flying golf balls and you'll find some of the most beautiful walks in town.

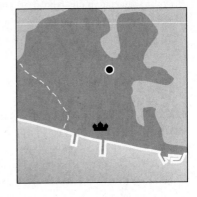

Ditchling Road, a long straight thoroughfare out to Hollingbury's bungalows and older community and on to the A27, hosts a motley collection of houses. The few detached houses with enormous gardens hover on the edge of the Friar and Surrenden areas, secluded off-the- main-drag communities with a 4WD parked on most of the driveways. The terraced Victorian homes perched on the wide pavements stretching down towards the Fiveways junction are home to middle-class, middle-income, thirtysomethings who spend their spare time doing up their houses and hanging out with parents of their children's friends.

The community is children-oriented with a lack of focal points from shops or pubs, largely because both parents tend to work, do the shopping once a week at Asda on the industrial estate by the A27 and come straight home to play with the kids before bedtime. But someone could (and will) make a fortune by opening a deli/café at Fiveways to scoop up the new parents and Saturday crowd who would otherwise get the bus to the North Laine or hang out at Seven Dials. Zel have already spotted the gap and filled it with The Open House, a lounge lizard of a pub with mosaic patio for Sunday barbecue lunches, nestling in the residential streets around Downs Infants and Junior schools.

● HOLLINGDEAN

Halifax agent, David Whittle points to Hollingdean as the area to watch around Fiveways. "It's all pretty full around here now" he says. "We've been waiting for months for properties to come on the market because of the huge demand in this neighbourhood. What we are finding is that roads like Stanmer Park Road which have traditionally been on the 'wrong side's of Ditchling Road, are being snapped up for around £200,000."

● HOVE

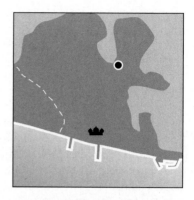

Brighton's quieter, more refined sister is only a stone's throw from the main action, but by the time you've marvelled at the Peace Statue and the manicured lawns which mark the boundary, an air of tranquillity really does seem to descend. The breathtaking architecture of Brunswick and Palmeira Squares leaves the showy, gaudy anomalies of Brighton's seafront such as the Brighton Centre and the tacky eateries paling into insignificance. It all looks impossibly grand and graciously residential. Hove prefers to do its shopping, eating and clubbing in Brighton, if only to keep hoi polloi off its doorstep. Its long stretch of high street is Church Road with its floral clock and

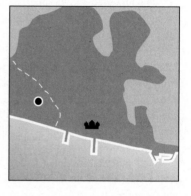

pretty trees silhouetted against the horizon, but don't expect to find anything much more interesting than a few nice clothes shops and a few reasonable restaurants until you get to George Street, the pedestrianised epicentre of Hove.

Many of the enormous houses you'll find in Hove have been converted into flats, and occasional ones will boast roof gardens with the best views in town. The original Hove was known as Brunswick Town, and these days Brunswick Square and Brunswick Terrace is still known to many as the centre of the universe. Since the 1850s and the development of Albany, Medina, Osborne and Ventnor Villas beyond Adelaide Crescent, Hove moved west as the Stanford family built its estate. Compared to Brighton, Hove is a baby, with few buildings dating back before 1825, meaning properties here can have the garages and gardens which Brighton's Regency town houses lack. Hangleton, Portslade, Aldrington and West Blatchington were former villages and even if they have been absorbed by the blanket of Hove, they still retain their respective identities.

● BRUNSWICK

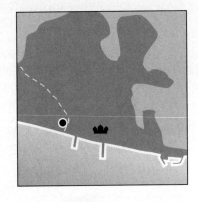

If you're young(ish), free and single with a bit of disposable cash, you're likely to go for the area north and south of Western Road around the Brighton/Hove boundary at York Road. The prices might have risen since Nigel Richardson immortalised the area in his book Breakfast In Brighton, but it's still well worth a look. Fantastically central, a few minutes walk to lots of great eateries and pubs and just back from the seafront. Most properties are converted flats - some with lovely little patio gardens.

In the last five years, most of the people who have moved to this part of town are likely to have sold their one-bed flat in London, made £100,000 on the deal and ploughed it into their £125,000 one-bed or £145,000 to £175,000 two-bed flat. They buy their interiors from the shoppers' heaven that is the North Laine and build an architectural garden out of nothing more than a slab of east-facing concrete and some serious creativity. But fear not: they may have moved from the designer-fest of Islington, but keeping up with the Joneses hasn't been encouraged in Brighton and Hove since the days when the Prince Regent first stamped his own individuality on the town. Finding your own style, making it rather than buying into it, being your own person is what life is about down here.

On the seafront itself, the Regency two-bed flats in Brunswick or Palmeira Squares, push the property prices into the 3% Stamp Duty over £250,000 bracket. A rare four-bed without a garden will easily go for £300,000. Bargains are not what they used to be but you can get a first floor flat with a balcony for £195,000, while a roof conversion in the same building will go for £155,000, and both will look out over the Channel. Seafront Hove is a different planet from Hillside Hove. Its streets are avenues - Grand, First, Second and Third, and The Drive and Upper Drive which are still the best addresses this side of the statue. Up the hill, the houses are slightly smaller, but the average price is in the £300,000 to £600,000 mark, with walled gardens and the kind of signals to the world that those who live here have arrived. (See Tongdean and Withdean.)

● CENTRAL HOVE

A year ago, Central Hove was stuck between cool Brunswick and family oriented New Church Road, but the Brighton Loft Company who gave Hanover a face lift last year with Hanover Lofts, is putting a firecracker under the few remaining blue rinses with sexy glass bricked flats in Tissbury Road, The Drive and Viceroy Lodge on the seafront at Kingsway. At £250,000 for a two bed light

filled flat with enormous garden in Tissbury Road, the prices are not going to break the bank for the contemporary living designer couples who are peeling off wads of tenners and throwing them at Carringtons Estate Agents. And where you find a bit of Gucci, the trendy bars and cafes are sure to follow.

● NEW CHURCH ROAD

The streets south of New Church Road which stretch down to the sea and look over the Western Lawns are where you'll find 1930s three bedroom semis with gardens and garages and large houses with gardens starting at £225,000 and heading up to £800,000 in Princes Square, with those north of New Church Road going for £200,000 upwards. It may seem a bit suburban, but the difference between buying in Hove and buying into Terry and June suburbia is that you can walk along the seafront to some of the best clubs in the country. Teenage kids can get a cheapish cab home, parents can walk their younger kids to school, and you can save a fortune on petrol because Brighton and Hove thinks it's a good deal bigger than it is.

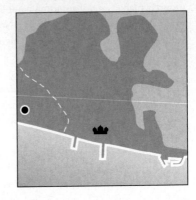

Portland Road, an underestimated street of character shops, a great bike shop, top video store, grocers, locksmiths, continental bakery, florists and the lovely old Lumley & Hunt bathroom shop, is around the corner. George Street, pedestrianised and planted with new trees to aid the soaring house prices, is not exactly the North Laine, but it'll do. The Dieppe Market with its French goodies visits it twice a year, once more than its festival trip to Bartholomews in Brighton, confirming the local interest in delis and all things cosmopolitan.

The wide, tree filled avenues off New Church Road are quickly becoming home to London relocators who have a bit more cash to spend on their kitchens than most. Some of the houses around Westbourne Gardens are enormous with four floors and endless rooms pushing prices up to £450,000 and beyond. Others such as Hogarth Road may be smaller inside but have huge gardens and are a bargain at around £295,000. "We've got a four bed in Middleton Avenue for £272,000 and a five bed on Derek Avenue at £365,000" says Paul Bonett. "But it's an odd area, this one. People moving from the Dials won't go beyond Sackville because they think the semis are too suburban. I've got one couple who are moving back to St Ann's Well after living here for six months. They thought it would be great, but they really missed the buzz of the city".

● POETS CORNER

The Bohemian area of Hove which leads from the station to Clarendon Villas, as far west as Alpine Road and down to Portland Road, is still up and coming. It is the place where the first time house buyer in Hove usually starts with a two-to three-bed Victorian middle terrace houses for between £155,000 to £195,000. You can pick up a small one bedroom flat for between £95,000 to £110,000 and two bedders are about £120,000.

East of Sackville are some two and three-storey Victorian houses which are going for about £165,000. It's a foothold on the property market, and the starting point for many families who might move to New Church Road when the kids get too big to share a room.

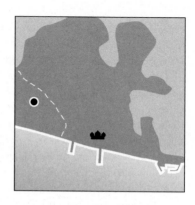

Hove has a few parks dotted around this area, and uses the beach as its playground. Davis Park is no more than a rose garden and a set of tennis courts belonging to Dragons Gym, Aldrington Rec is little more than a collection of rugby posts and a small children's playground while Wish Park is just big enough space to kick a ball around. Towards Portslade, Vale Park is also a nice place to take the kids but it's only when you get up to Hove Park and across to Preston Park and Queen's Park that you'll find the buzz, the trees, the bigger playgrounds and the cafes which a good park should be about. But Hove is a small town, and nowhere is too far from the glorious St Ann's Well Gardens with its café, tennis courts, winding paths beneath ancient elms, the enormous children's playground and heavenly scented garden.

● ST ANN'S WELL GARDENS

This is the area of leafy and not so leafy streets that border Montpelier, Seven Dials and central Hove. It is one of the genuine communities in Brighton and Hove, largely because at around 8.45am and 3pm, the streets are awash with parents and kids trekking to and from Davigdor, Somerhill, Brighton and Hove High School for Girls, Cottesmore, Cardinal Newman, Blatchington Mill and Hove Park. The area is dense with schools and

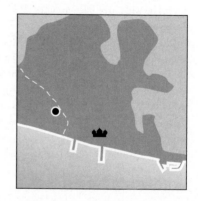

people rather than the shops, pubs and clubs which characterise the rest of Brighton and Hove, and its heart is in St Ann's Well Gardens where the community comes to play.

Houses here vary from late Edwardian semis to large, detached Thirties buildings. One of the best selling points of the area, apart from the school and the park, is the size of some of the gardens that average between 50 to 100 feet in Somerhill and Nizell

Avenues. But it does mean that they're not cheap, ranging from £290,000 to between £450 and 500,000. Around Highdown and Lyndhurst and a number of roads off there are the less expensive Edwardian four-bedroom houses with 20 foot square gardens which are currently on the market for between £230,000 and £375,000. The County Cricket Ground is a walk away at top of Selborne Road, as is Hove mainline station.

● HOVE PARK

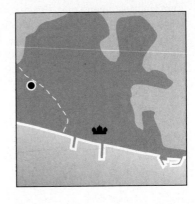

Above Withdean Stadium where Brighton and Hove brought back The Albion, the prices and the houses leave the real world behind. Hove Park, according to some estate agents and the people who live there, is the best place to live in Brighton and Hove. Safe, expensive, middle class, and not made up of the London types who are a feature of Preston Park railway station at 8am. "There's a lot of Brighton and Hove people who inherited properties in the Eighties, sold them and moved up here," Peter Gladwell of the Halifax told us. "It's a real community of butchers, bakers, candlestick-makers made good." Eighty per cent of the houses bought here are by local folk, according to Peter. "London people want London-by-the-sea. The people here are dentists, lawyers, people who've made a lot of money one way or the other. Airline pilots move here when they are based at Gatwick. That's the kind of person you'll find around here."

The park itself is a large, rolling, well-kept expanse of space hedged by the Old Shoreham Road. It is designed to please with a café, kiddies' playground split in two for the large and small, bowling green and recently revamped tennis courts. The miniature railway is run by volunteers and is open in the summer, and the cycle track makes it a perfect stroll for those with buggies and wheelchairs.

● TONGDEAN AND WITHDEAN

Tongdean Avenue has been described as the Beverley Hills of Hove. Houses here will go for an average of £600,000 to £750,000 with the odd beauty selling for more than £1million. According to Nigel Richardson in the Saturday Telegraph, their status is measured by the "inches of their Doric columns" although his snobby estate agent source added that he found this area "insufferably vulgar". The other most sought-after addresses are Tongdean Road, Dyke Road Avenue and Barrowfield Drive. The local choice of school here is not so likely to be Blatchington Mill or Hove Park, but the private Mowden School for boys, Brighton College, Hurstpierpoint College or Roedean. Surrenden Field, originally 5.65 acres of open space belonging to Home Farm (and once upon a time, Brighton and Hove Rangers, the forerunners to B&H Albion FC) runs across the bottom of Surrenden Crescent, neatly tying up the area with the boundary of Preston Park.

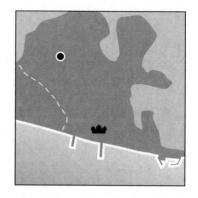

● *An ambulance siren can only mean one thing in Saltdean: another property on the Market (it's no coincidence the estate agent is next door to the funeral parlour). As oldies move out feet first, young families, wanting more garden and parking spaces for their money, move out of Brighton and into Saltdean. Gay couples have also discovered it, bringing a cosmopolitan vibe to what was once a sleepy retirement resort. It's still a resort (evident by every shop selling ice-cream), but with a strong community spirit. A dedicated group known locally as the Saltdean mothers run the pre-schools, toddler and baby sessions and support the excellent primary school. Their latest project involves transforming the oval park, the green heart of Saltdean, planting trees, replacing the slide and building a tea hut to sell even more ice creams.*

Marina Baker, *author of* Spells for Teenage Witches, *lives and works in a 1930s mansion in Saltdean*

07

● Choosing the right school is possibly the most important factor for parents, or would-be parents moving into or around Brighton and Hove. We've compiled a list of some of the schools in the area which parents have recommended to us. The list we've compiled and the information we're giving is based purely on the word of parents and children who chose them. It is not meant to be comprehensive, and has nothing to do with Ofsted reports or league tables. This information should be seen as complementary, to be used in conjunction with the official information. The Council (01273 293502) will give you a full list of State schools, and ABC magazine features a considerable number of advertisements for private schools and nurseries. If a particular school is not listed, that's no reflection on the school, it just means that no one recommended it to us. If you feel that we've missed out anywhere, please write in and we'll sort it out next time.

Officially, there is no catchment policy in Brighton and Hove; you choose the school you want whether it's in East or West Sussex, and nobody's going to stop you from applying. But as the best schools fill up with the locals, there's going to be precious few places for anyone living outside of the area. But remember that as good as a school is this year, it's only as good as its headteacher, and headteachers do move on. The good thing is that there are plenty of schools to choose from in Brighton and Hove, both in the public and private sectors.

● ALTERNATIVE EDUCATION

Finally it looks like pluralism in education is to get the seal of government approval, although in politics it's rare to find a solution without some kind of compromise. As they fight to keep the integrity of their educational systems, it may be some time before we can have a real choice in education, but at the moment, Steiner and Montessori are the most likely to get their state funding.

Brighton & Hove Montessori
67 Stanford Avenue, Preston Park
01273 702485
MontessoriBright@aol.com

For children of two and a half years old to eight. Montessori teaching is purposeful with activities very rooted in the real world; polishing shoes, washing up, cleaning, rather than water and sand play. The idea is that children learn how to be comfortable in their world and grow at their own pace. The teaching follows the individual's interest rather than the other way round, and reading and writing come naturally when the time is right. Keeping your child here to the age of five or six is a good alternative to the Reception classes for four-year-olds. Grants for three and four-year-olds accepted.

Montessori's sensitive handling of small children also has a greater impact on the whole family. Parents learn to respect their children's own ability, giving them the opportunity to dress themselves, get their own juice and organise their own games which tends to give them more confidence in the big wide world.

The Brighton Steiner School
John Howard Home, Roedean Road, Kemp Town
01273 386300
Children work in a disciplined environment but are allowed to learn about the world in an organic and non-competitive way, preserving their natural hunger for knowledge. In addition to academic success, the curriculum is consciously directed towards building social skills, creativity and the awareness of spiritual and moral elements in life. In the Nursery and Kindergarten, imagination and play are emphasised with formal learning starting around age seven. Children stay with the same class teacher from 7-14,

then enter the Upper School, taught solely by specialist subject teachers.

The Brighton School is a teenager in the world of Steiner and has attracted mixed opinion. But the parents are some of the most committed in the city and the shared vision tends to build a very cohesive community among adults and children.

Michael Hall, the oldest Steiner in the UK, is a school bus ride away in Forest Row near East Grinstead and a very different option to Brighton's own school. Far more established and set in the most glorious surroundings, it tends to attract a more middle class type of family. Both schools are very open to the public though and their Christmas bazaars are a must for a day out with the kids.

The Dharma School
White House, Ladies Mile Road, Patcham
01273 502055
In a big, old-fashioned school building on the edge of town, children follow the national curriculum in a Buddhist environment. There's a nursery and even the youngest kids learn to meditate in a morning 'puja'. The approach is traditional, with classes organised by age and going through to GCSE, but the feeling of calm is palpable and the kids have an uncommon courtesy to each other and adults.

Lewes New School
Talbot Terrace, Lewes
01273 477074
office@officelewesnewschool.co.uk

Whatever's in the air in Brighton and Hove, it's reached the noses of some of the country's most prestigious brands who are grabbing their plots and sticking their flags in while there's still space in central Brighton. Fish, Quod, Hotel du Vin, City Lofts, Conran and Partners... ooh, it's like the Goldrush.

They're all part of a bigger picture, these chains which spot the zeitgeist and move their interior designers in ahead of the rest. Oxford, Bristol, Brighton, Birmingham Leeds, Manchester and the 'burbs of London Town, they're all basking in the glow of their own makeovers. They'll bring employment, raise standards and encourage other quality names to move to Brighton and Hove and make this city an even Juicier place to live and work.

Samba Encounter by Carnival Collective,
part of the Where Else campaign

Contemporary City Living

at Saks House by Wasp

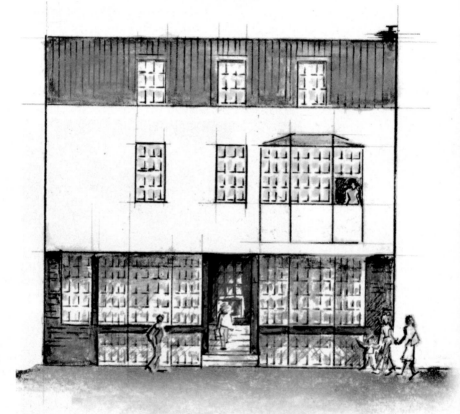

www.flats-in-brighton.co.uk

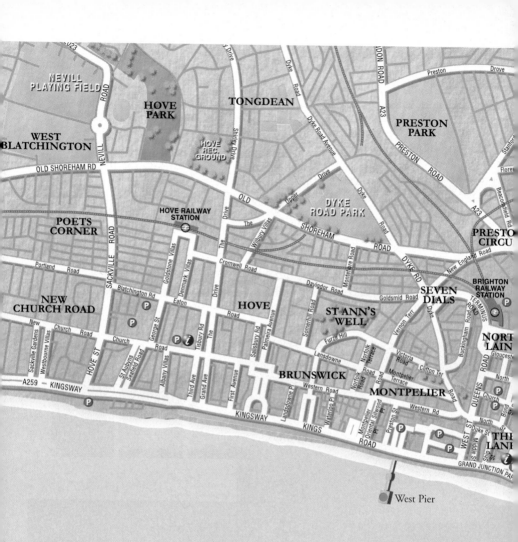

West Pier

FIVE WAYS

BEVENDEAN

Upr Hollingdean Rd

LEWES ROAD A27

Colombe Terrace

Lewes Rd

Bear

Road

Cemetery

Downs Crematorium

LONDON ROAD RAILWAY STATION

Gladstone

Lewes Road

UPPER LEWES ROAD

Cemetery

Woodvale Crematorium

Warren Road Warren Road Warren Road

Ditchling Rd

ELM GROVE

Union Road

Elm

Grove

WHITEHAWK

THE LEVEL

Ditchling Rd

St Peter's Place

Richmond Ter

Park

Road

Wilson Avenue

SHEEPCOTE VALLEY

St George's

St York Pl

RICHMOND PL

Whitehawk Way

HANOVER

QUEEN'S PARK

Queens

West Drive

East Drive

Freshfield

Sutherland Road

Manor Hill

GRAND PARADE

Royal Pavilion

Park Street

South Ave

Road

Wilson Avenue

Edward St

Eastern

Donald Hall Road

St James's St

OLD STEINE

New Rock Gdns

Upr Rock Gdns

Bedford St

Road

St Georges Road

Eastern Road

Church Place

Manor Rd

Bristol Gardens

Whitehawk Road

MARINE PARADE

KEMP TOWN

Eastern Rd

Arundel Rd

Marina Way

Madeira Drive

MARINE PARADE

Brighton Pier

MARINE

DRIVE

Roedean Road

A259

Brighton Marina

0 mile   ¼   ½

© Arka Cartographics Ltd. 2000   0 km   ½   1

brighton & hove

Hotel du Vin
&
Bistro

BRIGHTON

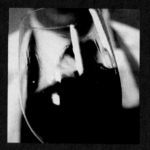

SHIP STREET BRIGHTON SUSSEX BN1 1AD

TEL 01273 718588 FAX 01273 718599

E INFO@BRIGHTON.HOTELDUVIN.COM

the juicy guide

fish! offers a combination of the freshest fish, cooked simply in vibrant surroundings with a relaxed atmosphere.

£9.95 set menu available
outside terrace seating

fish!

on - line booking: **www.fishdiner.co.uk**

165 North Street
Brighton
BN1 1EA

enquiries: **0845 100 45 55**

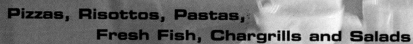

Felicia McGarry has taken what she considers to be the best of Steiner, Montessori and progressive education and designed this idealistic vision after years as a teacher in the State sector. Flooded only weeks after it opened in Autumn 2001, it could have been devastated before it began, but has already begun to earn a solid reputation.

● NURSERIES & EARLY CHILDCARE

● NURSERIES

With doors opening at 8am and closing around 6pm, with breakfast, lunch and tea provided, day nurseries are a godsend to thousands of working parents. But there are precious few which you'll find recommended in The Juicy Guide. Children are often palmed off with a weekly diet of convenience food, the kiddie-friendly names of Cowboy Casserole distracting parents from the fact that their children are unlikely to be given any fresh fruit or vegetables all week. Provide a lunchbox yourself, make sure staff will be consistent with potty training and ask about a high turnover of staff.

Blueberry Day Nursery

5 Davigdor Road, Hove
01273 733799 blueberry@tesco.net
A welcoming, happy environment with a strong emphasis on play, and good support for potty training. A big wholesome lunch is provided and they are happy to accept alternatives if your child has any allergies. Lots of information for parents and they will do a day book if you feel at all worried about anything. Blueberry has a full guide of their policies and a parents' guide and handbook. Beware the long waiting lists - it is so popular because it is so good! They take children from 18 months and go through to reception year. They are open from 8-6 but have a wide range of different sessions that you can chose at different times of the day".

Early Years Day Nursery

41 Dyke Road, Hove
01273 500151
www.earlyyearschildcare.co.uk
(Also at 44-46 Harrington Road, Preston Park. 01273 506455)
Open 8am-6pm with all-day care or half-day sessions available.
The nursery supplies nappies and has a full-time chef who cooks onsite. Paul lives in Hove, works part time at home and sends his daughter there: "Molly went to Early Years from the age of two to four. It's a really professional organisation, but can cost up to £30 per day. The building and facilities are fantastic and we now understand that there is a considerable waiting list to get a child in there. It's known as the 'American Express' nursery, as employees of Amex get some sort of subsidy from the company. Chris Eubank also sent his son there. All in all, we were very pleased with it, but sometimes it felt like dealing with

British Telecom - ie quite a lot of bureaucracy, and there does seem to be quite a high staff turnover of the carers. Though this did not affect us, some kids were getting new carers (mostly female 18-25) more than once a year. Molly loved it and misses it and her friends - which I suppose is the acid test."

Joyland Nursery
Grantham Road, Preston Park
01273 554 886

Open from 8.30am-5.30pm, with a number of different options of sessions. Lunchboxes only. Sharon's three-year-old's school care is split between Joyland Nursery, a term-time only nursery, and St Mary's Church Playgroup. "Joyland has a real family environment (being in a terraced house helps) and the children really feel like they belong. Educationally there is a reading/writing structure, but this is not enforced if the child does not feel ready for it. Learning through play is the key and activities are many and varied. What I also liked was the quiet area, which encouraged my sleepy head son to have a snooze in the afternoon if he felt like it. It also has a big garden and a pet rabbit"

The Orchard Nursery
89 Queen's Park Road, Brighton
01273 622883

Open 8am-6pm, with morning and afternoon sessions or all-day care available. Kids bring their own lunchboxes, but tea (beans and soup in winter, sandwiches and fruit in summer) is prepared and cooked onsite. Be aware that it has a very long waiting list.

● NANNIES AND AU PAIRS

The difference between a good nanny and a good au pair is price, professionalism, and if you don't work at home, peace of mind. Agencies like Bunnies in Preston Park (01273 505001) have been a consistent source of extremely reliable au pairs, but to avoid employing someone you've never met, ask them to find a girl (or boy) who is already in the area.

Jed's two-year-old is looked after at home and taken to toddler groups by a 22-year-old Slovak girl. "Au pairs are, I think, a fantastic option if your house has the space and you can deal with the idea of another person living with you. You've got to put down your boundaries, but when it works well, it's like living with a friend. Your children see them so much and become so comfortable with them that the childminding element is extremely comfortable. There's trust and friendship although it can be a little disconcerting to find yourself living with a 21-year-old blonde who walks around the house in a G-string, but these are sacrifices you've got to make. It's for the good of your kids"

Nick and Cathy work in the film industry which takes them all over the world - often at the last minute. Rachel was the only nanny who wanted to work their odd hours, so the job was hers. "To look back on it now, we were so lucky to find such a genuine, hardworking person who the kids took to very quickly. Nannies are normally a bit more mature than au pairs, and this was very important to us as Rachel is often left to look after them all day by herself. The kids benefit so much as they get undivided attention from her instead of a busy parent on the phone all day."

If nurseries are going to charge an arm and a leg to have your child sticking stars on to paper, you could spend that money on a school, particularly if they accept the three- and four-year-old grants. You could find yourself paying next to nothing for an excellent education at somewhere like Brighton and Hove Montessori School (01273 702485), or The Lewes New School (01273 477074) which uses a modern mix of Montessori and Steiner techniques (see Alternative Education section above).

Juicy Advice: Visit schools which have a specific philosophy such as Montessori, Steiner, The Drive and Lewes New School before you make a decision. Understanding the different options will allow you to make a more informed choice. Ask to sit in on a class and watch the practice rather than listen to the ethos - which could put you off.

● STATE NURSERIES

Tarnerland Nursery
St Johns Place, Kemp Town
01273 607651

The Royal Spa Nursery
Park Hill, Kemp Town
01273 607480

These two are worth a mention for being the only State-funded independent nurseries in the whole of East Sussex. Many of the primary schools have nurseries attached, but these two stand alone. Both The Royal Spa and Tarnerland come highly recommended and have fantastic locations with The Royal Spa nestling next to the playground in Queen's Park and Tarnerland situated just off the Queen's Park Road. The Royal Spa was purpose-built and the huge garden within the park provides a lovely environment for young children.

● PRIMARIES

Balfour Infants
Balfour Road, Preston Park
01273 500617
Balfour Juniors
Balfour Road, Preston Park
01273 553521

Academically, Balfour infants and juniors, situated in a largely middle-class area, do very well. Some Balfour Junior parents who prefer their children to be able to cultivate their artistic leanings, tell us that they have to spend a good deal on extra-curricular activities. But if art and music get pushed out to accommodate the highly structured curriculum, maybe Balfour can get away with it because its parents tend to be able to pay for the after-school art classes and the private piano or violin lessons. The clutch of arty types who fall into the Balfour catchment area are also more likely to fill in the gaps at home. But the schools do benefit enormously from parent power, with most local parents taking an extremely active involvement. The combination of their reputation, history and parent involvement means that it's hard to quibble about Balfour's place at the top of the tree, even though the value-added scores of the Junior school are actually less than some other less 'advantaged' schools. One note of caution: the junior school doesn't have space to take all the pupils in the top classes of the infant school, so every year some have to move on to other schools.

Cottesmore St Mary's Primary
Upper Drive,
Hove
01273 555811

The local infant and junior school in Upper Drive is a large-halled, stone building with a rather traditional interpretation of the school curriculum. It is one of the handful of Roman Catholic schools in Brighton and Hove and feeds the gorgeous-looking Cardinal Newman secondary school which sits on the other side of the road. (Incidentally, the only reason we haven't featured CN is because we couldn't find anyone who goes there.) Local Catholics get first crack of the whip if you're into the three R's, a highly moral framework and a rather stern approach to discipline.

Davigdor Infants School
Somerhill Road,
St Anne's Well, Hove
01273 731397

One of the reasons that young families are flocking to the deli and café community of Seven Dials and the borders of Hove is Davigdor and its junior school, Somerhill. The Council policy may be that you don't have to live in the area, but because the school is in such demand, the reality is that you do. It's a small, family environment that doesn't put children off education for life, and the head and teachers really do listen to parents. The kids make up their own rules, and the goldfish sitting in his open-topped bowl in easy reach for nicking in the entrance to the school is proof that they stick to them.

Downs Infant School
Ditchling Road,
nr Preston Park
01273 500146

Downs Infants and Junior schools have an artier profile than Balfour, being a little closer to Fiveways. The infant's school is impressive with art covering every wall, and class sizes kept to 30. Its exceptional education in art and music sells the school to the local arty community. The headteacher who used to sit naughty kids outside his door has now gone and has been replaced by the much more sympathetic Miss Kruger whose commitment to the children is shown through her lateral interpretation of the numeracy and literacy hours.

Downs Junior School

Rugby Road, nr Preston Park

01273 558422

Fortunes are changing at Downs Junior with a very active PTA group introducing money and ideas to an eager head. It's an enormous school by primary standards (500 pupils), and that can lead to some disorganisation and more traditional approaches to teaching and discipline. The numeracy and literacy is "coming on", according to one parent, and the playground is being upgraded - largely thanks to the PTA. A new £8,000 climbing frame, an amphitheatre for kids' own plays as well as the African tribal dancing and storytelling which is part of the cultural curriculum, and a plan for rubberised ball areas should improve the school tremendously. For working parents, the Breakfast and After School clubs are handy, and fun for kids with arts and crafts, chess clubs and basketball.

Elm Grove Primary

Elm Grove, Hanover

01273 708004

One of the most popular primary schools in Brighton. The previous headmistress transformed its ailing reputation by working in partnership with parents and the local community, and super-head John Lynch, now into his second year at the helm, is continuing to develop this, with parents' special needs support groups among the initiatives. Lynch is still preaching respect for each other and the environment as he did at Stanford, and the school's calm and peaceful atmosphere is a direct result. He's introduced a school council, new loos and even renamed the canteen "the restaurant"; "it's all about making the children feel like they deserve the best", he explains.

The school is part of the Children's University, which allows every child access to learning out of school hours. The Breakfast and After School are open from 8am to 6pm.

Goldstone Primary

Laburnam Avenue, Hove

01273 739730

On the north side of the Old Shoreham Road, Goldstone has an innovative legacy left by former headteacher with a good policy on the inclusion of music and arts in the numeracy and literacy push. Compared to some of the schools' take on numeracy for six-year-olds (reciting times tables - no really), the sight of children giggling as they lie down on the floor to measure each other is a joy. PHSE (Personal, Health and Social Education) is one of those newfangled subjects parents didn't have in their day, and at Goldstone, role playing, which forms its bottom line, seems to bring out a laudable confidence in its pupils. The school has recently merged with Knoll Infants under its new headteacher, Richard Sutton-Smith, and there are plans to move both schools onto the Goldstone site in the future.

Middle Street Primary School

Middle Street, The Lanes

01273 323184

Right in the heart of old town Brighton and serves a mixed community of media kids and inner city types. It also has a nursery for three to four-year-olds. Right-on and committed staff. The school achieves excellent results, and has a wide range of active links with the local community; Headteacher Gina Hutchins has successfully managed to integrate its very diverse mixed-ability multicultural intake which includes significant numbers of refugee and minority group children. It's currently one of five local schools selected by the DfES to participate in a prestigious national demonstration project about developing community schooling. Funds from this will start real progress on building a family/community room in a new upper storey to the school.

Queen's Park

Park Street, Queen's Park

01273 686822

Queen's Park school has a fantastic location, perched at the bottom of the park and within skipping distance of the park playground. Unlike St Luke's, Queen's Park has a separate nursery and a two-form entry. The school also has a lower intake than the others and so the class sizes are smaller, and since Queen's Park has become extremely popular, entrance is difficult unless you live very close by. Queen's Park and St Luke's have similar educational philosophies

and both work in close partnership with parents. The parent teacher's association is extremely active and their school fairs are always popular. Mrs Scott, the head teacher, has built the school's social and academic reputation, helped by a loyal teaching staff. The school exudes a cosy, close knit environment, which seems to appeal to both parents and children alike.

St Mary's CE, Rottingdean

Whiteway Lane, Rottingdean

01273 303109

Only a five-minute drive from Kemp Town, it has a very good reputation and is high on the league tables.

St Bernadette's
RC Primary School

Preston Road,

Preston Park

01273 553813

A highly recommended primary with, unsurprisingly, a heavy Catholic bias (99 per cent of the pupils are Catholic), where the teaching, discipline and ethos comes from the religion. Its policy towards special needs, for example, follows Jesus's model rather than the local education authority's. Academic achievement and social skills are also based on the Christian ideal with a good deal of support from the local parish and parents. Montessori has influenced much of the teaching, a legacy from the former deputy head who trained as a Montessori teacher, so expect a high level of independence from pupils.

St John The Baptist
RC - Aided Primary
Whitehawk Hill Road,
Whitehawk
01273 607924

St John the Baptist will appeal to those who want a traditional Catholic academic education with strong emphasis on discipline and the three Rs. Situated right at the top of Whitehawk Hill Road, it has wonderful views all over Brighton and has vast playing fields. The school has a one-class entry and an admissions policy, which gives preferential treatment to Catholics, but if you're a nice, middle-class, non-Catholic family, you stand a good chance. Acting head Ms W King has recently replaced Mr O Sullivan so expect some changes.

St Luke's Infants
Queen's Park Rise,
Queen's Park
01273 699924

Divided into infants and juniors, St Luke's is the largest primary school in the area with a three-class intake. Despite its size, one of the infant school's strengths is the gentle and caring approach adopted by both the staff and by Nesta Saunders, the headmistress.

St Luke's has long enjoyed an excellent reputation for the arts and has managed to successfully integrate it into the literacy and numeracy push. So good is the art, it was exhibited at the Gardner Arts Centre.

St Luke's Juniors
St Luke's Terrace, Queen's Park
01273 675080

The Junior School, headed by Ron Guildford, like the infants enjoys a steady academic reputation, and has recently been awarded Beacon School status which means that it's good enough for others to learn from. The school provides a range of extra-curricular activities, including athletics, football and chess. For those interested in league tables, St Luke's tends to be on a par with Queen's Park and Elm Grove.

Somerhill Junior
Somerhill Road, St Anne's Well, Hove
01273 739659

Keeps strong ties with its 'little sister' Davigdor Infants, sharing its huge field for football, baseball and other sports. Kids coming in aged seven join a 'family' made up of one child from each year to help them find their feet. It's a good example of the school's emphasis on pastoral care; the lack of classrooms, with an open-plan space divided off by curtains is another, allowing mixed-age groups to interact well. But on the whole, the feel is traditional, with children taught to write with ink pens. The headteacher is unusually candid in the way he presents children's work to would-be parents, picking up examples as she sees them rather than digging out the scholarly stuff. Good on art and music, with regular concerts. Another Beacon school, it's been identified as amongst the best performing schools in the country and represent examples of successful practice which other schools can take as their model.

Stanford Infants
Highcroft Villas, Hove
01273 555240

On the whole, Brighton is big on the arts, and at Stanford the infants make pottery masks in the school kiln and learn about multi-cultural arts within a broader curriculum. Arts include dance and music, and are used in numeracy and literacy hours. The school has had a major overhaul in the past few years; new head teacher, Mrs Wicker, now describes it is a parent-friendly school which encourages children to become confident enough to go on to the next, more formal stage of their education with a love of learning. The ethos of the school is an extremely supportive one, with staff encouraged to take courses, classroom assistants properly trained, and a staff room where teachers are recognised for their achievements. Recently inspected by Ofsted, had an excellent report.

Stanford Junior
Stanford Road, Hove
01273 565570

Stanford Junior verges on the hippie with its strong concentration on relationships, but that's fine by us and many people in Hove, Preston Park and Fiveways. Former superhead, John Lynch left two years ago after creating a happy school in which bullying is just about a thing of the past - a feat of Lynch's which the children recognise and appreciate. He has now gone on to Elm Grove leaving Mrs Robinson as acting head.

● SECONDARIES

Blatchington Mill School
Holmes Avenue, Hove
01273 736244

On the north side of the Old Shoreham Road in Hove, this is one of the better secondary schools and sixth form colleges, which was awarded performing arts status last year. Its Glenn Miller-style band, The Millstones, plays in the Brighton Festival and tours internationally, winning it enough financial support to build its brand new theatre that opened last autumn. Young musicians at Hangleton Junior and surrounding junior schools are often picked up by Blatchington scouts and encouraged to join the many ensembles and orchestras at the school. Parents report a strong sense of discipline, effective control of bullying and has an accessible attitude to pupils and staff. The school is also strong in English, IT and drama.

Dorothy Stringer High School
Loder Road, Preston Park
01273 557311

Dorothy Stringer has become one of the most sought-after secondary schools in Brighton, which means that it has become oversubscribed and its boundaries are receding. The school has a sound academic reputation and headmaster, Trevor Allen, leads the school in a disciplined but highly approachable way that appears to be very successful. The school is famed for its music department and Stringer children have sung both with The Brighton Youth Orchestra at Glyndebourne, and at the London Palladium. The sports facilities are excellent and include a swimming pool, tennis courts and large playing fields. Parents appear to have few complaints except that classes are too big as the school increases in popularity - a universal problem with the comprehensive system. It was recently awarded Specialist Sports College status.

Patcham High School

Ladies Mile Road, Patcham
01273 503908

Patcham High School has established itself as an award winning school with a reputation for innovation. The only secondary in the area to have achieved both the national GOLD Artsmark and GOLD Sportsmark (with a new recommendation for distinction), it is chosen frequently to pilot national initiatives such as summer schools. Headteacher Liz Fletcher and her team are known for being very approachable (Liz herself is reckoned to know each of her many students by name). Very much a local community school now, ex-students come back to help regularly because they still like to be part of

Patcham High's 'family' atmosphere.

Varndean School

Balfour Road, Preston Park
01273 561281

Varndean has an excellent reputation for secondary academic education. It shares a very large site with Dorothy Stringer and the Balfour schools, and has a healthy competition with Stringer. It has specialist Technology College status, and is also a Beacon school (good enough to be a role model for other schools). Andy Schofield, its headteacher for the past two years, has enhanced an already good reputation.

● SIXTH FORM COLLEGE

BHASVIC

205 Dyke Road, Hove
01273 552200

Brighton and Hove's sixth form college, where the brainiest kids from here and Lewes vie for places.

Varndean College

Surrenden Road, Preston Park
01273 508011

Varndean College is situated in the leafy suburbs of north Brighton with about 1,000 full-time 16 to 18-year-olds taking mainly advanced level courses. It has a national reputation for the quality of its exam results and, particularly, for its 'value-added' achievement where it was recently ranked as the top college in the whole country. The college is oversubscribed, thanks to the high number of students attracted to the college's great reputation for both good examination results along with the other opportunities arising from the excellent sports, music, drama and IT facilities.

As part of its important role in the Brighton community, Varndean College also offers courses for full-time adults - mainly in its one year Access to Higher Education and Office Administration courses. About 1,500 part-time adults are attracted to evening classes in IT, counselling, languages, and other areas, with a growing number taking up opportunities in 'outreach' centres in other parts of the City.

PRIVATE

Brighton & Hove High

Junior School: Radinden Manor Road, Hove
01273 505004
Senior School: Montpelier Road, Brighton
01273 734112

Placed firmly at the top of the Sussex league tables, Brighton and Hove was one of the first schools in the country to provide high quality education for girls, and early pupils were among the first women in England to go to university. Although it enjoys a brilliant academic reputation, the school also has vibrant art, music and drama departments. Brighton and Hove's academic reputation is famed, but one parent told us that she was impressed by the discouragement of personal competition. Despite this, it is worth pointing out that Brighton and Hove is deeply selective and will only take in girls who are already at the top of their class.

Brighton College Upper School

Eastern Road, Kemp Town
01273 704339
www.brightoncollege.org.uk

Brighton College is less selective than its main competitor, Brighton and Hove High although, academically, there's little to choose between the two schools. It beats the High School in some league tables, and has smaller class sizes and a broader curriculum. Contrary to popular opinion, parents report that it is neither traditional nor disciplinarian but lively and progressive and very family oriented. Headteacher, Dr Anthony Seldon is extremely involved in the community and pioneering initiatives with state schools such as the under-resourced COMA (College of Media Arts) in Whitehawk. Music, drama, dance and sport are exceptional with former national coaches teaching rugby, hockey and cricket (including a former Ladies cricket captain).

Newlands School

Eastbourne Road, Seaford
01323 892334/490000 www.newlands-school.com

An independent day and boarding school from 3 to 18 set on a picturesque site in Seaford. The school has excellent sports and recreational facilities and has recently introduced a superb theatre arts programme offering a full range of dance, drama and music lessons enabling children to develop their talents and receive a thorough academic education simultaneously. A fleet of mini-buses transports day children across Sussex. The school does not select pupils but achieves very good academic results and the Gannon Centre on site provides extra tuition and support for children with a range of special needs.

Roedean

Roedean Way,
Rottingdean
01273 603181

The famous ivory tower on the hilltop with its own tunnel down to the sea has managed to keep hold of its reputation as top gels' school, while joining the 21st century. Set up by early feminists, it has always been keen to encourage girls to get ahead and provides exceptional facilities to help them get there. An indoor swimming pool, theatre, dance studio, design technology and language labs lead off corridors connecting bedrooms to classrooms and individual studies. The environment inside is cosy while the wind of the outside world hammers against its impenetrable walls. Roedean gels never even need to leave the building, apart from a little community service every week to give them a sense of the real world they were born to rule. Day girls, weekly boarders and full-time boarders come from all

over the world, and there are probably more Chinese and African faces here than anywhere in Brighton.

Stonelands School of Ballet and Theatre Arts

170-172 Church Road,
Hove
01273 770445

Stage school for day and boarding boys and girls aged between 6 and 16 with small class sizes, and steep fees.

St Aubyns

76 High Street,
Rottingdean
01273 302170

The children at St Aubyns enjoy the peaceful and relaxing location of Rottingdean village set between the sea and the downs. It is a traditional Christian prep school, but has every modern facility imaginable from a computer suite to a performing arts studio with music, art, and extensive sports facilities. Fencing lessons and horse-riding are popular choices. The emphasis on small classes and good behaviour means its pupils are successful academically. The school provides all that you would expect for fees that reach £2,800 for day pupils and £3,765 for boarders, per term. It's recent conversion to co-education and the enthusiasm of the headmaster, Mr Gobat, also contributes to its popularity. Don't be put off by its out of town location, day pupils of all ages commute from Brighton and Hove on the school bus.

St Mary's Hall

Eastern Road,
Kemp Town
01273 505004

St Mary's Hall in Kemp Town is a Christian, independent, day and boarding school for children of three to 18. The Junior school accepts boys but after the age of eight it focuses solely on girls. St Mary's Hall doesn't have a selection policy, which is unusual in the private sector. The policy of welcoming all abilities attracts parents who like the idea of private education but don't want their offspring to be pressurised. St Mary's prides itself in its caring approach, enjoys a reputation for being a gentle but academic school and the class sizes are very small. As you would expect from an independent school, the music, art, drama and sports facilities are all extensive.

Windlesham School

190 Dyke Road, Hove
01273 553645

A homey environment for 3 to 5-year-olds extending out the back into a warren of classrooms, lawns, swimming pool and sports courts for the older ones, Windlesham is led by Mrs Bennett-Odlum, a shiny happy sporty type whom the kids flock to. Specialist drama and music teachers coach the boys and girls through impressive school productions, and a choir practices twice a week. An unusually good understanding of alternative forms of education among the teachers means

that children from outside poshschoolville are accommodated comfortably, but at £1,200 per term fee for the over 6's, scholarships to Brighton College and Hurstpierpoint, Brighton and Hove High and St Mary's are the traditional route out at 11.

● SPECIAL SCHOOLS

Amaze

01273 772289

Local parent helpline and advocacy group which helps parents find their way through the maze of options and obstacles surrounding children with special needs.

● AUTISM

There are four special units at State schools in B&H, for children with autism: West Blatchington Infants, and West Blatchington Juniors; Downsview School and Downs Park School.

ASD Support

01273 424963

● HEARING IMPAIRED

There's a special facility for children with severe hearing impairment at Bevendean Primary, and an ICAN centre (for children with speech and language difficulties) at Carden Primary school.

Pre-School Special Needs

Jeanne Saunders Centre
01273 294944

● FINDING YOUR SCHOOL

League Tables will only give you a guide, so consider this advice compiled from a number of teachers from alternative to State education. When looking around, check the following - and watch out for sales flannel.

● NURSERY, PRIMARY AND JUNIOR

- What training do the staff have? If Montessori or claiming to be part of another educational system, check they belong to and are inspected by the correct outfits.
- Who inspects them? Are Ofsted reports visible?
- How do the adults interact with children? If very small children, do they talk down to them or ask parents about them when they can answer for themselves? Do they get down to their level?
- How many children in classes? How many trained and experienced staff to look after them?
- Is it colourful and homely inside?
- Is the environment calm or rowdy? If it's full of exuberant kids, check to see it's not disorganised, and that the quieter kids are being cared for. If it's too calm, are the kids happy or constrained?
- What happens in the course of the day? How formal/informal?
- What are the aims of the school? What is its ethos?
- What records are kept on the child?
- What equipment/activities does the school have?
- How much space is there for bigger children, and how safe is it?
- Do children have free or restricted access to each other, to toilets, snacks etc?
- What is the settling in procedure?
- What is the supervision procedure over lunch/playtime?
- What is our gut feeling about the place and the staff?
- Imagine your child there; would he/she be comfortable, safe and happy?
- Do you like the staff? Can you imagine having an open and frank relationship with them if your child goes to this school?

● SECONDARY

- Past results at GCSE and A level. Ask if there's a difference in results between boys and girls.
- Truancy rates - not just from school but from lessons; some children may make the register, but spend their days wandering around the school.

- What's the take up at 6th form?
- Extra curricular activity. Duke of Edinburgh for example. School trips.
- When looking around, look at the displays; are they marked, or are they there to look good?
- Look at textbooks to see how new they are
- Look at exercise books to see how well they've been marked; how long is the comment? What is being rewarded?
- Ask about reward systems.
- Check the pastoral approach. Do year heads rotate so that they can maintain their relationship with the children throughout their schooling, or do they end at the end of each year?
- Staff morale. What's the relationship between staff and head? Do they call each other by their first names? Do the heads go on school trips? How involved are they? What's the turnover of staff?
- Homework - what happens if it isn't done?
- What's the discipline policy? Why would a child by excluded or suspended? How many cases?
- Do they have plans for extension? What will they do with it?
- How active is the parent/teacher association?

● **With summer approaching, the obvious reason to be glad to live in Brighton is the beach. In the summer I meet up with friends and we retire to the beach in our denim skirts and sleeveless tops. There we have a day of relaxation and attempted tanning. Everyone wanders down, and eventually there'll be loads of us, staying into the warm evenings talking and laughing. In the winter we stick to places with radiators. The nightlife is good, and whatever you are looking for it's bound to be somewhere in Brighton. If you're not feeling up to it (or is age a problem?) there are also cinemas, bowling alleys and restaurants everywhere. Everywhere is just a bus ride away, and you can walk most places. I'm glad I don't live in a place like London where friends are scattered far and wide. If you are new here, you're bound to feel how eager and able the city is to provide for everyone.**

Zenobe Reade, 15, Brighton College

08.1

● ANTIQUES & COLLECTIBLES

Brighton Architectural Salvage

33 -34 Gloucester Road, North Laine
01273 681656

If you're looking for a beautiful restored fireplace this is the place to come. Sometimes you many find the odd cast iron bath or railings but the rest is a lucky dip.

J S Carter Antiques

9 Boundary Road, Hove
01273 453382

With eight rooms of furniture, among the restoration there are some beautiful Edwardian mahogany pieces. Although it can be expensive, expect to find designs that you wouldn't see in any usual antique shop.

The Lanes Armoury

26 Meeting House Lane, The Lanes
01273 3211357

Voted the best antique and collectibles shop in Great Britain by the Miller's Antique Guide. Mark, the owner, has all types of military armour and weapons from every period. A real haven for little and big boys alike and children are very welcome.

Penny Lane Gallery

33 Upper St James's Street, Kemp Street
01273-686869

Beatles memorabilia, collectibles, vintage film posters, original Rock photography, animation art, rare vinyl, books, ceramics, glassware, cards and coasters all lovingly collected by Kemp Town's art eccentrics Meg and Jane.

The Old Postcard Shop

38 Beaconsfield Road, Preston Park
01273 600035

Go on. Guess.

Snooper's Paradise

7-8 Kensington Gardens, North Laine
01273 602558

Two floors of flea market heaven, browse through the endless stalls of bric-a-brac and collectibles and you're sure to find exactly what you're looking for and more besides. Furniture upstairs and Tuff Tarts clubbing gear on the ground floor.

● ART AND DESIGN

Art Republic

13 Bond Street, North Laine
01273 724829

Fine art poster, print and framing

gallery. Check out the latest exhibitions online and what's on worldwide. You're welcome to check out a picture at home to see if it suits you first. Expert advice and friendly staff.

Artworker

27 Kensington Gardens, North Laine
01273 689822
Grand Parade, Old Steine
01273 675461

Not your run of the mill art shop. Sells all the top range of artist materials for the serious artist.

B.A.G.

108a Dyke Road, Seven Dials
01273 711016

Brighton Artists Gallery provides an outlet for local artists to exhibit, sell and develop their work. New exhibitions every month. Fabulous place to tap into all the talent Brighton has to offer. Open Tuesday -Saturday 11-6pm.

Brighton Bead Shop

21 Sydney Street, North Laine
01273 675077

Bead kits for all ages and skills plus rows and rows of individual beads to suit all budgets for your own individual design. Mail order service - 01273 740777

Brighton Designers & Makers

39 Sydney Street, North Laine
01273 671212

Fantastic local talents abound in this shop and gallery. They have monthly exhibitions with the artist of the month

working downstairs. Over 140 local artists sell their wares here at very reasonable prices

CJ Graphic's

32 Bond Street, North Laine
01273 734400

Bursting with specialist paints, pens, paper and all things arty.

Clarke's Stationers

11 Bond Street, North Laine
01273 728811

The largest selection of stationery and art supplies in Brighton. Arranged over two floors. They also have a nice line in handmade papers and photocopying services.

Economy

82 St George's Road, Kemp Town
01273 682831

The best place to go for all your handicraft needs and everything you need to entertain your little ones come rain or shine. Pens papers, glue, stickers, you name it they've got it.

Pen to Paper

4 Sydney Street, North Laine
01273 676670

All the usual pretty funky accessories and stationary. Specialists in handmade paper.

TN Lawrence

208 Portland Road, Hove
01273 260266

Specialist arts shop for printmakers and

artists. Mail order catalogue available.

White Gallery

86-87 Western Road, Hove
01273 774870

Contemporary gallery covering all mediums of ceramics, glass, jewellery, painting and print. Affordable works of art for home or office. Local and national artists. (See Arts section)

● AUCTION HOUSES

Raymond P Inman: Fine Art Auctioneers

35 Temple Street, Central Brighton
01273 774777
mobile 07769 697747

● BOOKSHOPS

Bookmarch

91 Dyke Road, Seven Dials
01273 735577

Books bought and sold. Modern first editions. Large cross section of books and annuals. Book service available.

Borders

Churchill Square,
Central Brighton
01273 731122

The ground floor stocks magazines, books and CDs, you can even listen to the new sounds before you buy. Upstairs has an enormous selection covering all topics imaginable and the children's section has storytelling for the little ones at 11am on Saturdays.

Brighton Books

18 Kensington Gardens, North Laine
01273 693845

One of the best second hand bookshops in town. Paul and Catherine buy and sell top quality titles covering topics such as biographies art, design and 20th century literature.

City Books

23 Western Road, Hove
01273 725306

Voted by the locals as the best shop around. Their excellent fiction department has lured authors like Louis de Bernieres, Nick Hornby and Will Self. It's well worth having you name added to their events mailing list. They also have excellent sections devoted to children's books, travel, music, poetry, local history and alternative health.

Colin Page Antiquarian Books

36 Duke Street, The Lanes
01273 325954

Walk through the doors into a library offering a great selection of antiquarian books on architecture, antiques art and rare books.

David's Book Shop

3 and 5 Sydney Street,
North Laine
01273 690223

David and Ann have a huge stock of clearance books. The children's section is especially good from 50p upwards. They also sell Pokemon and Harry Potter trading cards.

Kemp Town Bookshop

91 St George's Road, Kemp Town

01273 682110

Small good quality bookshop with a wide range of topics and gift wrap and cards. Their ordering service is second to none.

Oxfam Books

30 Kensington Gardens, North Laine

01273 698093

Wide cross section of good quality second hand books, plus vinyl records and CDs. Good children's section.

Practical Books

14/14a Western Road, Hove

01273 734602

Great selection of foreign language books and mind, body and spirit. Beautiful crystals and cards.

Read and Fed Books

94 St James's Street, Kemp Town

01273 625006

www.readandfedbooks.co.uk

Shamelessly nicking the idea from Books for Cooks in Notting Hill, Angela and her gourmet gang decided that Brighton was gagging for a bookshop dedicated to the foodie, with coffee and armchairs lending an air of indulgence to the shopping. More than just Nigella's and Jamie's latests, what you get here are cookery books as well as books about food, and lessons upstairs on how to create the perfect dinner party. The two to three hours lessons cost £20-£25 (including the food), with local chefs taking you through the ropes.

Sandpiper

34 Kensington Gardens, North Laine

01273 605422

Good quality bargain books to adorn any self-respecting coffee table.

Savery Books

300 Ditchling Road, Five Ways

01273 503030

Two shops in one selling a wide selection of good quality second hand books.

Sussex Stationers

55 East Street, The Lanes

01273 328032

114 St James's Street, Kemp Town

01273 608229

50 Western Road, Hove

01273 204700

A Sussex institution and excellent local stationery chain that also sells popular fiction, non-fiction and children's books.

Two Way Books

54 Gardner Street, North Laine

01273 687729

This shop always has a throng of people browsing. They have a fantastic collection of old comics, paper backs and collectibles for both children and adults.

Waterstones

71-74 North Street, Central Brighton

01273 206017

The largest book shop in Brighton covering five floors and every subject imaginable.

● CHILDREN'S THINGS

Abstract
35 North Road, North Laine
01273 693737
The extremely friendly owner, Bernadette started off with a sewing machine and a market stall and now has a successful and beautiful line in fleece outfits and blankets. Custom designed Moses basket blankets and linings. Linen cotton range for the summer. Stockists of the Baby Hut cotton sling by Chetana Parmar (01273 245864) which allows blissful babies to be carried around in ultimate comfort.

The Animal House
12 Bond Street, North Laine
01273 206836
Every animal cuddly toy imaginable plus toys and gifts.

Blue
20 Church Street, Central Brighton
01273 700370
Arts and crafts made by local artists. Ceramics, cards, jewellery, natural earth coloured clothes. Beautiful handmade kiddies shoes.

Cat and Mouse
17 Sydney Street, North Laine
01273 600145
Designer wear for children aged 0-16

They have their own designs as well as Oiliy, Kenzo, Quik Silver and French Connection to name a few.

Cup Cake
104 St George's Road, Kemp Town
01273 634134
Family run small business selling continental children's clothes and beautiful accessories. All the toys are nostalgic wooden toys not found anywhere else in Brighton and remind you of when you were young. Clothes range from 0-8 years

Cutie
33 Kensington Gardens, North Laine
01273 697957
Barbie girl collection of t-shirts, dresses etc and a fabulous selection of funky pants . In the back you'll find the beanbag boudoir stocking every kind of beanbag and throw imaginable.

Daisy Daisy
33 North Road, North Laine
01273 689108
Traditional wooden toys, adorable little fairy outfits, miniature toy soldiers, cowboys and Indians a huge hit with little boys. New clothing range was so successful second hand clothes had to go. Kit out your little darlings in the chicest of outfits such as beautiful suede dresses.

Dials
86 Dyke Road, Seven Dials
01273 823003

Ever so cute collection of children's clothes and accessories and toys kids up to seven. They produce their own brand of cool funky t-shirts and now supply stuff for the mum's too like shoes, bags, cushions and homeware. Next time you're looking for something for the little darlings pick something up for yourself too.

The Discovery Store
Churchill Square, Central Brighton
01273 322500
www.thediscoverystore.co.uk
Airborn helicopters, Monsters Inc that roar as you pass by, mini pool tables and inflatable sofas, this is kid heaven - however old you are.

The Disney Store
Churchill Square, Central Brighton
01273 778842
Oh go on - your kids will love you forever. The staff and their prefect manners are straight out of Disneyland too

Early Learning Centre
Churchill Square, Central Brighton
01273 722189
On a wet rainy day in Brighton, there's nowhere like Churchill Square if you've got young kids. And The Early Learning Centre really don't seem to mind if your toddlers make a giraffe family on the floor or hide in Postman Pat pop up tents all day long. Someone should get wise and put a café at the back for the parents.

Gamleys Toy Shop
64-68 Church Road, Hove
01273 733002
Good quality toy shop since 1965. Stockists include Matel, Galt, Lego, Playmobile etc. for all ages. Far better than their sister store in Churchill Square, but to be fair they have been open longer.

Girl Heaven
Churchill Square
01273 737376
Or nightmare for the parents who watch their little darlings' faces light up and book themselves in for a hair braiding, make over or girly party. First stop on the search for any self respecting Barbie girl.

Gymboree Play and Music
Churchill Square, Central Brighton
01273 772900
Once upon a time, this was the crèche where shopaholics would happily leave their little monsters to play Wendy houses and watch Snow White and the uproar that followed its closure you don't want to know about. These days Gymboree, once the name of posh kids clothing in Churchill Square, has brought its creative mix of learning, fitness, positive parenting and fun to the Mall. The classes are designed to stimulate progress through the all important early years, with activities developed for six separate age groups from new-borns to under-fives. Led by trained instructors, each 45 minute class

is about encouraging your child and helping them build confidence, competence and self-esteem. Apparently Kate Winslett takes baby Mia to her North London local.

H&M
Churchill Square, Central Brighton
01273 729743
Kids clothes that are astonishingly inexpensive, dead trendy and last forever.

Havelock Road Post Office
107 Havelock Road, Preston Park
01273 552002
Friendly local post office, also stocks a good selection of Orchard toys.

Ju-Ju
24 Gloucester Road, North Laine
01273 673161
Funky casual and club gear for the young.

National Schoolwear Centres
40 Blatchington Road, Hove
01273 739676
schoolshop@lineone.net
www.n-sc.co.uk
The only shop that sells the generic uniforms for all the schools in the area, although the odd thing you may need to go to John Lewis for. Accessories too, plimsolls, bags ballet and swimming kit.

Nursery Stars
01273 306240
Mail order company selling beautiful

cringe-free children's music. Over the Moon featuring traditional nursery rhymes with modern ambient arrangements is a great chill album both for post clubbing parents and a soothing bedtime solution for cranky kids.

Pine Secrets
65 East Street, The Lanes
01273 729271
Largest selection of Beanie Buddies and Babies and now Pokemon collectibles. Great prices.

Poundland
Western Road, Central Brighton
Everything for £1 shops seem to be springing up everywhere but this one is by far the best with a huge selection of items for the home, gifts, toiletries, biscuits and cakes. The entire upstairs is devoted to toys.

Toby Tiger
15a Montpelier Place, Montpelier
01273 710610
Zoë sells her own brand fleece children's clothing here in her shop for a fraction of what you would pay in the London stores. The shop also stocks little handmade leather shoes, traditional toys and t-shirts and baby-grows. Even little Woody Ball-Cook wears Toby Tiger.

Toys and Togs
94 Boundary Road, Portslade
01273 880808
Second hand and seriously cheap goods for infants and toddlers. Bikes, prams,

three-wheelers and Little Tyke type cars. They also have good second bikes for grown ups.

Wig Wam
267a Preston Drove, Preston Park
01273 55504
Sells everything from pre-pregnancy stages to kids clothes, accessories and toys (including wooden) for little ones up to age eight. Joanna also stocks, all natural washable nappies, the fantastic Tripp Trapp highchairs and cool locally designed t-shirts.

Yamama
92 Trafalgar Street, North Laine
01273 689931
Fun stylish clothes for the younger set. Good basics at good prices.

● CLOTHES

Badger for Men
25 Bond Street, North Laine
01273 722245
Upmarket trendy shop filled with designer men's clothes and shoes. Stockists of Camper, Hackett, Schott, Hush Puppies plus Timberland, Rockport and Birkenstock.

Badger for Women
26 Bond Street,
North Laine
01273 325421
Same stockists as above but women's lines. Other designs include Great Plains, Duffer, Evisu and Diesel.

Design4Nation
Archway, Duke Street, The Lanes
01273 747339
Tucked away off Duke Street is a new courtyard filled with designer labels and fashion heaven for anyone out for a bargain. There's massage, coffee, flowers, jewellery, interiors and the clothes.

East
25 Kensington Gardens, North Laine
01273 622282
Sister company to the Badger shops stocking similar upmarket casual wear. Same labels as Badger including the popular Evisu.

East
51 East Street, The Lanes
01273 776711
Not to be confused with East in Kensington Gardens this is more classical suits and separates for the elegant woman, with eastern style accessories to match. Helpful and friendly staff.

Farnsworth
55-56 East Street,
The Lanes
01273 321218
Don't be deceived by the shop's exterior. They sell a great line in country clothes and sweaters and stock Barbour but they also have a large selection of traditional toys for children, cards and Crabtree and Evelyn smellies. Downstairs houses the cook shop for all your culinary needs.

Garden

39b Sydney Street, North Laine
01273 692691

Brand new designer outlet so new we barely got a glimpse as Juicy fled to its own designer and off to the presses. The fashion is local and exclusive to B&H.

Glass House

East Street, The Lanes
01273 326141

Stylish and creative clothing range for women all sizes looking for arty and elegant designs something of a cross between Ghost and Armani. At last designs for real women without model figures who have (physically and spiritually) outgrown Top Shop. Particularly good for taller women too.

Greenwich Village

Bond Street, North Laine
01273 695451

New York's namesake in one shop. A labyrinth of stalls for the bohemian in all of us. Imports from India, Africa etc. Great selection of ethnic colourful clothes at reasonable prices. Jewellery and artefacts such as Bhuddas are popular.

The Hemp Shop

22 Gardner Street,
North Laine
01273 818047

It's amazing what you can make out of hemp. Beautiful stylish clothes in earthy hues and accessories and bags. Plus perfumes and beauty products.

Igigi

37 Western Road, Hove
01273 734160

Zoë the owner has an eye for classical yet fashionable clothing. All her pieces are collectibles to build a wardrobe that is unlikely to date. Designs are limited and change often.

Inside Out Design

34 Upper St James's Street
01273-674819

Unstructured clothing made and designed by Inside Out Design, Oska, Out of Xile, Adini, East and Animale.

Jump The Gun

36 Gardner Street, North Laine
01273 626777

A shrine to the Mod age. The Vespa in the window gives you a good idea of what you can find and the Paul Weller lookalike will guide you around his fantastic good quality clothes designs.

Long Tall Sally

10 East Street, The Lanes
01273 731791

A range of casual and classic clothes for the taller woman. Now a range for the taller teenage too.

Mambo

37 West Street, Central Brighton
01273 323505

California cool. Sweats, swimming costumes and casual gear for men and women, plus accessories and fantastic Hawaiian shirts.

Minky

26 Sydney Street, North Laine

01273 604456

32 Sydney Street, North Laine

01273 604490

Both shops sell men and women's street wear from London, each shop has different stock. 26 Sydney Street has Glitzy Tarts stock upstairs.

Moist

20 Dukes Lanes, The Lanes

01273 2205544

Super cool and trendy gear for the young who've got a bit of cash.

Motto

12 and 15-16 Duke Street, The Lanes

01273 326633 (women)

01273 771093 (men)

Upmarket designer duds. Stockists include Nicole Farhi, Fake London, Ted Baker and John Smedley.

Old Village

7 Duke Street, The Lanes

01273 204747

Stunning collection of designs with that Vintage feel but definitely new and hot off the rack but the prices are steep and the service sullen and unfriendly. If you've got £200 to blow and want a fabulous shirt to turn heads then this is the place for you.

The One 40 Five Store

27 Sydney Street, North Laine

01273 571145

Streetwear items like hoodies, sweats, jeans, t-shirts and jackets from labels such as Stussy, Silas, Mecca and Freshjive is what you'll find here. And there's a ladies department in the basement too!

Profile

3,4 and 25 Dukes Lane, The Lanes

01273 733561

Designer clothing for men and women. Stockist of Armani, Hugo Boss, Joseph, Prada and Helmut Lang. The women's shop is at Dukes Lane. 01273 323275

Urb

40 Middle Street,

The Lanes

01273 325336

As the name suggests - urban wear for boys. Complete the look with backpacks, sunglasses and baseball caps.

WOW

23 Market Street,

The Lanes

01273 689931

Previously known as Way Out West. Up to the minute fashions for women, stocking shoes, clothes and accessories. Everything from day wear to club wear.

Yellow Submarine

12 Kensington Gardens,

North Laine

01273 626435

Sister shop to the one in Covent Garden. The two girls who run this one are young and fun. They stock great retro men and women's gear and furniture with new accessories such as bags. They also promote local bands and have big plans for the future, watch this space...

● SHOES

Buffalo

33 Duke Street, The Lanes
01273 738866

Very clever mix of trendy casual trainers and elegant kitten heels. Something for both day and night.

Ecco Shoes

Churchill Square,
Central Brighton
01273 732195

Italian designs at reasonable prices

Ghita Shuy

17 St George's Road, Kemp Town
01273 885275

Ghita's shop is also her work room so if you're lucky you'll catch her working on new designs. Her shoes are exquisite, beautifully made -particularly the pointed toed appliquéd flats, and the designs come to her in her dreams. All shoes are made to order for children and adults.

Jones

20-21 East Street, The Lanes
01273 32874
80 Church Road, Hove
01273 733016

Elegant and contemporary shoes for men and women. Stockists of Camper.

Pullingers

9 Bond Street, North Laine
01273 725476
5 George Street, Kemp Town
01273 670187

Good old fashioned shoe shop, selling Church's for men and everything comfy for ladies and gents, Dr Martens for the young.

Vegetarian Shoes

12 Gardner Street,
North Laine
01273 691913

Guilt free, animal friendly footwear. Fashionable hard-wearing styles and the closest look to leather you'll ever find.

● DEPARTMENTS

Debenhams

95-99 Churchill Square,
Central Brighton
01273 326531

Manoeuvre your way past the boring frumpy lines and you'll find Morgan, Pineapple and their own fantastic Red Herring label. Elvi is excellent for fashionable clothes for larger women.

Primark

188 Western Road,
Central Brighton
01273 205211

You would be forgiven for mistaking this store for Marks and Spencer next door because it looks and feels just like it, but note the price tags and buy, buy, buy.

TK Maxx

32-28 North Street, Central Brighton

01273 727483

Discount Designer clothing outlet for all the family. If you're expecting high end designs this is not for you but it's definitely worth a trawl to find a bargain or two. Good leather section.

● SECOND HAND CLOTHES

30a Upper St James's Street

Kemp Town

01273 681384

Open Thurs, Fri, Sat otherwise by appointment.

Be careful not to miss this jewel in Kemp Town. Margaret and Kim have the most beautiful collection of vintage textiles and clothes. Textiles include curtains, linens and lace in fabulous condition and at very good prices. The vintage clothes are affordable and good quality. Otherwise you'll find vintage shoes and children's wear. Pop in for a browse and a chat.

Camden Traders

Bond Street, North Laine

01273 699165

Watch out for the change in name. Loads of trendy second hand clothes mainly from the 1970's.

D and K Rosen

Church Street, The Lanes

01273 326931

Mr Rosen will kit you out to be a king.

A genuine local character, he'll rabbit your ear off, but he's got loads of quality old fashioned second hand clothes for men. Knitwear, coats, hats and accessories from days gone by.

Marie Curie Cancer Cure Charity Shop

99 St George's Road, Kemp Town

01273 673695

One of the best charity shops. Good selection of good quality clothes, books, kids toys etc.

Poppets

50 Blatchington Road, Hove

01273 770449

They stock only good quality second hand clothes, toys and nursery equipment. A definite for some top quality bargains.

Revisions

3 Pool Valley, Old Steine

01273 207728

Designer nearly-new. Great styles at reasonable prices. Stuart and Angela will kit you out in the perfect Armani, Chanel, Gucci or Prada number (to name a few) for a fraction of the price. They even have a good selection of beautiful Voyage cardigans at rock bottom prices.

Starfish

25 Gardner Street, North Laine

01273 680868

Second hand retro clothing and accessories.

To Be Worn Again

51 Providence Place, London Road
01273 624500
24a Sydney Street, North Laine
01273 680296

Largest second hand clothing warehouse in Brighton. At the Sydney Street shop you'll find a great selection of quality second hand clothes, including leather, fake fur, shoes, coats and knitwear. Upstairs houses the Brighton Retro Furniture which stocks everything you'll need to recreate the perfect 1960's/1970's home.

Walk in Wardrobe

89 Western Road, Central Brighton
01273 775583

Alongside the rental section you will find beautiful good quality second hand clothes for sale plus new French designer clothes for sale. The owner has fantastic taste and is on hand to help you choose.

● RENTING CLOTHES

Masquerade

40 Preston Road,
Preston Circus
01273 673381

Fancy dress and costumes and the best selection of masks in town.

Walk in Wardrobe Rental

89 Western Road,
Hove
01273 775583

Rental of prom gowns and evening gowns for that special occasion.

Revamp

11 Sydney Street, North Laine
01273 623288

Vast collection of fancy dress for sale or hire plus accessories such as wigs, masks and boots. They have a good children's section and all the usual party gear like balloons, banners etc.

● DIY

B&Q

Pavilion Retail Park, Lewes Road,
Brighton
01273 679926
43-61 Brighton Road,
Shoreham by Sea
01273 463423

National superstore so you should know what to expect...

Brewers

49 New England Street,
Preston Circus
01273 570243

Brewers exceptionally knowledgeable staff and fantastic stock make it the decorators' paint shop. Not only do they sell Fired Earth, John Oliver and Farrow and Ball, but if you find a paint range that you like they will order it for you.

Homebase

Holmbush Farm Retail Park,
Upper Shoreham Road
01273 871403
Old Shoreham Road, Hove
01273 729637

Nationwide DIY superstore.

MacDougall Rose

12 Richmond Parade, Central Brighton
01273 606482
Do not be fooled by MacDougall Rose's appearance of being only for professionals, they welcome all and sundry. Dulux specialists and the staff are knowledgeable and friendly.

Paint Magic

31 Western Road, Hove
01273 747980
Jocasta Innes' shop stocking her own paint range as well as John Oliver and Fired Earth. There's a gorgeous selection of mosaics and they run courses in decorative paint effects and furniture making. If that's not enough, they also sell handmade kitchens to die for.

The Stencil Store

15c Prince Albert Street, The Lanes
01273 721216
Colour wash, scumble glaze, acrylic-based paints and a wide range of stencils and stencil sticks.

Sutton's Furnishings

56 Church Road, Hove
01273 723728
A beautiful paint range, including Designers Guild, Zoffany's and Osbourne and Little.

Wickes

Davigdor Road, Hove
01273 207766
Aisles and aisles of just about everything you'll ever need if you're doing up your house or decorating the Christmas tree.

● FABRICS

The Fabric Warehouse

42 George Street, Kemp Town
01273 620744
Fantastic selection of unusual and discount fabrics sold at very reasonable prices including an excellent curtain material selection. Top service too.

Fabric Wear

51 Gardner Street, North Laine
01273 605512
All the usual zips, silks, needles and fabulously cheap and exotic sari materials for your individual creation.

Saffron

21 Bond Street, North Laine
01273 694919
Fabulous collection of hand woven cottons and silk from a family run mill in India. All fabrics are fair trade. Textiles include tassels, tablecloths, cushion covers and cloth on the roll. Friendly expert advice.

Southern Handicrafts

20 Kensington Gardens, North Laine
01273 681901
If you can't find it here chances are you won't find it anywhere. The one stop shop for serious dressmakers.

Velvet

Gardner Street, North Laine
01273 670007

27 Bond Street, Central Brighton
01273 326007

Homing fearlessly into the mass of Brighton's hippy chics who can run up a skirt out of a net curtain (and do), Velvet is a pleasuredome of fabrics and harberdashery happiness. They've even got the pattern books that your mum used to wade through in John Lewis, but with enough sequins and sew-on rose buds to make sew-your-own a thoroughly trendy experience.

● FLOWERS

Bonsai KO
45 Sydney Street, North Laine
01273 621743

Such a tranquil little shop. The owner is friendly and knows all there is to know about caring for Bonsai trees. He has worldwide orders and stocks books and tools to help you along.

Botanica
47 Gardner Street, North Laine
01273 686377

There's no sign on the door but you can't fail to spot this great florist in the North Laines. All the usual arrangements, functions etc plus exotic blooms and the deepest red roses you'll ever see.

Flowers by Best
42a Ship Street, The Lanes
01273 205040

Very pretty blue and yellow shop selling a lovely array of fresh flowers and designer hand tied bouquets.

The Flower Stand
Outside St John's Church,
Palmeira Square, Hove
01273 711711

Open from 9.30am to 8pm 7 days a week, this buzzy flower stand is a real find. Expect Kangaroo Paw, Proteas and Gingers next to Irises and Tulips, all served with the kind of passion that you don't find in the average florist.

Gunns
13 14 Sydney Street, North Laine
6 Castle Street, Central Brighton
Western Kiosk Churchill Square
01273 683038 (for all shops)

Large family owned florist selling a wide selection of plants and flowers at really good prices.

Tiger Lily
01273 708977
07787 531199 fax. 01273 571554

Flowers by order for people who want wedding flowers with a difference, this Hanover-based florist will design something extra special for the big day, right down to the last button-hole.

● FOOD AND DRINK

● BEAUTIFUL BAKERS

Cantors of Hove
20 Richardson Road, Hove
01273 723669

Tiny little shop selling a good selection

of rye bread, bagels and salt beef.

Truffles Bakers and Confectioners

21 George Street, Hove

01273 725686

More than your run of the mill bakers. Great selection of cakes and fresh baked bread, pies and pasties.

● BASICALLY BOOZE

Brighton Malt House

North Road, The Lanes

For whisky connoisseurs. Ring the bell. It's only open at the weekends.

Brighton Wine School

01273 721353

ella@brightonwineschool.co.uk

Original and informative ways to de-mystify wine and selection. Anything from one off local tastings to four-week courses held in the historic wine cellars of the Old Ship Hotel.

The Butlers Wine Cellar

247 Queen's Park Road, Queen's Park

01273 698724

Henry Butler sells speciality wines for connoisseurs he is also one of the Brighton Wine School tutors.

Latin Spirits and Beers

PO Box 3092, Littlehampton BN16 1TW

01903 856223

Colin Bradshaw comes to Brighton and Hove three times a week to deliver his wide range of speciality spirits and beers

Altai vodka is a big seller as are the tequilas and schnapps.

Le Grand Fromage/ L'Espirit Du Vin

8-10 East Street, Shoreham

01273 440337

L'Esprit du Vin has a selection of fine wines (including organic) while Le Grand Fromage stocks unusual and quality cheeses for that perfect accompaniment.

Southover Wines

80 Southover Street,

Hanover

01273 600402

Obscure and eclectic collection of wine, ales and beer from around the world.

● CORPULENT CHOCOLATE

Choccywoccydoodah

27 Middle Street,

The Lanes

01273 381999

A veritable chocolate nirvana. The most fabulous and innovative designs in chocolate for all occasions and to order. The shop resembles a gilded boudoir and is not to be missed.

Montezuma's Chocolates

15 Duke Street,

The Lanes

01273 324979

Organic, orgasmic chocolate. Great children's range and their famous truffles. Mail order available.

● CHOLESTEROL CORNER

The Cheese Shop
17 Kensington Gardens,
North Laine
01273 601129
The name says it all really, although they do have a nice line in veggie pizza and focaccia and ciabatta bread to compliment your cheese.

● DEAD GOOD DELIVERIES

Beans and Things
01273 477774
Organic deliveries to your door.

Can be slow in sending you their catalogue but once they do we hear they're worth it.

b.right.on Food Co
01273 705606
Miranda and Pete deliver home cooked organic meals to your door. Fantastic selection of cuisines and cultures available for example, wild salmon teriyaki, fragrant rice and wasabi/soy dressing, Thai fishcakes, or a host of vegan and vegetarian delights. Exceptionally good value. Try out their vast range of chillies too.

Kudos Foods
01323-811118
www.kudosfoods.co.uk
Home delivered food delivered to your door the night before your dinner party, hassle free, nutritious. A bargain at the price.

The Organic Oasis
01444 459596
Organic deli which provides homestyle organic catering for dinner parties and bigger fish if you join their Sussex Good Food Club at £20 per year.

Real Food Direct
01273 621222
Local organic produce home delivered.

● DELICIOUS DELIS

Bona Foodie
21 St. James's Street,
Kemp Town
01273 698007
A deli with a difference. Selling the usual range of meat, cheeses and fancy foods they also have a good range of organic products and items for people with allergies. You can choose to take away the prepared meals or indulge yourself in the small but pleasant café at the back. The range of marmalades, curds, chutneys, pickles, and relishes is reason enough to take a peak. Champagne mustard is recommended for those with expensive taste.

The Cherry Tree
107 St James's Street,
Kemp Town
01273 698684
Mediterranean delicatessen specialising in produce from Italy, Turkey and Greece. Pasta, speciality canned foods, organic bread and cakes. Fabulous olives, cheese and jams from Turkey.

Cullens

102/4 Church Road, Hove

The famous chain of London speciality mini-markets has found its way to Hove. Good quality deli stuff, fruit, veg, freshly baked bread and hot meals made daily. Open seven days a week.

Deb's Deli

4 Gardner Street, North Laine
01273 604925

Their display of pies, pastries and quiches etc in the window will tempt you in. They have a great selection of English and continental delicacies.

Kemp Town Delicatessen

108 St George's Road, Kemp Town
01273 603411

The queues at lunchtime spell out the popularity of this store. They sell fresh juice, croissants and pastries, homemade soups and the usual deli stuff. They also have a cappuccino bar.

The Italian Shop

91-94 Dyke Road, Seven Dials
01273 326147

Owner Giovanni is a sweetheart and will sell you genuine Italian delicacies and takeaway foods.

Le Gourmet

159 Dyke Road,
Seven Dials
01273 778437

Good quality European deli selling goods from Italy and France. Freshly prepared take-away food available too.

Lanes Deli and Pasta Shop

128 Meeting House Lane, The Lanes
01273 723522

Step into Little Italy and forget you're still in England. Wonderful fresh pasta and all the usual deli stuff , expensive but definitely worth it.

Spaghetti Junction

60 Preston Street,
Central Brighton
01273 737082

Currently under refurbishment. Wonderful deli foods, paninis, and hot pastas to eat in or take away.

● EXQUISITE EASTERN

Embrotrap

19 Church Road
01273 733246

Chinese supermarket selling the most extensive range of soy sauces plus products from all over Asia.

Ryelight Chinese Supermarket

48 Preston Street
01273 734954

Sells everything you need to create the perfect Chinese dish.

Taj Mahal

21a/b Bedford Place, Brunswick
01273 325027

The place to shop for Asian and Oriental, their exotic fresh produce section of mouth watering delicacies as is their selection of olives, feta and halal meat.

Yum Yum

22-23 Sydney Street
01273 606777
Oriental supermarket stocking all you need to recreate the perfect Asian meal. Cheap and exceptionally good noodle bar upstairs.

● FRANKLY FISH

Fish At the Square

2 St George's Road,
Kemp Town
01273 680808
You can't miss this fishmonger as there's a beautiful fish sculpture hanging in the window. Fish arrives fresh everyday and they make their own scrumptious fish cakes and other fishy products.

Kevin's

17 Richardson Road,
Hove
01273 738779
Fresh, high quality fish served by the charming Kevin who is always ready with a smile. You can order in advance.

Kings Arches

Brighton
As recommended by Rick Stein. Buy freshly caught local fish at a tiny window next to the Fishing Museum.

Shoreham Fish Market

Shoreham Lagoon
Buy the widest selection of the local fisherman's catch including lobster, crab and bream.

● FRUIT'N'VEG

Proto Greengrocer

St George's Road, Kemp Town
01273 681518
Top quality fruit and vegetables open Mon-Sat They also sell flowers, plants and organic foods. Open Sunday morning until 12.00

● MAINLY MEAT

Brampton's Butchers

114 St George's Road, Kemp Town
01273 682611
One of the few remaining old-fashioned family butchers around. Quality assured Scotch beef, free range chickens etc. People travel far and wide for their produce. Their adjoining shop sells a fantastic range of cheeses and salamis.

Canhams of Hove

48 Church Road, Hove
01273 731021
Deli style sandwiches, quiches, pies, pasties and patisseries made on the premises. Suppliers of local jams. Small butchers with one of the best selections of free range meat in town.

Gibson and Coe

49 George Street, Hove
01273 731407
Good quality family butchers and fishmongers

Sensational Sausages

57a George Street, Hove

01273 723200
International and English sausages of any flavour imaginable, plus an extensive range of mustards, chutneys and continental provisions. Vegetarian sausages available.

● OSTENSIBLY ORGANIC

Archers Organic Butchers
128 Islingwood Street, Hanover
01273 603234
Locals flock to this organic butchers famed for its quality.

Choice Cuts Organic Butchers
95 Preston Drove, Preston Park
01273 381616
Organic produce such as veg, chutneys as well as meat and eggs.

Choice Cuts Deli
94a Preston Drove, Preston Park
01273 381616
Same owners as the butchers next door. The produce is every bit as organic and yummy as the stuff you find next door.

Home Grown Organics
01903 879541
An organic gardener who can set you up to grow your own goodies, including herbs and flowers, a taste of the Good Life.

Middle Farm
Firle (on the A26 to Eastbourne)
01323 811411
More than just a place to take the kids as the shop also sells a huge range of organic products including English wines and ciders (01323-811324) There are 70 different types of cheese to chose and taste from plus organic and additive free meat.

Old Spot Farm
01825 722894
Originally set up by farmer Ray Gould in the 70s to provide good quality organic produce for his children. The farm sells everything from free range, additive free, organic chickens, beef and pork to their own homemade sausages.

Ridgeview Estate Winery Ltd
Fragbarrow Lane, Ditchling Common
01444-258039
Organic sparkling wine that tastes as good as champagne.

● VIRTUOUSLY VEGETARIAN

Golchin Food Store
132 Western Road
01273 324514
A vast array of international vegetarian produce that you just can't find anywhere else and the best range of juice from all over the world. Vegan and gluten free available.

Infinity Foods
25 North Road
01273 603563
This supermarket is always busy. They have a fantastic selection of high quality organic produce. Luscious vegetables,

bakery and a good range in alternative medicines. Friendly and knowledgeable staff. There's a café round the corner in Gardner Street.

● GIFTS

A Lot of Gaul / Belle Boutique

32 Kensington Gardens, North Laine
01273 621135

Get your balls here if you fancy a game on the petanque terrain near the West Pier. All things French for sale from Bretton shirts to Asterix and Tin Tin collectibles and the latest in French dance music. Belle Boutique occupies the back room of the shop and offers French food and smellies, the 3 types of garlic are very popular.

Appendage

36 Kensington Gardens, North Laine
01273 605901

Fabulous collection of unusual contemporary jewellery and gifts made by local artists at affordable prices, handmade bags, copper heart key rings and John Castle's reclaimed wood lamp bases and painted shades.

Bazar

58 Church Street, Hove
01273 737121
32 London Road, Preston Circus
01273 628435

An amazing collection of jewellery, gifts and home accessories imported from 28 countries. Unusual, quirky and reasonably priced one-offs that you're unlikely to find anywhere else.

Brighton Peace and Environment Centre

Gardner Street, North Laine

A shop, library and education centre. Fair trade gifts, clothing, books, the list is endless in the pursuit of giving peace a chance.

Departure Shop

19 Gardner Street, North Laine
01273 572100

Everything for the traveller. Beautiful contemporary luggage and accessories. Books, maps, beauty kits, sunglasses and seasonal accessories.

Em Space

20 Sydney Street,
North Laine
01273 683400

Cool cards and gift wrap. Check out the local artists work while you're there.

Fossil 2000

3 Kensington Place,
North Laine
01273 622000
www.fossil2000.co.uk

Nothing in glass cabinets here, everything on display and ready to be touched and handled. Huge array of A grade crystals and ammonites. Everything for the collector large or small. Dinosaur teeth and eggs. Exclusive fossilised seabed stone with orthoceras inlaid crafted into bowls, plates goblets etc. Children friendly.

The Gadget Shop
Churchill Square, Central Brighton
01273 737767
For the man or woman who has everything.

Malarkey
34 Bond Street, North Laine
01273 722339
Individual gifts and cards and one-offs for those who want something different.

Planet Gadget
39 Gardner Street, North Laine
01273 603800
19 Meeting House Lane, The Lanes
01273 227778
This is the place to come for that silly gift you've been looking for. Inexpensive selection of knick knacks and gadgets plus bags, novelty lighting and chrome accessories.

Rin Tin Tin
34 North Road, North Laine
01273 672424
The ultimate in ephemera. Rick the owner has a fabulous collection of tins, toys and prints plus a framing service.

Tsena
6 Bond Street, North Laine
01273 328402
Original limited edition gifts. Personalised embroidered cards made by local, Laura Windebank. Bob and Blossom t-shirts for kids. Leather and suede books in pastel hues. Personalised ceramics for weddings etc. Plus

glassware, pewter and cards all designed by local and national designers.

What's New
12 Brighton Square, The Lanes
01273 777373
Great innovations shop stocking the best seller 'warmys', a reusable hand warmer that at a click of a button warms to 45 degrees, a must for every winter. Other amazing inventions include the cordless light bulb, the doggy dosh moneybox and the water dispenser. If you're looking for an unusual gift this is the place to come.

● HI-FI

Jeffries
69 London Road, Preston Circus
01273 609431
High end stereo equipment - Rega decks and the like - sold and repaired by people who care.

Powerplant
40 Church Road, Hove
01273 775978
Incredible top of the range hi-fi and entertainment systems, home cinema, multi room systems, lighting control and the ever-popular plasma screens. Everything trendy and bang up to date.

● INTERIORS AND EXTERIORS

Acme Art
40 Gloucester Road, North Laine

01273 601639

www.acmeartshop.com

A unique gallery housing artist and owner Chris Macdonald. Chris uses reclaimed furniture and old technology to fashion beautiful one off sculptures such as a table top made from an old Singer sewing machine, a lamp with the reflector being an old Volvo hub cap and a bird made from a cycle seat. Fantastic craftsmanship and innovation.

Ananda

24 Bond Street, North Laine
01273 725307

Furniture and textile gallery stocking wonderful items from south east Asia.

Antiques et Cetera

190 Portland Road, Hove
01273 746159
antiques.etcetera@btinternet.com

With a passion for costume jewellery and unusually shaped jugs, Ken really knows his stuff. There is a good selection of items from the 18th century through to the modern day including small pieces of furniture and collectibles. He is happy to part-exchange.

Aquatech

23 New Road,
Brighton
01273 607766

Better known as The Fish Furniture shop, Aquatech sells coffee table fish tanks, long, thin fish tanks, fish furniture and well, all things fishy, but at a price.

The Arts and Crafts Home

28 Gloucester Road, North Laine
01273 600073

If you need inspiration for your home then this is the place to come. Repro furniture, wallpapers, fabrics, designer paints and arts and crafts.

Bamboozled

41 Prestonville Road, Seven Dials
01273 220055

Eco-friendly furniture. Design your own, they can make it to order or chose from the many items in the shop ranging from beds, sofas, to coffee tables and wardrobes. Bring a little of Indonesia into your home.

Blackout

53 Kensington Place, North Laine
01273 671471

Tucked around the back of the North Laines lies this little bit of the Orient. There is no sign on the door but the shop window of Chinoserie will definitely pull you in. Oriental goodies and trinkets for a bit of fun.

Blue-Bell

28 Kensington Gardens, North Laine
01273 699456

Everything for the chic garden - tables, stools, planters bamboo benches, tranquil fountains and, of course, garden gnomes.

Bo Concept

Churchill Square
01273 730008

A sort of Ikea without the range, this is cool furniture and earthenware objets for minimalists. The prices are a bit steep compared to the Ikea equivalent but by the time you've worked out how much the petrol, time and effort would cost you to get to Croydon, you might as well as buy the cupboard.

Boudoir
13 New Road, The Lanes
01273 710818
Antique and contemporary furniture. Beautiful bed linen, accessories and gifts, French crystal chandeliers, nightwear and everything the name suggests.

Brick a Brick
25 Gloucester Road, North Laine
01273 697300
Beautiful selection of second hand furniture that looks good as new. Wonderful leather sofas at great prices.

Brighton Pottery Workshop
94 Trafalgar Street, North Laine
01273 601641
The place for that special gift. Traditional ceramics fashioned on the work found in Brighton in the 18th century. Resident potter Peter Stocker is more than happy for you to sit and watch whilst he creates.

Brunswick Interiors
27 Western Road, Hove
01273 206982
Full interior design service offering a large range of fabrics and furniture. Known for their re-upholstery service.

Caz Systems
18-19 Church Street, Central Brighton
01273 326471
Contemporary lighting and furniture. Beautiful Philippe Stark glass stools. Colourful plastic chairs and designer styles.

Chairmaker
54 Western Road, Hove
01273 777810
Beautifully made contemporary sofas, chairs and dining chairs.

Cissymo
25 Church Street, Central Brighton
01273 205060
38 Sydney Street, North Laine
01273 607777
88 Western Road, Hove
01273 202008
Funky stuff for your bathroom, cool loo seats, shower curtains etc. plus an array of cards, kitsch accessories and gifts.

Decorative Arts
27 Gloucester Road, North Laine
01273 676486
Stripped chunky oak handcrafted furniture, leather sofas and contemporary soft furnishings.

Dermot and Jill Palmer Antiques
7-8 Union Street, The Lanes
01273 328669

Definitely worth a browse, somewhere amongst the three floors you'll find something to suit your budget. European, mainly French antiques for the home and garden. They also have a warehouse of furniture to tempt you and your purse strings further.

Domus

2 Union Street, The Lanes
01273 737356
Stylish contemporary homeware and kitchenware, 1950's tin toys and children's accessories. Large selection of Alessi products.

Egg and Spoon

15 St George's Road,
Kemp Town
01273 608884
Stylish contemporary kitchen and tableware. Stockists include Rosle, Francis Francis espresso cups and saucers in fabulous designs, and Eva if you're looking for something outside the norm. The silicone oven gloves are amazing.

Elephant

1 Duke Street, The Lanes
133 Ship Street, The Lanes
01273 731318 (for both shops)
The Duke Street store stocks elegant and tasteful colonial style furniture. This vast store spanning five floors stocks everything you need for the elegant home. A little hint of Conran resounds through the products. Fine lighting, textiles, furniture and accessories.

England At Home

22 and 32 Ship Street, The Lanes
01273 205544/738270
Contemporary funky furniture and a super cool accessories such as heart shaped leopard print cushions.

Enhancements

1 Cavendish Street, Kemp Town
01273 677303
Refurbished furniture, lovingly restored and in Shabby Chic and country styles. Everything for your home and garden.

Evolution

42 Bond Street, North Laine
01273 205379
Helps Buddhists work together with their profits going to charitable projects. Beautiful array of Indonesian goodies including brightly coloured wooden mobiles and toys, ceramics, glass, textiles and everything for the tasteful eclectic home. Gifts include books and cards.

Fired Earth

15c Prince Albert Street,
The Lanes
01273 719977
Friendly and knowledgeable women only team guide you through choosing the ultimate in natural stone tiles and natural flooring. Fabulous bathroom accessories including the amazing stone basin. Be prepared to spend some money - quality and individuality doesn't come cheap. Installation service available.

The Floor

32 Gloucester Road, North Laine

01273 602894

As the name suggests, here you'll find a vast array of floor coverings tiles include terracotta, slate and limestone and floor coverings include jute, seagrass and sisal.

Gaff

66 Trafalgar Street, North Laine

01273 819202

If you're tired of run of the mill flooring this is the place to come to. Design your own, any shape and style is not a problem. They also have their own designs if you're stuck for inspiration and a colour matching service.

Habitat

Churchill Square, Central Brighton

01273 324831

Always packed, always expensive and somehow always getting our cash out of us.

House

82 North Road, Central Brighton

01273 571674

Best described as a mini Heals and as the name suggests stocks everything you would need for your home, cushions, leather bound stationary, mirrors, lights, shades etc and beautiful Mongolian skin cushions.

Jezebel

14 Prince Albert Street, The Lanes

01273 206091

The ultimate for the Art Deco enthusiast. Furniture and accessories, the clothes have since gone to make room for the fabulous furniture, lamps, glass and china. Fabulous Art Deco clocks too.

Jugs

44 Blatchington Road, Hove

01273 719899

Unusual furniture made from Indian hardwood has made this place a real find. It also sells those little extras you need to call a place home. Unique gifts such as photo albums covered with palm leaves are also on the menu.

Kemp Town Terracotta

5 Arundel Road, Kemp Town

01273 676603

Plenty of seconds at this little mews pottery studio at the edge of the city.

The Kensington Yard

77-78 North Road, North Laine

01273 689405

Specialists in 1930's stripped oak and Art Deco furniture plus decorative objects and textiles from the 1920's and 1930's. A great place to go if you need a new dining table and chairs.

Lindorf

100 Trafalgar Street,

North Laine

01273 691936

More Italy than Scandinavia, but these kitchens are very chic. Our reviewer said "Think Prada winkle pickers and you're almost there". Don't quite know what that means but it sounds cool.

Master Tiles

121 Portland Road, Hove
01273 770723
www.mastertiles.co.uk

Tile heaven for those who are re-decorating. The wide selection may make you indecisive but there are many that are beautiful and interesting so you can't go wrong. Designs range from the traditional to the more exotic and are mostly made of natural materials.

Mojoe

24 Church Street, Central Brighton
01273 208708

If you're into minimalism, this is for you. Mojoe sells anything from handmade greetings cards to the latest sunlounger to unique pieces of art for the wall. Moses (Mr Mojoe) is as an interior designer and worked at Muji (the Japanese home/office - very minimal chain of stores throughout the world) and has an excellent eye for design and fashion.

Nona Samini Boutique

3/20 Brunswick Square, Central Brighton
01273 206639

Invitation only on a monthly basis for private views or by appointment. Nona uses her home as a showroom. Show casing furniture and home accessories from Italy. Truly beautiful mirrors, chandeliers, paintings, cushions etc.

Oki Nami shop

York Place, London Road
01273 677702

Japanese shop and deli bar which suffers only for its location off London Road. Takeaway sushi sets and delicious Japanese tit bits make a delightful option to a sarnie at lunchtime and for wheat intolerancers, Japanese is the way to go. For those who can linger longer, there's a seating area on the first floor where you can get stuck into your wasabe and lust after the collection of Hello Kitty crockery at the same time. Happily, for the trillions of Japanese students from St Giles who make it their spiritual home, it's a hop and a skip.

Orientasia

9 East Street, The Lanes
01273 748698

If you are searching for a genuine oriental carpet they have the best selection in town. They also have a good range of cushions, rugs and kilims

Oxfam Fair Trade

146a North Street, Central Brighton
01273 326364

Beautiful selection of textiles, cards, and items for the home all made by fair trade workers from around the world.

Painted House Interiors

12-12a Boundary Road, Hove
01273 414069

Bringing the concept of window shopping into the literal sense, you can look at this bizarre collection but then you have to ring them up to purchase anything. There is a lot of junk but if you wander past regularly you may be pleasantly surprised. They also specialise in painted furniture but it's usually strange things like glass blocks and novelty items that catch your eye.

Parker Bathrooms
66,68,70 Dyke Road, Seven Dials
01273 329829
Family run shop selling contemporary and traditional bathroom furniture. They have the largest range of taps, showers and bathroom equipment in East Sussex and a lot of it is made especially for them.

Pure Design
20-21 Chatham Place, Off Seven Dials
01273 735331
Owner Rachel scours the country for classic original furniture from the 1950's through to the 1980's. She offers a design service and will source for you. Designs include works from Arne Jacobson, Robin Day and Vernerpanton. Glass and ceramics available too.

Pyramid
9a Kensington Gardens,
North Laine
01273 607791
Beautiful 1940's cards, inlaid loo seats, gifts, cards and watches.

QVS
Olive Rd, Hove
01273 421300
Lighting which our kitchen man (Justin) at MFI reckons is the business.

Rapid Eye Movement
23 Gardner Street, North Laine
01273 694323
Contemporary home accessories. Funky Japanese items, watches and sunglasses. Add a bit of colour and fun to you home.

Roost
26 Kensington Gardens, North Laine
01273 625223
Contemporary collection of design items for the home, funky lights, kitchen accessories and paper items.

SF Cody Emporium
186 Western Road, Brighton
01273 328207
Brightly-coloured, mass-produced, cheap and sometimes stylish gifts and home accessories.

Shop
28a Gloucester Road, North Laine
01273 600477
Stunning collection of furniture, textiles and accessories from the Swat Valley in Pakistan and North and East Africa. Affordable as well as beautiful.

Silver
38 St James's Street, Kemp Town
01273 606909
Bespoke, original glass furniture, often with driftwood from the beach framing the mirrors, costing between £200 to thousands is the core stock here. Paul Lewis says that he can make anything out of a piece of glass. "They're all

unique" he tells us. "If I don't take a photo and delete the design off my computer, I'll never be able to reproduce that piece again. People love the idea that they've got their own original work of art in their living room - especially when it doesn't cost them a fortune."

Sofa and Futon Shop

11 Gardner Street, North Laine
01273 0677017
Beautiful collection of sofas and futons, extensive coverings available, especially good quality leather.

Souk

4 Little East Street, The Lanes
01273 776477
Everything imaginable from Morocco, a most beautiful line in ornate lamps, furniture, ceramics, tiled tables, kilims, accessories, each piece guaranteed a topic of conversation in your home.

Steamer Trading Cook Shop

35 Ship Street, The Lanes
01273 227705
Everything you could need for your kitchen. Spread over three floors, Steamers specialises in shiny things - Alessi and the like.

Suttons Interior Design

56 Church Road, Hove
01273 723728
Quality soft furnishings and accessories. Fabrics and textiles from leading designers like Osborne and Little, Zoffany, Designer's Guild etc. Complete interior design service available.

Vanilla

23 Ship Street, The Lanes
01273 725538
Contemporary ultra sleek leather furniture, lighting, ceramics and mirrors.

Tab

07904 404055
www.tab-wallpaper.com
The shop has gone but Catherine is planning to open up again later in the year. In the meantime drool over her extensive designs and order any one of her original 1960s and 1970s wallpapers.

Tucan

29 Bond Street, North Laine
01273 326351
Brightly coloured home accessories and gifts from Latin America. Children's wooden toys, funky furniture, jewellery and much more.

Wallace McFarlane

14 St George's Road, Kemp Town
01273 297088
Wonderfully friendly and helpful owners who stock an array of delicious gifts and goodies for your home. Chose from the wide selection of soaps and smellies and work your way through the artistic talents of local artists, whether you're looking for cushions, stationary or ceramics you'll find it here. They also sell Cocoadance chocolate which is one

of the finest handmade chocolates money can buy.

Yashar Bish
96 Gloucester Road, North Laine
01273 671900
Wide selection of rugs, kilims and textiles from Turkey. There are also fabulous lamps, beads, ornate inlaid backgammon sets and village soaps. Upstairs you'll find antique Turkish pots and Anatolian village artefacts.

● IT'S A GIRL THING

Boutique
7 Trafalgar Street, North Laine
01273 600206
A heaven for girly underwear. Heart print bra and knickers sets, black lacy knickers with pink bows, scented and flavoured lipgloss like... chocolate?

Brief Encounter
Brighton Square, The Lanes
www.brasbras.com
01273 208404
Beautiful lacy designer underwear and a huge choice of great swimwear. Stock includes La Perla, Lejaby, Chantelle, Cotton Club and Aubade.

Magick
1-2 Sydney Street,
North Laine
01273 686568
The place to go for underwear with a difference. Choose between sexy corsets, babydolls, teddies etc.

Pussy
3a Kensington Gardens, North Laine
01273 604861
Everything for the girly girl. Satin sheets and pillows, Babycham pyjamas, books, bags and accessories...

She Said
13 Ship Street Gardens
(between Ship Street and Middle Street)
01273 777811
www.shesaid-uk.com
Owner Nic Ramsey has just opened an erotic lingerie boutique that is best described as an upmarket Ann Summers. High quality lingerie at affordable prices, select couture partywear, leather and latex. Sumptuous. Exclusive bags and jewellery and some of the world's finest adult toys. Mail order available.

Tickled
15 Gardner Street, North Laine
01273 628725
Gifts and gadgets just for girls. Satin sheets, inflatable husbands (aren't they all?), orgasmatrons and sensual personal pleasures for women.

● JEWELLERS

Jewellers in The Lanes
The Lanes is synonymous with antique and contemporary jewellery shops. There are too many jewellers to mention them all here, but all have a fabulous selection of jewellery from Art Deco pieces to more modern 60's and 70's

pieces. The prices are considerably lower than in London and you'll always get a good chat.

Conberts

16 Sydney Street, North Laine
01273 625222

An unusual combination of olde worlde tea shop and contemporary jewellers. Christian designs the jewellery and sells other designers work too and Ray runs the tea room. All jewellery is mounted in ornate gilt frames, and you can browse as you sip.

Grains of Gold

50-52 Meeting House Lane, The Lanes
01273 777197

Specialists in platinum and contemporary jewellery with quality certified diamonds. Design service available.

Jeremy Hoye

22a Ship Street, The Lanes
01273 777207

Contemporary designer jewellery, mainly in silver. Wedding bands, engagement rings with diamond and semi precious stones available too.

Little Gem

31a Meeting House Lane, The Lanes
01273 721198

The owner says that he's got the best prices in Brighton. Whether that's true or not, the service is very good and if you can't pay right now he'll set up a plan for you. The jewellery is to die for .

Shorer's Workshop

01323 894140
www.big-gems.co.uk

Mike Shorer's family has been designing and making unique and exquisite items of jewellery, trophies and objets d'art for over 250 years. And he can remodel old items too so don't get rid of the family jewels.

Silverado

30 Meeting House Lane, The Lanes
01273 326756
3b Kensington Gardens, North Laine
01273 676676

Large selection of silver rings at rock bottom prices, plus contemporary silver jewellery.

Soma

24 Meeting House Lane, The Lanes
01273 321332

Contemporary silver and semi precious jewellery, supporting local designers. Recently introduced engagement and wedding rings with precious stones set in platinum or white gold.

● LOTIONS, POTIONS & WITCHES

Green Buddha Bookshop

15 Bond Street,
North Laine
01273 324488

A tranquil oasis of relaxation and inner peace. Music, crystals and incense fill the air. They specialise in eastern philosophy and self help books.

Hocus Pocus

38 Gardener Street,
North Laine
01273 572202

Encourages the work of quality crafts people. This New Age store sells tarot cards, crystals, incense and has tarot consultations available. Everything for the alternative with an open mind.

Neal's Yard

Kensington Gardens,
North Laine
01273 6014464

Heavenly apothecary. Medicinal herbs, lotions and potions in the famous blue and purple bottles. Alternative music books too.

Winfalcon

28 Ship Street,
North Laine
01273 728997

Tarot readers on hand to tell you your destiny. This shop sells all things alternative as in crystals, incense, dream catchers, books etc. Friendly and knowledgeable and just so Brighton. Also a healing centre to put you back on track after a day at the sales.

● MARKETS

BHASVIC College Car Boot Sale

open Sat 8am; Sun 9am

Free for all selling toys, children's clothes, second-hand home accessories and junk.

Brighton Station Sunday Market

open Sun 6am-12pm

Brighton's very own Portobello Road. Get up early, stroll around the stalls and check out the variety of junk, CDs, records, bikes, books, old clothes and retro furniture.

North Laine Junk Market

Upper Gardner Street, Brighton
open Sat 10am-2pm

Old junk, clothes, records and tat, but there are real antique bargains to be found so it's always worth having a look.

The Open Market

Behind Somerfield on the London Road
open Mon 7am-1pm; Tue-Thurs 7am-5pm; Fri 7am-6pm

Cheap, permanent market selling fruit and vegetables, plastic toys, sweets, meat, fish and a continental food stall.

Upper Gardner Street

North Laine
open Sat 10am-2pm

Mostly junk, clothes and records, but some gems can be found lurking if you search long and hard enough.

● MONEY

The Brighton Coin Shop

38 Ship Street, The Lanes
01273 733365

If you are going on holiday or have just returned don't go to a bank to change your money, come here. Their exchange rates are the most competitive and they don't charge a commission, you'll save a lot of money.

● MUSIC

The Acoustic Music Company
39 St James Street, Kemp Town
01273 671841
A startling array of imported guitars and stringed instruments including things you've probably never have heard of such as members of the entire mandolin family (mandola, bouzouki, dulcima, mando bass). Owner, Trevor Moyle travels from Hawaii to Oregon to find the best examples of these in the world and bring them, bizarrely enough, to Kemp Town.

● OPTICIANS

Bromptons Opticians
32 Gardner Street, North Laine
01273 697711
Not your run of the mill average opticians. They have an extensive selection of designer frames and are still the only stockists of Booth and Bruce which are their best sellers.

Specs Opticians
22 Kensington Gardens,
North Laine
01273 676796
Once through the fabulous iron gates you'll find all you'd expect from a top opticians, a vast selection of designer glasses and sunglasses. Eye testing too.

● PAMPERING

Aveda
22 East Street, The Lanes
01273 720203
Leaders in haircare products including vegetable hair colours. Travel sized bottles to try if you need convincing first. Great line in quality inexpensive make-up.

Barber Blacksheep
18 St George's Road, Kemp Town
01273 6234083
A hit with Brightonians especially those with kids. Friendly, fun relaxed salon with excellent service. Ladies cuts from £12. Children £7.

Bay House Aromatics
88 St George's Road, Kemp Town
01273 601109
The place for essential oils at great prices. They also sell dolphin massagers (which is useful if you've got a dolphin), tinctures, flower remedies and wooden massagers. Very friendly and helpful.

Bristol Gardens Health Spa
Bristol Gardens, Kemp Town
01273 698904
Naturist's dream spa with four floors of naked folk happy to dispense with their modesty in return for a no-looking policy. The relaxation rooms on the fourth floor allow for some naked reclining and ... Well? This is Brighton. Mixed singles during the week and couples at weekends.

Catwalk Studio
69 Western Road, Hove
01273 735948
Spanish owner, Maria has both a boutique and treatment rooms, so you can shop and be pampered at the same time, and sells Balenciaga perfumes, evening gowns, European designs and accessories. Facial and body masks are £25 per treatment.

Just Gents the Barbers
121 Dyke Road, Seven Dials
01273 700338
Haircuts for boys of all ages starting at £6.

L'Occitane en Provence
23 East Street,
The Lanes
01273 719171
www.loccitane.com
Christmas presents a plenty at this new branch of the gorgeous Provencal goody chain. Soaps, shower gels, massage oils, hair and skin stuff - all made out of the best lavenders and essential oils Provence can produce.

Lush
41 East Street,
The Lanes
01273 774700
Chances are if you're heading down East Street Lush will find you. Heavenly scents of fresh hand-made products waft down the street. Chose from deli style face packs and scrubs to soaps and the ever-popular bath bombs.

MAC
6 Dukes Lane, The Lanes
01273 720026
This sleek shop is more of a make-up studio than a store and has the goods to make a supermodel out of all of us. Inexpensive prices and helpful staff.

The Nail Bar
Churchill Square, Central Brighton
01273 736303
New York comes to Brighton. Once you've done your shopping, treat yourself to a manicure and watch the world go by. Basic manicure £15.

The Nail Studio
1 Brunswick Road, Hove
01273 327274
Everything imaginable for false nails. I'm not sure what you'd imagine about false nails, but whatever it is, you'll find it here. Booking is essential.

Pecsniff's
45-46 Meeting House Lane, The Lanes
01273 723292
Specialist aromatherapy shop selling soothing and effective blends of essential oils.

Pee Wees
5 Kensington Gardens, North Laine
01273 604030
At long last a hair salon where the client finally calls the shots. They offer great advise on homecare and take your lifestyle into consideration. Friendly service, caring consultations and

comprehensive after care philosophy. All staff have extensive training and offer free tea and coffee.

The Pink Pamper
74 St James Street, Kemp Town
01273 608060
Hair, beauty, manicures, massage, tanning, nail extensions, aromatherapy, Reiki and much, much more. Mostly for men.

Saks Hair And Beauty
David Lloyd Fitness Centre,
Brighton Marina
01273 666426
Mark and his top team of tress-trimmers come with a Vidal Sassoon pedigree and beauty salon to match. In the spirit of the New Millennium, there's plenty of aromatherapy and chakra balancing at the salon.

Shrine
83 Dyke Road, Seven Dials
01273 205605
Beauty treatments offering Dr Hauska holistic facials, plus all the usual massage, waxing, nail treatments etc. Reiki sessions available, alternative health referrals given and wedding/party make up. Beautiful new salon and friendly staff. Closed Monday and Sunday.

Stage One Hairdressing
36-37 Bond Street, North Laine
01273 734225
Friendly salon with unhurried consultations. Craniosacral therapy on

offer for the complete mind and body experience.

Sundials Tanning Studio
116 Dyke Road, Seven Dials
01273 770500
Brand spanking new, up to the minute state of the art tanning. £2.50 buys you six minutes of sweat free, vertical tanning (with some funky music thrown in) to give you a healthy glow or top up your holiday tan.

The Treatment Rooms
21 New Road, The Lanes
01273 818444
A true oasis and shrine to pampering the body. State of the art equipment and fantastic service offered unhurried in tranquil surroundings. A definite must. Holistic treatments and beauty therapy at very good prices. Go on treat yourself.

Vital Touch
www.vitaltouch.com
Ok, so they're not exactly in Brighton or Hove, but they're our mates and it's our book and their products are so gorgeous that you need to know about them. Katie Whitehouse is a natural therapist who has been teaching and practising aromatherapy massage and reflexology for years. Her range of ready to wear and bespoke aromatherapy products includes pregnancy, labour and post-natal kits. Deep Action inspiration gels and any number of massage oils. Wrapped and schlepped to your door, they make great gifts.

● PETS

Doggy Fashion

1 Grafton Street,

Kemp Town

01273 695631

www.heavypetting.co.uk

A truly camp shopping experience for your pooch. Gordon Fletcher not only primps and preens the neighbourhood's best friends, but can clothe them for anything from Sunday brunch (a spotty neckerchief collar perhaps?) to a night out with the boyz (leather studded waistcoat or crop top T shirt?). Check out the website for the full, glorious range of accessories, including dog bowls designed to coordinate with the most fashionable of kitchens...

● PHOTOGRAPHICS

Jessops

78 London Road

01273 693500

154 Western Road

01273 323784

125 Queens Road

01273 321492

Stocks all leading brands, new and second hand. Developing and printing.

Monolab

10 Upper Market Street,

Hove

01273 731116

As the name suggests, everything for black and white printing and developing.

Spectrum

Unit 10, Hove Business Centre, Fonthill

Road, Hove

01273 708222

sales@spectrumphoto.co.uk

Right behind Hove train station, this is where the increasing number of professional photographers who move to Brighton and Hove are taking their work. They offer a range of traditional photographic and digital services including E6 processing, hand printing and high res scanning. Unlike some of the other labs, the staff here are passionate about photography and happy to offer help and advice.

● RECORD SHOPS

Across the Tracks

110 Gloucester Road, North Laine

01273 677906

Packed with boxes of second hand vinyl, from 60's rock to 90's old skool hip-hop to what is perhaps the best collection of country music in town. Take time to browse and you'll unearth a gaggle of forgotten classics, usually at good prices. It's a little grubby in here and could do with a lick of paint, but don't let that discourage you.

Bang

16 Bond Street, North Laine

01273 220380

www.bangmusic.co.uk

Lots of hip-hop discs can be found here, along with a few soul and funk classics, break beats, and drum'n'bass. There are turntables and accessories to keep the mixers and scratchers happy, and a listening post where you can listen to the staff recommendations, who are sweet and warm and helpful. Look carefully and you'll dig up a few bargains, although new releases can be a little pricey and there's little here that you wont find elsewhere.

Black Grass

39b Sydney Street, North Laine
01273 677772
info@blackgrass.com

Black Grass is for hip-hop aficionados, Brighton's answer to New York's Fat Beats. Alongside new and old skool hip-hop can be found classic breaks and funk, all on vinyl for the turntablist. Also on offer are Shure needle and Vestax mixer products, widely considered to be amongst the best for hip hop DJ's, and Montana spray paint for the graffiti artist courtesy of Worms Paint Store.

The Borderline

Gardner Street, North Laine
A tiny place, you can find quite a mixture here. They are well stocked with spoken word stuff, including the ranting satires of the late, great Bill Hicks and some readings of cult novelist Jack Kerouac. If you're after something a little unusual, there's also an avant-garde section and although some CDs are a little expensive, there are quite a few budget CDs of old crooners like Mel Torme, Dean Martin and jazz goddess

Nina Simone. Also a decent choice of jazz, blues, rock, and punk.

BPM

4 Bartholomews, The Lanes
0700 446 639
www.bpm-music.co.uk

All the very latest discs will be found in here. There's a nice mix of US house, nu-nrg and techno. It's loud and bright, and has eight turntables to test those tunes on, so it's often busy in here. The web site is well worth a visit too, as you can sample some MP3's before you buy. They also do free deliveries within the UK.

Charlie's Orbit

95 St George's Road, Kemp Town
01273 571010
charlie@charliesorbit.fsnet.co.uk

Nestled away from the hustle and bustle of the town centre, you'll find Charlie's Orbit in the relative quietness of Kemptown. A refined shopping experience for used CDs and vinyl ranging through film soundtracks, rock and pop and oldies, as well as a few from the hip hop and house genre. Well ordered racks are home to rows of vinyl with little descriptive labels telling you the about the track and its condition, and playing of records before you buy is warmly welcomed.

The Classical Longplayer

31 Duke Street, The Lanes
01273 329534
classicallongplayer@hotmail.com

This is the first stop for classical music

fans. Its extensive selection is very well categorised, providing all the old masters and more; Mozart, Puccini, and Elgar will be found alongside a collection of spoken word, the vintage comedy of "The Goon Show", and classic radio productions like Radio 4's definitive "Lord Of The Rings" from the early 80s.

Covert Records

39a Sydney Street, North Laine
01273 624774
info@covert-records.demon.co.uk

Vinyl only underground music shop. Specialists for techno, house, breakbeat, electro and electronica.

Dance 2 Dance

129 Western Road, Hove
01273 220023l fax: 01273 329459
info@dance2.co.uk
www.dance2.co.uk

If you're serious about vinyl, turntables, and all the accessories to go with them then you'll feel right at home here as they have sound and lighting equipment for hire, record bags, and tickets for Slinky, Superfish, and other dance music events that don't begin with the letter S. There's trance, drum'n'bass, trance, techno, trance, hard house and trance on vinyl. Top tunes, nice people.

Essential Music

16 Brighton Square, The Lanes
01273 202695

Essential Music proudly claim to have "the largest selection of soul, jazz and reggae in Brighton". Whether you like the scratchy blues of Charley Patton or the bebop of Coleman Hawkins, you'll find something to suit. There are great bargains, and an unusual soundtracks section where you can buy jazz from Woody Allen's films, or Serge Gainsbourg classics. It's often crowded in here and the staff are busy but helpful.

Fine Records

32 George Street, Hove
01273 723345

You should find something in here that appeals to you, as there's quite a mixed bag of vinyl, CDs and tapes to be found. We managed to uncover an old copy of a Paul Robeson concert on vinyl (which we've never seen elsewhere), a collection of orchestral works, Mario Lanza, Glenn Miller and an organ music section. There's also some rock and pop scattered around too, but that's not really the game here.

Music Meltdown

10 Sydney Street, North Laine
01273 608806

One or two collector's items in here. There's a nice little selection of original Beatles and Stones' vinyl, and lots of old and new house discs with a turntable to try before you buy. It's reasonably priced with quite a few CDs too.

Rounder Records

19 Brighton Square,
The Lanes
01273 325440

A neat and tidy shop packed with a wide variety of vinyl and CDs from rare Smiths 12-inch singles, the latest drill'n'bass sounds from Warp records, and some punk, Latin funk and nu-jazz. The well-organised layout makes finding what you want quite easy, and there are a few cut-price CDs too. This is also probably the best place in town to get information and tickets for gigs,

Urban Records
24 Gardner Street,
North Laine
01273 620567
Vinyl only shop specialising in house and garage, with some hip-hop, rare groove, and DJ promo's thrown in. A smart and clean place with very friendly staff. Serious DJs will feel at home here

Wax Factor
24 Trafalgar Street,
Brighton
01273 673744
This shop is great for collectors and those wanting to just browse in the hope of finding a surprise. Tucked away at the end of the North Laine, it's easy to miss but well worth a visit for those who have some time to kill. There are hundreds of original 7" and 12" classics on two floors, from Led Zeppelin and The Beatles to Sinatra and Benny Goodman for big-band swingers. But if you want to buy a book on feminism or philosophy or get a tape of Dire Straits, before sitting down for a quick coffee? It's all here. A gem.

● SPORT & STREETWEAR

Air Born Kites
42 Gardner Street, North Laine
01273 676740
Kites, hot air balloons, stomp rockets and all you need for the massively popular kite surfing. Repairs and orders available.

RE-AL
7 Dukes Lane, The Lanes
01273 325658
Everything for the skateboard and rollerblade crazed kid, and all the cool accessories needed to make you even cooler.

Reload
6 Kensington Garden, North Laine
Skate clothing for young boys and girls. Accessories and bags, culture stuff.

Route One
3 Bond Street,
North Laine
01273 323633
Street wear and alternative sports equipment. DC Trainers, skateboard hardware, maps and videos.

Zunamee
80 Church Road, Hove
01273 202000
Trampolines, marine and chandlery equipment. Inflatable swimming pools. All can be ordered on line in the store. Nice line in casual and sports clothes and equipment too.

● SUPERMARKETS

ASDA
Brighton Marina Village
01273 606611
1 Crowhurst Road,
Hollingbury
01273 541166
Both now open 24 hours a day.

Co-Op
(Some are open from 7am-10pm and
8am-8pm on Sundays)
London Road and Baker Street
01273 606722 (department store)
76-82 Blatchington Road, Hove
01273 73394
124 Dyke Road, Hove
01273 206553
56-57 Lewes Road, Brighton
01273 684610
Nevill Road, Hove
01273 205481
33-39 Old London Road,
Patcham
01273 552001
269 Preston Drove, Brighton
01273 562315
3-5 West Way, Hangleton
01273 732741
Whitehawk Road, Brighton
01273 682763

Sainsbury's
93 Lewes Road, Brighton
01273 674201
1-4 London Road,
Brighton
01273 685461

Old Shoreham Road, Brighton
01273 439257
Home delivery on the Net:
www.sainsburystoyou.co.uk

Somerfield
119 London Road, Brighton
01273 601521

Tesco
Upper Shoreham Road, Shoreham
(Holmbush Centre)
01273 367600
Boundary Road, Portslade
01273 367500
Tesco Metro, Dyke Road, Brighton
01273 369400

Waitrose
130-131 Western Road, Hove
01273 326549

● TOBACCONISTS

Burkitts
117 Church Road, Hove
01273 731351
Old fashioned tobacconist family run since 1873. Extensive range of cigars, lighters etc. and all things for the serious smoker.

Taylor's
19 Bond Street, The Lanes
01273 606110
Tobacconists to the stars. Wide range of products including Havana cigars. The walk in humidified cigar room is popular with the celebrities.

● VIDEOS

The Video Box

107 St George's Road, Kemp Town
01273 670469
New releases on video and DVD plus an extensive back catalogue. A large kids section plus games. The best art house cinema collection in town. Also at:
122 Elm Grove, Elm Grove
01273 623313
64 Goldstone Villas, Hove
01273 821469
1 Surrey Street, Shoreham
01273 823455
69 Western Road, Hove
01273 204325

88 Preston Road, Preston Park
01273 230075

Videostar

125 Western Road
01273 776335
This chain of shops has all the latest videos and DVD's for that quite night in and the guys who work there make spot on selections for you. Also at:
253d Ditchling Road, Five Ways
01273 507055
229 Queen's Park Road, Queen's Park
01273 623464
60 St James's Street. Kemp Town
01273 690935

● *I love being able to meet people for coffee at The Meeting Place on the lawns at Hove on a spring afternoon; you can listen to a jazz band playing on the lawns and watch the waves roll in. It's a friendly place, Brighton and Hove, where anyone can be whatever they want to be. I came across The Sanctuary about 10 years ago and started hanging out there because it was the kind of place where you didn't have to worry about what you looked like to get a friendly welcome. I told the owner that if he ever wanted to sell it, I was his woman, and last year my dream came true. The food's much better these days with Oriental and Mediterranean vegetarian food and fresh fish on Fridays, but the feel's the same; we still do Junk TV on Thursday nights, but we also have poetry readings, an open mic on women's night, storytelling and buzzy live performances. And it all goes on while the other two floors are serving fantastic food and late night cake and coffee. I think The Sanctuary is about what Brighton and Hove does best - it's eclectic, laid back and indulgent, just like the people who live here.*

Sharon Gordon, *proprietor of The Sanctuary Café, Hove and lives in Hove.*

08.2

sponsored by

DUKE OF YORK'S *Premier Picture house*

● CINEMAS

The Duke of York's Picture House

Preston Circus, Preston Park
01273 602503 (advance booking and box office) 626261 (recorded information)

An independent cinema to rank up there with anything London's got to offer, Brighton's most popular art house is a proper carrot cake independent with all that implies. 'One-night only' showings are its speciality, so make sure you paste its calendar of events on your front door to avoid missing such favourites as *Brighton Rock*, *The Italian Job* or an Almodovar retrospective. *The Brighton Jewish Film Festival* is on here in November with some screenings at the Cinemateque. There's a bar upstairs serving booze and proper coffee.

Brighton Cinemateque

Media Centre, 9-12 Middle Street, The Lanes
01273 384300

Showing everything that you won't find in any other cinema, from Russian films to early silent movies and digital shorts. Only open a few nights a week, so ring for details or pick up their brochure around town.

Gardner Arts Centre

University of Sussex, Falmer
01273 685447

Arts films and seasons - similar to the sort of things you'd find at the Duke Of

York's but with more of a student slant. Basically, if it's got subtitles and lacks a coherent narrative, it's in.

Odeon

Kingswest, West Street,
Central Brighton
0870 5050007

A big, old-fashioned, multi-screen cinema that boasts a built-in Haagen Dazs café, so at least if the film's rubbish, you can enjoy the ice-cream. Just remember to add 15 minutes to your timing - the ice-cream queue can take its time.

UGC Marina

Marina Village, The Marina
08701 555145

A mega-screen multiplex showing all the latest blockbusters. The main joy here is that it shows films at a remarkably civilised time; most evenings the main show doesn't start until 9pm. A UGC card allows you to see an unlimited number of films for £9.99 a month. The downside is that to qualify, you have to commit to a year's worth of visits.

● ART GALLERIES

Brighton Museum & Art Gallery

Church Street, Central Brighton
01273 290900

Re-made and re-modelled, the Brighton Museum & Art Gallery is reopening just about... now. The refurbishment includes of the permanent galleries and

the opening temporary exhibition is *Kiss & Kill: Film Visions of Brighton.*

Burstow Gallery

Brighton College,
Eastern Road,
Kemp Town
01273 704229

Part of Brighton's most famous public school.

Fabrica

Holy Trinity Church, 40 Duke Street,
Central Brighton
01273 778646 www.fabrica.org.uk

Art installations housed in a beautiful old church in the heart of Brighton's shopping area. Art gallery, artists resource centre and network, Fabrica is supported by South East Arts to help artists of all disciplines find their feet. It's also just a fantastic place to relax in if the shopping gets too much. Fabrica is also the home of the Art Network - see Business chapter.

Fourwalls Art Promotion

01273 383616 / Mob: 07909 511159

Lara Bowen has gone from cocktail waitress to art impressario in less than a year, persuading restaurant and bar owners to show off the level of local talent on their walls. Tony Clarke could be seen at the brand new Blanch House restaurant earlier this year with his enormous portraits of Jackson, Ali, Beckham and Bowie fitting setting off the Blanch leather minimalism to perfection.

Gardner Arts Centre

University of Sussex, Falmer

01273 685447

Outside the theatre is a large space often given over to massive sculptures, installations and conceptual art for theatre goers to enjoy.

Phoenix Arts

10-14 Waterloo Place, Central Brighton

01273 603700

www.slab-o-concrete.demon.co.uk/

exhibitions.htm

open Sat-Tues, 11am-5pm.

Artist/charity/collective/co-op in an enormous Sixties building to the east of St Peter's Church in Waterloo Place. Workshops for adults and children open days dotted throughout the year, plus exhibitions in the rooms that used to be home to huge mainframe computers in the Seventies.

Preston Manor

Preston Drove, Preston Park

01273 290900

Edwardian home of the Stanford family who once owned the whole area around Preston Park. It dates from the 1600s, but most of the furniture and fittings are more Upstairs Downstairs with mangles and smoothing irons, tin baths, as well as a butler's pantry. Check out the eccentric pets' cemetery in the walled gardens.

Royal Pavilion

Pavilion Gardens, Old Steine

01273 290900

Possibly the most sumptuous, ostentatious and hedonistic piece of architecture in the UK. Originally the holiday home for the Prince Regent, it became the place for aristocratic hangers-on and the Prince's arty entourage to spend their spare time in. Make sure you get a guided tour through the fabulously over-the-top palace for a feast of gossip and information. Kids love the stuffed swans in the kitchen's baking tins and Queen Victoria's princess-and-the-pea bed and expect to bump into The Beast or Aladdin around every corner. Storytelling and art sessions for kids during half-term.

The University of Brighton Gallery

Grand Parade, Old Steine

01273 643012

Originates, shows and tours an eclectic range of international and national art as well as local and student work from its parent, The University of Brighton. It features wide-ranging exhibitions, including multi-media and art installation pieces, but the highlight of the year has to be the graduate shows in June where you can pick up some real steals from the big names of the future. Some exhibitions also tour.

White Gallery

86-87 Western Road, Hove

01273 774870

A must for art lovers, with a loan scheme subsidised by South East Arts to allow your money to go directly to the artist while you take your time paying the gallery interest free. Look out for established painters such as Paula Rego, Picasso and Lucian Freud, as well as emerging young artists.

● COMEDY

The Barn Theatre
Saxon lane, Seaford
01323 490001
Off the beaten track, but an enthusiastic comedy venue.

The Hanbury Ballroom
83 St Georges Street, Kemp Town
01273 605789
Kemp Town Crack is the regular Thursday comedy night, but there's always something happening.

The Krater Comedy Club @ Komedia
44-47 Gardner Street, Brighton
box office: 01273 647100
The best smallish comedy/performance art venue in town. A lot of acts try out their shows here before going up to Edinburgh - and the successful ones come back. The Krater Comedy Club, a stand-up fest, is on Saturday and Sunday nights. Watch out for the monthly News Revue.

The Prince Albert
48 Trafalgar Street, North Laine
01273 730499
Another regular comedy venue. But, as

with most venues, things change here too often to start giving you lists.

Sanctum @ The Sanctuary Café
51 Brunswick Street East, Brighton
01273 770002
www.thesanctuarycafe.co.uk
A comedy club every last Tuesday of the month. 9pm kick-off. For details, see www.priestess.co.uk/sanctum

● LIVE PERFORMANCE

Akademia
14 Manchester Street,
Old Steine
01273 622633
Forms part of the University of Brighton's Student Union, Akademia only open to students and their guests during term time. Thursday night is the exception when it hosts a comedy club. A venue throughout the Festival and open for rep companies during the holidays.

The Brighton Centre
Kings Road, Brighton
01273 290131
Big and cavernous and squatting on the seafront in all its ugly Seventies concrete glory, the Brighton Centre is a good illustration that what's good for trade shows isn't necessarily good for gigs and shows. In terms of acoustics and atmosphere, the Centre is about as appealing as platform 4 at the train station. The poor bar service only

exacerbates the situation, but (and there's always a but) it is the only place in town for big bands to play and if it wasn't there then they wouldn't be there either. All though is not lost. There are plans to build a new Brighton Centre on the same site but - it's promised - one that'll be less of an eyesore.

Brighton Little Theatre Company

Studio Theatre,
9 Clarence Gardens, Brighton (opposite Pavilion)
box office: 01273 205000.
www.the-little.co.uk
Formed in 1940, this amateur repertory company stages some 11 productions a year, running the full gamut of the theatrical genre with Sir Donald Sinden its founding president. Catch its annual outdoor performance at Lewes Castle.

Carnival Collective

01273 625617
The Carnival Collective is one of Brighton's local assets, a voluntary community samba organisation that gets the city by its ghoolies with a fabulously infectious stomp. They've been part of the festival scene for years and are one of the big Where Else campaign shows this year with Samba Encounter. Their grand design is to develop it into a yearly carnival to rival Rio! Happily they do 10 week courses in samba drumming and dance leading to performance (if you want) so you'll be able to join in.

Concorde II

Madeira Drive, Kemp Town
01273 606460
An excellent booking policy and a bar almost as long as the walk home along the seafront make it the best live venue in Brighton. Known as the home of the Big Beat Boutique, all kinds of acts also play here from Badly Drawn Boy to Asian Dub Foundation, Courtney Pine, Mr Scruff and Fila Brazilia.

The Dome

Pavilion Gardens, Old Steine
01273 709709 www.brighton-dome.org.uk
Brighton's stunning centre piece has been lovingly restored to the tune of squillions and is back in time to host the best of the festival and to become the leading venue for arts in the South. With state of the art acoustics and the ability to turn itself into just about anything the event demands, it should provide a welcome boost to our arty happenings. The Juicy Awards on June 24th will be one of the first events after the festival with a feast of theatrical surprises and celebrities to help us celebrate the massive amount of talent in Brighton and Hove.

Free Butt

25-26 Albion Street, Old Steine
01273 603974
Along with the Pressure Point, this is indie heaven. If having the band playing in your face and sweat running down the walls is what you're looking for then the delightfully-named Free Butt is for

you. Essentially a pub venue, the Free Butt is a loud and beery place where you're likely to see esoterically named bands that will test your eardrums and your hardened gig-goer's credentials to the limit.

Gardner Arts

Lewes Road, Falmer

01273 685861

Sussex University-based arty theatre with a strong emphasis on the avant-garde. Kids' pantos here tend to be particularly worth a visit. Its venture into kids' drama and interactive theatre is a must for everyone under the age of 10.

Komedia

44-47 Gardner Street, North Laine

box office: 01273 647100

Komedia was set up in 1994 to bring European-based visual and physical theatre to Brighton. Specialising in fringe productions, the Komedia is the place to go for comedy, performance theatre or kids' drama. Komedia's International Theatre in Edinburgh has just been awarded by The Institute of International Theatre for Excellence.

The Lift

11-12 Queen's Road, Central Brighton

01273 779411

Above the Pig In Paradise pub in the centre of town, The Lift has a well earnt reputation for putting on eclectic nights of left-field music ranging from the sublime to the ridiculous and back again - often on the same night. Entry is

usually fairly cheap, so don't worry if you haven't heard of the names on the bill. This is what gig-going should be like.

The New Venture Theatre

Bedford Place, Brighton seafront

01273 746118 www.newventure.org.uk

This training ground of new writing and directing allows Brighton and Hove to witness some breathtaking new theatre and, natch, a few duds along the way. The food there is top notch too.

Pressure Point

33 Richmond Place, North Laine

01273 235082

Traditional indie venue above the pub. The walls are black, the floors are sticky after years of beer abuse... you know the sort of place. A good venue, one of the stalwarts. If it's a guitar band you want, this is the place to look.

The Sallis Benney

Grand Parade, Old Steine

01273 643010

The University of Brighton's own theatre, it's rarely open to the public except during the Festival. Also look out for summer-term student shows.

The Sanctuary Café

51 Brunswick Street East, Brighton

01273 770002

www.thesanctuarycafe.co.uk

If kitsch is your thing then The Sanctuary's your place. Hosts "Creative liquid" every other Thursday night showing cult movies and classic television programmes in its beatnik basement.

Theatre Royal
New Road, Central Brighton
01273 328488
www.theambassadors.com/brighton
The oldest theatre in Brighton dating back to 1774 and scene to many a luvvie from Marlene Dietrich to Sir Larry himself, The Theatre is in a bit of transition at the moment; 2001 had a series of triumphs under chief exec Mark Courtice with one offs like Miller and Armstrong bringing the 30 somethings flocking back to the theatre. These days Chris Haylett, fresh from head office at Woking is holding the keys and has plans for a mix of high art (La Traviata, Don Giovani) and good old fashioned entertainment like Boogie Nights.

● MUSEUMS

Remember to take local ID to most of these museums and you'll get in at reduced price.

Booth Museum of Natural History
194 Dyke Road, Preston Park (oppo Dyke Park Road)
01273 292777
home to more stuffed birds than there are in a stuffed bird shop, the Booth is full of insects, beasties and all manner of things to do with natural history. It's a spooky old place to hang around, the

sort of place where Peter Cushing plays the curator.

Brighton Fishing Museum
201 Kings Road Arches, Brighton
01273 723064
Most people check this out during the Brighton Festival, but this sweet museum keeps the spirit of this one-time fishing village alive.

Brighton Sea Life Centre
Marine Parade, Madeira Drive, just by the Palace Pier
01273 609361
The perfect place to take anyone from little Johnny to Granny on a rainy day. Creatively designed, it's a joy on the eye and is filled with more fish than there are stars in the sky. The rays can be fed and stroked, the seahorses are beautifully displayed in magnified glass and the shark tunnel is a treat for anyone scared of the misunderstood little loves.

The Engineerium
Nevill Road, Hove
01273 559583
This small boy's dream of a museum is set in a beautifully restored Victorian station, housing an impressive collection of steam engines, from small toys up to a 10-metre-high beam engine. Exhibits include the Giant's Toolbox, an interactive exhibit explaining all the major principles of mechanical engineering, plus the giant has thoughtfully left belongings around the

building for younger kids to spot. The staff are knowledgeable and very helpful.

Foredown Tower
Foredown Road, Portslade
01273 292092

Hove Museum and Art Gallery
19 New Church Road, Hove
01273 290200

Sussex Toy & Model Museum
52/55 Trafalgar Street, North Laine
01273 749494
It's easy to miss, but it would be a shame. Lurking under a bridge just below Brighton station is the recently renovated museum of toys and er, models.

● ARTS TO DO

● WORKSHOPS

Brighton is mad about drumming, and there are few events more stirring than the sight and sound of the Carnival Collective leading a procession of drummers and dancers through town to the beach for the symbolic Burning of the Clocks ceremony to mark the end of the year. Throughout the Festival, there are plenty of music, arts and dance workshops. After last year's Festival, when Zap trained most of the kids in Brighton to beat their own drums, adults might want to sign up to keep ahead of the pack.

BA Spurr
01273 884226
Art workshops for adults.

Bucarr Ndow
07960 478360
Master drummer teaching Djembe drumming.

Fern Keita
01273 607238
African drumming workshops for women.

New Holistic Health Centre
Beaconsfield Villas,
Brighton
01273 696295
Offers a myriad of workshops.

Peter Evans
01273 733773
Singing teacher.

● SALSA (CUBAN-STYLE)

Philippa King
tphilking@lineone.net
Philippa teaches individuals and short courses, and even holds corporate salsa evenings.

Sussex Arts Club
Ship Street,
The Lanes
01273 727371
Piru and Mary run the Thursday Salsa nights at The Sussex Arts Club.
Leo, who used to run the night at the

Sussex now operates out of The Gap Club in Hove. Contact him at leocubano@hotmail.com for details.

● BRIGHTON STORYTELLERS

Pub With No Name
58 Southover Street, Hanover
01273 601419

Brighton Storytellers are a mixed bag of folk who tell and perform stories of all kinds. During the winter they usually book a programme of well-known and gifted narrators. Stories told can be traditional or modern, comforting or scary, or bizarre. Brighton Storytellers weave their tales wintry magic on the first Sunday of every month.

● *There are at least 20 yoga classes taking place at any given time of the day in this city; I can bend my body into contortions for less than a fiver, in a Buddhist Centre, an African artefacts warehouse, a church hall, a healing centre, a front room. At any time of day, I can go out for a loaf of bread and be gone for hours, simply because Giovanni, the Italian greengrocer in Seven Dials has decided to sing the five verses and four choruses of Santa Lucia whilst serving me with olives. And I can walk back from the beach ,with my towel under my arm on a late summer's evening, smugly content in the knowledge that all those "trippers" are stuck in a traffic jam in Croydon on their way back to the metropolis.*

Joanne Good, *breakfast presenter, BBC Southern Counties*

08.3

● Brighton and Hove is a haven for kids. The Council has spent a fortune on sandpits and playgrounds on the seafront, as well as the Summer Fun in the Park programme which provides free storytelling, African drumming and face-painting every day in different parks across the city throughout the summer holiday. During the rest of the year, a new programme of art clubs and extremely imaginative pre-school sessions takes place at the libraries and museums in Brighton and Hove at around £3 per child. Acting and telling nursery stories at Preston Manor for four years and up, seaweed and sand play for two-five-year-olds at the Booth Museum, astronomical observation of Jupiter and Saturn at Foredown Tower and food sculpting at Hove Museum both for eight years and up, were just some of the sessions which went on in February this year. Check with each Council venue for what's on - especially during the school holidays. See the Arts section for details of Brighton and Hove's museums.

● LIBRARIES

Brighton Central library

Vantage Point,
New England Street,
Preston Circus
01273 290800
children's lending, music and reference
library: 01273 296957

Stuck in what used to be the DVLC building, this is a far cry from the days when it was part of the Brighton Museum. Still, it's only a stop-gap until the Council get the go-ahead to start building the Jubilee Project which will amalgamate the Prince Regent swimming pool.

Hove Library

182-186 Church Road, Hove
01273 290700

● REGULAR DATES

Borders Bookshop

Churchill Square Shopping Centre,
Central Brighton
01273 731122

Special children's storytime events on weekend mornings - readings complete with balloons, music and refreshments. The café's a refuge for the parents. The place to sip coffee, rest your tired toes and browse through the best stocked magazine section in Brighton while the kids sit cross legged and listen to what Harry Potter did next.

The Duke of York's Picture House

Preston Circus, Preston Park

01273 602503/626261

Junior Dukes, the cinema's kids club, opens its doors on Saturdays at 11am for competitions before the film, and birthday boys and girls even get to start the film in the projection room. And if you've got bigger kids, you can leave them while (if you've got any sense) you go and sit in a café and relax.

UGC at the Marina

Marina Village, Brighton

08701 555145

Saturday morning pictures for £1.50. It's not quite as carrot cake as our beloved Junior Dukes, but it'll do.

Kids@Komedia

44-47 Gardner Street, Brighton

box office enquiries: 01273 647 100

On Saturday and Sunday mornings, the arty Komedia puts on kids' shows which will inspire a new generation of puppeteers. Take them to the Junior Dukes Film Club on Saturday and the Komedia on Sunday, and they'll look after you when you're old.

● INDOOR ACTIVITIES

Badgers Mini Tennis

Church Place, Kemp Town

01273 671622

Coaching for four years and up at Manor Gym in the winter and Badgers Tennis Club in the summer.

Brighton & Hove Gymnastics Club

St Agnes Church, Hove,

01273 776209

Older kids have to book regular sessions.

Candy Castle

Enterprise Point

Melbourne Street, Lewes Road

01273 276060

Bouncy gyms and ball ponds. Not quite as friendly as it used to be since the scowly girls took over from the jolly giant, but it's a lifesaver when it's blowing a gale outside.

Paint and Pottery Café

31 North Road, Central Brighton

01273 628952

Another painting studio for would be artists, and a treat for a quiet afternoon with even the littlest of kids. The studio fee is £4, and you can stay as long as you like. The items start at £3 (tiles, little ornaments, little bowls etc) The firing and glazing is done by the pros, and you collect 24-48 hours later. They also do kids parties for a minimum of six children where the birthday child gets a piggy bank which their mates have painted for them.

Paint Pots

39 Trafalgar Street, North Laine

01273 696682

Paint your own pottery for a two hour studio fee (£3 for kids) plus the raw material for a variety of prices (a cereal bowl will cost £5). The idea is for the kids (or hen parties etc) to paint it while you have a cup of tea. Owner, Vicky Rawlinson, bakes and glazes the pottery and you collect a couple of days later.

Sealife Centre
Marine Parade, Old Steine
01273 604233
The ballpond here is free and open for kiddy parties and coffee hungry parents. The sealife centre itself is an expensive but worthwhile treat.

Wacky Warehouse
The Saltdean Tavern, Saltdean Park Road, Saltdean
01273 302863
More bouncy gyms and ball ponds. And there's a pub attached and they let you take drinks into the kiddie bit, so if you're thirsty...

● MUSIC, ARTS AND DANCE

Beacon Arts
Knoyle Hall, Knoyle Road, Brighton
01273 557124
Tap, Ballet, Jazz and drama classes. Jo Alderson runs art workshops for kids here as well as at Balfour Infants School.

Children's Music Playhouse
Brighthelm Centre, North Road, North Laine 01273 267834

Jackie Chase and her band of musicians have finally found a home at the Brighthelm Centre where parents and toddlers flock to clap their hands and wiggle their fingers to real musical instruments proper singing. Ring for details about piano, guitar, drum and singing lessons as well as music and movement classes for older kids. Also Practical Science Club and Drama, French and Music Theory.

Dance Art Studio
01273 556313
Principal Lynda Forster is everything you would expect a ballet teacher to be - small, neat, dressed in black and devoted to her 'gels'. Real grown up ballet for little girls

Helen O'Grady Drama
01273 881440
Helen O'Grady believed in boosting self esteem through drama and spawned a network of groups all over the world. They're also all over B&H and there tends to be a waiting list but if your kids love acting, improvisation and all without a hint of competition, this is their bag.

Ittaikan Aikido Club
Dorset Gardens, Brighton
01273 696383
paulb@beel.fsnet.co.uk
Paul Bonett (3rd Dan) and Brian Stacey (4th Dan) take a special juniors version of the Aikido class on Sunday afternoons from 4.30 to 6pm.

Phoenix Arts

10-14 Waterloo Place, Central Brighton
01273 603700

Activities for kids include Colourbox, a six-part course for 7-11-year-olds in design, collage and drawing.

Sama Organisation

01273 698781
www.samaorganisation.co.uk

Kids' after-school karate clubs at many schools in the area.

Stagecoach Theatre Schools

01273 747072

Ring Kate Bennett for formal but fun approach to drama, singing and dance for 4 - 16-year-olds with shows

Yoga for kids

01273 461541

Liz Warrington teaches yoga to 5-9-year-olds and 9-12-year-olds at Natural Bodies (see Health chapter for details) and at Balfour Infants for 8-14-year-olds.

● OUTDOOR ACTIVITIES

Brighton Pier

Madeira Drive, Brighton
01273 609361

Amusement arcades, dolphin derbies, simulators and rides to scare the hardiest and sweeten the littlest.

Stanmer Park

Lewes Road

The garden at the disused Stanmer House is a natural activity centre for kids, with wooden swings hanging from the cedars and fallen tree trunks sculpted into badgers (or are they moles?) for kids to scramble over. The dairy farm always seems to have calves in the barns, and the duck pond, café and vast open spaces are a winner with kids all year round.

Pells outdoor Swimming Pool

The Pells, Lewes
01273 472334

Saltdean Lido

Saltdean Park Road,
Saltdean
01273 305155

This is a good, proper lido just like they should be.

The Triangle swimming pool

Burgess Hill
01444 876000

Flumes and waves worth travelling for.

● PARENT AND BABY/ TODDLER GROUPS

Brighton and Hove Gymnastics Club

St Agnes Church,
Hove
01273 776209

Fiddlesticks Music

Stanford Avenue, Preston Park
and Southover Street, Hanover
01273 882951

Kemp Town toddler group

The Krypt,
St George's Church,
Kemp Town
drop in: Tuesdays and Thursday 10am

Little Dippers

67 Upper Gloucester Road,
Central Brighton
01273 328275
Remember the babies swimming underwater on the opening title sequence of Tomorrow's World and the British Gas ad? Lauren Heston encouraged them to use the breathing reflex babies rely on in the watery womb, and can do the same with yours. Her half hour classes are only for babies of 12 months and under.

Mini Music

Number Portland Road,
Hove
01273 327509

Mosaic

Community Base,
13 Queens Road,
Central Brighton
01273 234017
Cultural activities for children of mixed and ethnic races. Every 3rd Sunday, a bring a dish social invites older children and their families, but at the moment, it's only the under fives who get to take advantage of the 9.30-11.30 soft room play every Tuesdays. Members only - although membership is free for black and mixed parentage.

Rum a Tum Tum

Hanover Community Centre, Southover
Street, Hanover
01273 710896

Steiner Parent and Toddler Group

Whitehawk Road, nr Kemp Town
01273 386300
Breadmaking, singing and a calm, creative environment for the under 3's. Steiner also has regular bazaars, fetes and creative workshops. Highly recommended for kids of all ages and all educational choices.

Tumble Tots

Various venues in Brighton, Hove,
Hassocks, Cuckfield and Worthing.
Phone 01273 723511 for details.

Twinkle Twinkle

Phone 01273 272501 for details.

Whitehawk Toy Library

Whitehawk Road,
nr Kemp Town
01273 296924
Lends toys and has indoor activity days during school holidays.

Wam

The Parent Network
01444 230043
Enables parents to make friends with other parents and it is split into local groups. Events include children's activities, coffee mornings and playschemes.

● PLAYGROUNDS

Blaker's Park
Tiny little park between Preston Drove and Stanford Avenue with Council tennis courts and a young children's playground.

Hollingbury
Playground for younger and older kids (but beware the hideous teenagers coming out of Varndean and Stringer for a fag behind the slide at 3.15). Tennis courts and wide open space for a good run around.

Hove Park
Hove Park is a delight for buggy pushing dog walkers, with circular paths, playgrounds, squirrels and a sweet café complete with veranda, even if the owner doesn't like kids running around.

Preston Park
Large space with cycle tracks, bowling green, tennis courts and young children's playground. Two cafes.

Queen's Park
Kiddy dream of a park with pirate ship and café with mini milks and homemade cakes. Parents take picnics and make friends with their kids' friends' mums and dads. Duck pond and tennis courts too.

St Ann's Well
Tree lined and packed with squirrels with a sweet little well in the middle. Two playgrounds for toddler and bigger kids.

Seafront Playground at the Ellipse
Brand new playground which was still being built when we went to press.

● CHILDREN'S BIRTHDAY PARTIES

The Sea Life Centre, Bowlplex, Monkey Puzzle, Candy Castle and all the sports centres organise their own. You can take your own food and let the kids run riot at St Gabriel's Family Centre on Wellington Road in Elm Grove, Hopscotch on Portland Road, or The Whacky Warehouse next to the Lido in Saltdean as well as virtually all the church halls in the city. Bowlplex is particularly well organised for older kids. Most places will work with you to organise what you want; an art teacher at the Beacon Arts was willing to do art work to a theme, arrange songs and a little show with the kids while parents got the tea.

The Magic Rabbit (01273 206562) is a big favourite as a visiting show, appealing to adults with his dry sense of humour while the kids go gooey over the rabbit. Mr Pineapple Head (01273 473913) is a clown for young kids and Dandelion Puppets (01273 857482) provides lovely nature stories in Punch and Judy style.

08.4

● A BIT OF A FLUTTER

Brighton Racecourse
Manor Hill,
top of Whitehawk Hill
01273 603580
From April, flat racing kicks off three days a week at The Racecourse normally on Wednesday or Friday afternoons. If you've got kids, make sure you get to the Amateur Race Days where you can flutter on the Arab stallions on Sundays while the kids bounce on the bouncy castle.

● THE DOGS

Coral Greyhound Track
Nevill Road,
Hove
01273 204601
Racing takes place Tuesday, Thursday and Saturday evenings (£4 and £5), Wednesday afternoons (free) and Sunday lunchtimes (free).

● BASKETBALL

Brighton Bears Basketball Club
Gemini House,
136-140 Old Shoreham Road,

Hove
01273 778520

● BOWLS

Adur Indoor Bowling Club
Recreation Ground
Old Barn Way,
Southwick
01273 870670
Membership is £60 a year with a £20 joining fee, but anyone can play for £1.60 a session.

Bowlplex
Marina Way, Marina
01273 818180
Like walking inside a pinball machine - a right sensory attack - but for most of the kids who go there, that's cool. Still, it's a fun night out, and remember to phone and book a lane. Open till 12.30am from Monday to Thursday, with a late license till 2am on Friday and Saturday, and from 10.30 to 12.30 on Sundays. Prices range from £3.45 to Friday and Saturday nights when everyone pays £4.25. Shoe hire is free and there are special student nights on a Sunday, when bowling cost £1.50. If you're interested in joining a team go along on a Monday or Thursday.

Hove & Kingsway Bowling Club

The Beach, Kingsway, Hove
01273 734386

Curiously open to men only and membership is required. There's a women's club next door, but they don't have an office, so send membership applications to the men's club and they'll pass it on.

● CRICKET

Brighton and Hove Cricket Club

Nevill Playing Fields, Eridge Road, Hove
01273 555534
www.brighton-hove-cc.co.uk

They have men's, women's and Under 16's teams. Membership costs between £25 and £40 a year. Matches are played every Saturday and Sunday form late April to early September.

Sussex County Cricket Club

The County Ground, Eaton Road, Hove
01273 827100

This year's season runs from April 10 to late September. Prices vary depending on the type of match Sussex are playing, but it's between £10 and £15 for adults, £3 and £5 for under sixteen's, £7 and £12 for seniors. Under fives are always free. Seasonal memberships also vary in price but range from £10 for juniors to just under a hundred. There are also coaching courses for children in the Easter and summer holidays, they last for two or three days and cost between £20 and £30. If you want to get involved in village cricket and want advice on how to contact your local team, the Sussex Cricket Board at the County Ground will be able to help you.

● FOOTBALL

To find out about playing the local leagues, phone the Sussex County Football Association on 01903 753547.

Brighton & Hove Albion Football Club

Withdean Stadium, Tongdean Lane, Withdean, Brighton
admin offices: 5th floor, 118 Queens Road, Brighton
01273 778855
ticket office: 5 Queens Road, Brighton
01273 776992

There ain't no stopping The Seagulls. Depending on when you're reading this, they'll either be lording it at the top of Division Two or having a sharp taste of nosebleed reality in Division One. And who does Bobby Zamora play for now? Questions, questions. And then there's the question of the ground. Whatever the answers, the only thing that's sure is that tickets will be hard to come by.

Southwick Football Club

Old Barn Way, Southwick.
01273 701010

If you're looking for a cheap but fun day out come and pay £3 and watch a match, kids get in for £1.

● GOLF

There are six golf clubs in the Brighton & Hove area which are all listed below, but if you need any further assistance, or you want to know about clubs in the county, contact the East Sussex County Golf Union on 01273 589791.

Brighton and Hove Golf Club

Dyke Road, Brighton
01273 556482 - office
01273 507861 - bar/restaurant

Dyke Golf Club

Devils Dyke Road, Brighton
01273 857296

East Brighton Golf Club

Roedean Road, Kemp Town
01273 604838 - office
01273 603989 - pro shop

Hollingbury Park Golf Club

Ditchling Road, Hollingbury
01273 552010

Rottingdean Miniature Golf Course

Marine Drive, Rottingdean
01273 302127

Waterfall Golf Club

Saddlecombe Road, Devil's Dyke
01273 508658

West Hove Golf Club

Church Farm, Hangleton, Hove

01273 419738 - office
01273 413411 - lounge
01273 413494 - shop

● GYMS

Alive

25-27 Castle Street, Brighton
01273 739606

Fitness and natural health centre with gym, sauna, sunbed and an extensive range of classes, including yoga, aerobics, dance, flamenco, salsa and tango. Virtually every complimentary therapy is also on offer: aromatherapy, massage, shiatsu, homeopathy and cranial therapy. Membership starts at around £30 a month, but there are loads of different options.

Brighton and Hove Gymnastics Club

St. Agnes Church, Goldstone Lane, Hove
01273 776209

Gymnastics for all ages including adult lessons and 'mums and minis' sessions for children aged 1-3 years. Six months membership and insurance costs £10.50, then it's £3.75 per session. If you feel competitive they have in-house competitions twice a year.

Brighton Health & Racquet Club

Village Way, Falmer
01273 667800

Enormous and supposedly the best gym in town. It's a bit of a drive for anyone who doesn't live on campus at the

University of Sussex, but with its top-of-the-range tennis and squash courts, gym and swimming pool, it's probably worth it. There are crèche facilities, children's swimming lessons and kiddie yoga on offer while you work out.

Cheetah Gym

King Alfred Leisure Centre, Kingsway, Hove
01273 206644

Claims to be the most comprehensive weight-training facility in the south. It's a favourite among Hove's gay men and also has a ladies-only section. There's no crèche, but next door at the King Alfred Leisure Centre they have and they'll take your little ones.

Coral Health and Fitness Centre

Orchard Road, Hove
01273 731262

The gym here opens from 7am-10pm during the week, 9am-8pm on Saturdays and 9.30am-8pm on Sundays, but the squash courts are available from 9am. Facilities here include cardiovascular and weights area, squash courts, aerobics, crèche, sun beds, sauna, health suite and lounge bar. Memberships for off peak visits are £18.50 a month, and £185 a year or £27.50 a month, and £275 a year in peak time (5pm-9pm Monday to Friday). Average prices for aerobics classes are £2 for members, £3 for non-members and squash courts are £3.50 off peak and £5 in peak hours.

David Lloyd Centre

The Marina, Brighton
01273 666400

Well-equipped gym where you can pump your inner thighs while looking out to sea. The swimming pool is enormous and often empty and kids are welcome at most times of the day (Mon-Fri 9am-12.30pm and 1.30pm-8pm). The café, which maybe isn't the best café in town (unless you think paying over the odds for a ham sandwich a good deal), also has a seaview and is a perfect place to watch the sunset. There's a crèche, as well as its own expanding nursery school.

Dragon's Health And Leisure Club

St Heliers Avenue, Hove
01273 724211

Said to be a favourite among young singles (isn't that what gyms are for?), the swimming pool and beauty therapies attract a less iron-pumping crowd off-peak. Crèche facilities, ballet classes for members' kids, resident osteopath and sports massage mark it out.

Gym and Tonic Training Studio

47 Queen Victoria Avenue, Hove
01273 505459

A fully equipped gym and weights room for one-on-one training programmes. Appointments must be made but the studio is open from 7am-9pm, Monday to Friday, 8am-6pm on Saturdays and occasionally on Sundays if a session has been booked. It costs £20 per session.

Riptide Gym

150 Kings Road, Brighton
01273 725444

Situated on the seafront between the piers at the bottom of West Street, and open seven days a week from 7am to 10pm there is a fully equipped gym, classes including circuit training, crewing, Tai Chi and Yoga, sauna and a TV lounge area. There's no pool, but spinning classes (aerobics on a bike) and crewing classes (aerobics on a rowing machine) are a speciality. In the summer, the windows open on to a seaview. Which is nice. Prices vary depending on when you want to visit - £262.50 a year or £25 a month if you want to go anytime, £187.50 a year or £18 a month for off peak (7am - 4.30pm) or £150 or £14.25 for early sessions (7am - 10am). Trial visits are free and you can just go along for the day rate of £9.50. Riptide also offers sun beds for £4 a session.

Shape Health Studios

38 Devonshire Place, Kemp Town
01273 234500

Possibly the cheapest gym in town and offers a fully equipped gym, sauna, spa, steam room, cardio-vascular room and weights room. You can also arrange your own training programme with a personal trainer. The indoor swimming pool is just big enough to hold a gaggle of naked grannies (we didn't try - it's just a guess). The downside is that it's members only: membership costs £295 a year or £160 for six months. Students

get reduced prices - £195 per year, £160 for nine months, £120 for six months and no joining fees. Open from 8am to 10pm Monday to Friday, 9am to 8pm on Saturdays and closed on Sundays. Also at Fonthill Road, Hove, 01273 232300.

Sky Gym

Enterprise Point, Melbourne Street Brighton
01273 383007

Memberships here cost between £20 and £32 a month and allow you to use the fully equipped gym and sauna without any extra charge and take advantage of their full time martial arts school which has classes in kickboxing, judo, tai chi and soo bahk do. There are other classes, available for non-members, which include aerobics, yoga, tai bo and circuit training and cost £4.00 a session. Sky gym is open from 7am-9.30pm, Monday to Friday, 9am-4pm on Saturdays and 10am-2pm on Sundays.

● HOCKEY

Brighton and Hove Hockey Club

Preston Park Cricket Ground, Brighton
01273 389945
www.brightonandhovehockeyclub.net

Open to all ages and abilities, whether you're an expert or just have dim memories of playing at school. If you're interested in joining phone the number above or go along to meet them at

Sussex University, where they play on astroturf every Wednesday night 8-10pm.

● HORSE RIDING

Horse Riding
Southdown Riding School, Race Hill, Brighton
01273 679299

Rottingdean Riding School and Livery Yard
Chailey Avenue, Rottingdean
01273 302155
Offers a great selection of lessons, all taken by British Horse Society trained instructors. Prices range between £12 - £15 per hour for a group lesson, £15 for half an hour for a private lesson, £15 for an hour hack and £6 for a half hour lead. They also offer an 'own a pony day' for children. This costs £35 and they get a hack, lessons in how to look after a pony and lots of competitions.

● ICE SKATING

Sussex Ice Rink
Queen Square, Brighton
01273 324677
Open in sessions - 10.30-12.30, 3.30-5.30 and 8-10pm Tuesday to Friday, and 10.30-12.30, 2-4, 4.30-6.30 at the weekends, with an extra session of Saturday nights from 8-10pm. It costs £3.25 a session for children and students, £3.75 for adults and hiring skates cost £1.25. They also organise

lessons for children, beginners, intermediate and advanced skaters for £25 for a 5 week course and there are opportunities for 'Baby Bladers' (up to 5 years old), ice hockey sessions and discos on Friday and Saturday nights.

● LEISURE CENTRES

King Alfred Leisure Centre
Kingsway, Hove
01273 290290
Open seven days a week but times vary each day and there are adults only, ladies only and kids fun sessions throughout the week. One of the draws is the swimming pool, complete with bridges and some serious (and we mean serious) flumes. There is also a cardiovascular gym and a sports hall for aerobics and badminton. Membership costs around £40 a month.

Moulsecoomb Community Sports Centre
Moulsecoomb Way, Brighton
01273 622266

Portslade Sports Centre
Portslade Community College, Chalky Road, Portslade
01273 411100
Open from 9am to 11pm, Monday to Saturday and 10am-11pm on Sundays. Available here are sports halls, squash courts, aerobics, a floodlit pitch, snooker room and a bar lounge. Memberships cost about £24 a year for an adult and there is coaching in most

sports played here. Aerobics classes cost between £2.60 and £4, squash courts are £4.90 for 40 minutes.

Southwick Leisure Centre
Old Barn Way, Southwick
01273 263200

Stanley Deeson
Wilsons Avenue, Whitehawk Hill
01273 694281

In an unfashionable location on Whitehawk Hill just set into East Brighton park but the Stanley Deeson is one of the few places where you can get a walk in squash court.

University of Sussex Sports Complex
University of Sussex, Falmer
01273 678228
www.sussexsport.com
info@sussexsport.com

Extremely well equipped sports centre with two sports halls, a fitness room, dance studio, martial arts room, 7 squash courts, 6 hard tennis courts, grass football, cricket and rugby pitches... all it lacks is a pool. Students and University of Sussex staff get a discount, but it's open to the public as well. There's a wide range of classes including break dancing and three types of yoga. Average price is £32 for 8 weeks.

Withdean Sports Complex
Tongdean Lane, Withdean
01273 542100

● MARTIAL ARTS

Genbu Khan Ninpo Bugei
Brighton Ki Centre, 12 Queens Square,
Central Brighton www.genbukhan.org
01273 415774

Portslade Sports Centre
Chalky Road, Portslade
01273 411100

Zeb Glover is the instructor of this particular club, Nyojo Dojo, where they practise Ninpo Taejutsu and Kokusai Jujutsu. Classes are held in the evenings on Tuesday and Thursday at the Ki Centre and on Wednesday at Portslade Sports Centre but if you want to get involved you must contact Zeb before hand. He will talk you through everything that is involved and enrol you onto a free introductory course which they hold once a month. After that initial class it is £5 every time you go.

● KARATE

Sama Organisation
01273 698781
www.samaorganisation.co.uk

As well as adult karate and kicikboxing classes, Sama runs very popular kids' after-school karate clubs at many schools in the Brighton & Hove area.

● TAEKWON-DO

Hove Park Upper School
Nevill Road, Hove
01273 670415

You can drop in here and have a go, even if you've never heard of Taekwon do. Classes are held on Mondays and Wednesdays; juniors from 6 - 7.30pm, adult beginners from 7.30 to 9pm and advanced adults from 8.30 to 10pm. It costs £3 for your first lesson to see if you enjoy it and £4 a time after that.

● RUGBY

Brighton Rugby Football Club
Waterhall Playing Fields, Mill Road, Westdene
01273 562729

Hove Rugby Football Club
Park View Road, Hove
01273 505103

● SWIMMING POOLS

Lewes Leisure Centre Swimming Pool
Mountfield Road, Lewes
01273 486000
Swim while looking out over the Downs.

Pells Outdoor Swimming Pool
The Pells, North Street, Lewes
01273 472334
An outdoor lido with plenty of room for lounging.

Prince Regent
Church Street, Central Brighton
01273 685692
A swimming pool in the middle of town

where there's a free crèche Tuesday and Thursday mornings - and that means you can get a stress-free swim. There are four swimming pools and a health and fitness suite. Open from 7am-10pm on weekdays and 9am-6pm at weekends, but the times and types of sessions vary for each pool. There are lessons, exercise classes, sunbeds and a sauna. Adults pay £2.70 for a swimming session, children (between 4 and 17) £1.40. Memberships cost between £38 and £70 a month, with a joining fee of either £50 or £80.

Saltdean Lido
Saltdean Park Road, Saltdean
01273 305155 (or 01273 880616)
Opened in the 1930s by Johnny Weismuller, this is a good, proper lido just like they should be. There's also the Shape Fitness centre, complete with gym and sun beds. The swimming pool is open from the end of May to the end of September, 7am-9pm Monday to Friday and 9am-6 at the weekends. There is a day rate of £10 but memberships cost £200 a year and £120 for 6 months, student memberships are cheaper at £125 a year.

Surrenden Swimming Pool
Surrenden Road, Preston Park
01273 504858
This pool is mainly used for schools, swimming lessons and clubs but open to the public for adults only between 8 and 9am, on Sunday mornings, for all ages, between 9 and 12, and during the Easter

and summer holidays on weekdays from 1.30pm to 4. A swim costs £1.85 for early mornings, £1.75 for children and £2.45 on Sundays and during the holidays. On weekends, you can hire the pool for your own personal use at £43 per hour on Saturday and £46 on Sunday. Not such an extravagance if you share it with up to 30 mates.

● TENNIS & OTHER THINGS WITH RACQUETS

Council courts are in just about every park in Brighton and Hove. You can't pre-book, but most of the courts have clubs attached. The best bet is to turn up and someone will either kick you off or collect payment. The city is extraordinarily pro-active in promoting tennis to budding young Henmans and even has its own tennis development officer at the Council. Call Nicky Salmon: 01273 292570 for a list of clubs attached to the council courts.

Badgers Tennis Club
Church Place,
Kemp Town
01273 671622
Four tennis courts in a hidden little corner of Kemp Town. Membership is £120 pa or £275 for a family of four plus a joining fee of between £10 and £50. Kids can learn to play mini-tennis from 4 years old, with indoor coaching up the road at the Manor Gym. Members can take guests in for a fiver per session up to 6 times a year.

Brighton Health and Racquet Club
Village Way, Falmer
01273 667800
See Gyms section in this chapter.

Brighton Squash Club
Withdean Sports Complex, Tongdean Lane
01273 383071 www.brightonsquash.co.uk
Club sessions are every Monday, Wednesday and Thursday from 6-9pm. Anyone can play between these hours for £3.00 or £1.50 for students, just turn up and challenge someone. The club has four men's and one women's county league teams for those who have the skill.

Dragon's Health & Leisure Club
St Heliers Avenue, Hove
01273 724211
See Gyms section.

First Tennis - Individual and Group Tuition
Church Place, Kemp Town
01273 671622
A training organisation is linked to Badgers Tennis Club, found in the same place so you can be coached here or they will come to you, any time of year. They train all ages in groups or individually, wherever you want to play. Prices for members of Badgers are £10 for half an hour, juniors are £7 for the same amount of time and non-member prices start at £12.50.

Grasshoppers Lawn Tennis Club

The Drive, Hove

01273 771934/330130

www.grasshopperstennis.co.uk

A small club with three floodlit courts. Membership (from May to May) costs £12 for under 18's, £33 for students and £126 for adults, but non-members can attend for £3 a day. Tournaments are held during the summer.

Pavilion and Avenue Lawn Tennis Club

Preston Drove, Preston Park

01273 506087

A members club, but new people are always welcome, and members can bring guests along for a small fee. Yearly memberships are £151 for seniors, £75 for juniors and £250 for a family. The ten courts are open all year round and coaching is available for £12 and hour for children and £18 for more advanced players, non-members can take advantage of this but just have to pay an extra £1.50. They're in the middle of building a swanky new clubhouse that will be finished in may and can be used by all members.

Preston Lawn Croquet Club

Preston Drove, Brighton

01273 505731

Memberships cost £159 per year for adults, £32 for 15 to 18 year olds and £16 for under 15s. Coaching is available in group or individual sessions for about £13/£14 an hour. There is a clubhouse

for members to use and a whole host of social events to enjoy.

Sussex County Croquet Club

Victoria Road, Southwick

01273 591874

Sussex County Lawn Tennis Club

Kingston Lane, Southwick

01273 593644

Withdean Sports Complex

Tongdean Lane

01273 542100

Pay and play at these Council-run indoor courts.

● THE WATER

Hove Lagoon

If you're a complete beginner in seagoing activities, it's probably best to learn the ropes at Hove Lagoon (01273 424842; windsurf@hovelagoon.co.uk) which - and this the reassuring bit - is only four feet deep. Their fully-trained staff teach RYA courses in sailing, windsurfing, canoeing and just about any other watersport you can think of. Local schools make good use of the facilities for their older kids. Varndean School spends the last week of its summer term down at the Lagoon, Thomas A Beckett teaches its kids to build rafts there and St Christopher's puts it's pupils through sailing courses. This summer, there are multi-activity week breaks on offer to kids and parents will be able to leave their children with trained staff from 9am-5pm. Hove Lagoon is open to anyone over the age of six, and it's a good opportunity for holidaying parents with older kids to get some time to themselves.

● DIVING

Sport divers report that the diving in the area is for the hardy, but visibility can get up to ten metres; seven metres is the average though, and if you lose sight of your buddy, you're on your own. There are a good deal of wrecks to explore, although they tend to be quite deep, and plenty of fish - even if they are the grey, edible kind. The English Channel is not the Red Sea, but if you want to keep your diving up in this country, it's not as bad as you might think. From July, the sea can be quite warm (17 celsius last year), and a 5mm suit will do you just fine. Beware the strong currents and join a dive club; the following have been recommended by our diving chums. Sunstar (01903 767224); Newhaven Scuba Centre (01273 612012) and Scuba Diving GB (01273 383444). If you don't want to go with a club, the Marina can offer you a boat and skipper.

● SAILING

Brighton Sailing Club
109 Kings Road Arches
01273 321802
www.brightonsailingclub.org.uk
You don't need your own boat to join,

but as there are few crew places available it helps. The club meets every Wednesday after 8pm and races on Sunday mornings from late March to early November, so pop down to meet the members and find out how to join.

● SURFING

Throughout the year, the sea is awash with surfers; that Surfers Against Sewage has opened its only branch outside Cornwall tells you how popular it is here. To the uninitiated, the waves don't look enticing enough to get your kit off for in the middle of winter, but there are enough bottoms being hauled into wetsuits on the beaches east of the Marina, around the West Pier and at Hotpipes behind the Old Power Station at Shoreham to prove us wrong. Fanatics report that it's only because it's the nearest surf to London - and because the apres-surf is suitably cool. According to the papers, the waves can get up to 12ft, but on an average surfing day, they don't get higher than your chin. Surfing around the West Pier is probably the most laid-back, with the longer established East Marina surfies least likely to share their breaks. For a tide timetable, ring the Marina (01273 819919). A useful website to use for Brighton surfing is www.sharkbait.co.uk

● *I am a true Brightonian, born and bred. Well, OK. I was born in London and brought up in Rottingdean village, but compared to most of today's residents it's enough to claim genuine roots. I went to live in London as soon as the guards on the train would let me on without ringing my mother to come and collect me, but after ten years in Soho, I came back to Rottingdean where where we're lucky if the Co-op stays open past six. For me, that's the appeal of Brighton; you've got everything you could want in the centre, but ten minutes on a bus and you can be walking on the South Downs, and not see anyone for hours. Try doing that in Hyde Park.*

Amanda Sangorski's a TV producer and lives in Hove.

● Brighton and Hove may be a throbbing metropolis but it only takes ten minutes or so to get into the heart of the countryside. Flanked by the South Downs on all sides, and Devil's Dyke at its centre, Brighton and Hove's country garden is a breath of fresh air for anyone from the hardiest of rambler to the idle stroller. And if you're not into doing the trek yourself, you can always borrow a horse or even a llama to do it for you.

The number of quintessential English country pubs within a 20-mile radius is enough to make you forget the city, with roaring fires and locally brewed beer in winter, or villages alive with the scent and sound of the English summer. Go east down the A27 to Firle and you'll find The Ram Inn bursting at the seams with Brightonians and Hoveites and their families, or turn off to Glynde and feel the spirit of the country at The Trevor Arms, with green wellies piled at the door. Well dear, we are in spitting distance of Glyndebourne. The Jolly Sportsman offers finer cuisine if you fancy a real culinary treat after an afternoon of yomping, while the idyllic Hungry Monk in Polegate is where the Banoffi pie was born. If you want proper rambling information, check the South Downs website: www.vic.org.uk

For those seeking to fill more than their stomachs, Charleston, the home of Vanessa Bell and her Bloomsbury entourage, is a must on the cultural tour, while youngsters will prefer Ashdown Forest, the original Hundred Acre Wood. And if they want to see real small animals, Drusilla's Park is only 20 minutes drive from Brighton.

As always, send your suggestions through the Opinion button on the website www.juicyguides.co.uk if you've found pubs which you think should be Juiced and we'll put them in the monthly newsletter and into next year's guide.

● PUBS

● VAGUELY NORTH

The Bull
2 High Street, Ditchling
01273 843147

Dating back to 1569, this is the kind of beamed hostelry you can take your American friends to and watch them faint. The garden is sweet with apple trees groaning with fruit in the summer, and the food has plenty of vegetarian options.

The Griffin Inn

Fletching, nr Uckfield

01825 722890

Owned by yet another London refugee, James Pullan formerly of Draycotts and Joe's Brasserie, The Griffin is where the likes of Helen Baxendale and Raymond Briggs who managed to save up for a pile in the country, spend their spare cash on a plate of organic veal or smoked chicken and olive salad. Using produce from local farms, much of which is genuinely organic, the food here is worth making the half hour trip for, and as one of the few restaurants in the area which can boast a wine list featuring 50 bottles of great wines under £20, it's good value at around £30 a head. The Sunday lunch in the garden with spit roast and live jazz over views across Sheffield Park might even make you think about packing your bag and buying a pad in the Sussex countryside. There are rooms at the inn too for those who can't bear to leave.

Half Moon

Ditchling Road, Plumpton

01273 890253

Walkers retreat and Sunday lunch favourite, but arrive before 12.30 if you want to eat before 2pm. The bar is always packed, hiking boots piled outside the door, and if you're late, you'll have to suffer the blaring TV and billiards crowd in the annex. The garden is paradise for children, and possibly the best in the area. If its raining, the smoke's too much and the bar is full, it's

only a five minute drive to The Jolly Sportsman at East Chiltington, but the kids won't thank you.

The Jolly Sportsman

Chapel Lane, East Chiltington,

nr Plumpton

01273 890400

Posh, rustic restaurant with an eclectic selection of neeps, tatties and ciabattas mixed in with fine Modern British dining. A few locals still huddle the bar, while the Guardian and Telegraph readers (and writers) laze over the papers and ponder whether to go for the haggis (£6.90) or the chicken liver parfait with onion marmalade (£4.85), while parents consider what on Earth to feed the kids. The garden may be a haven for kids, but feed them before you leave home. Expect to pay around £25 per head for dinner.

The Royal Oak

Poynings

01273 857389

Always packed, it might take an age for your bangers and mash, Sunday roast or Salmon Hollandaise but what's the hurry? The kids can play on the climbing frame in the large garden and you can plan your walk across Devils Dyke while you wait.

The Sandrock Inn

High Street, Ditchling

01273 842777

A warm welcome from Val and Vern in a lovely village pub. There's a bizarre Tex

Mex theme inside, but people do eat the strangest things in villages.

The Shepherd and Dog
Faulking
01273 857382
If the Royal Oak is full (or vice versa), try this lovely old pub just down the road with little poo sticks stream running through the garden perched on the back of Devil's Dyke. A lane next to the garden leads up onto the top of the Dyke and affords some breathtaking views of the area. Book if you want a table for a weekend lunch. But parents beware they will not let kids into the bar even to buy a packet of crisps, so if you are a family don't go in winter.

Vinyard Lodge
42 High Street,
Hurstpierpoint.
01273 835000
vinyardlodge@btopenworld.com
www.vinyardlodge.com
Large sofas and enough toys to keep anyone under the age of 7 amused throughout a South Down Roast Lamb lunch, a garden with swings and views, and an ambience laid back enough to keep the punters in until closing time, the Vinyard Lodge (sic) is a welcome addition to the Sunday lunch chapter. During the week, the food is more varied than the staple 2 roasts (pork or lamb? That's the country for you) with steak sandwiches and posh bangers and mash for under £8. With 26 wines on offer and locally sourced produce, come

Springtime, there'll be a queue of food loving young parents up the A23 before you can say "Mine's a Chardonnay".

● VAGUELY WEST

Pulborough
The Old Priest House
London Road,
Coldwaltham
01798 873642
Reports have been coming in about this new place near Pulborough. The late kitchen and simple cooking with the best organic and locally sourced ingredients sounds good enough for the 40 minute trek from Brighton, and we've heard good reports but we haven't done it yet. Subscribe to the newsletter via www.juicyguides.co.uk and read the review when we've been. Or click on Opinion and tell us what you think.

● VAGUELY EAST

The Anchor Inn
Barcombe
01273 4000414
If you fancy a good walk to and from your pub lunch, park at the carpark on right hand side of the A275 just before Barcombe, and follow the river to the pub, crossing over at the only possible place. On a summer's day, it's heaven; in winter, it's a muddy but serene 40 minute walk. Boat rides and ice creams at the pub's kiosk, and good food at the pub wait you. And it's child and dog friendly.

Firle Place

Firle (off the A27 on the way to
Eastbourne)

A beautiful old house, full of history. Right in the courtyard there's a cute little tea rooms where you can get your smoked salmon sandwiches and teas. Perfect after a walk on the Downs.

The Gun Garden in Ypres Castle

Rye 01797 223248

On a Sunday evening, this little smugglers' haunt is throbbing to the sound of local bands as Rye's Bohemian old town brings its weekend to a close.

Hungry Monk

Polegate
01323 482178

Gorgeous old thatched pub with beams, roaring fires and the business for a full on romantic evening with your true love. Set in the middle of a picturesque Sussex village, it's also a good bet for a Sunday lunch and walk. Said to be the originator of the very first Banoffee Pie.

Littlington Tea Gardens

Littlington

Established over a 100 years ago, the tea gardens are the perfect place to go after a stroll in Seven Sisters Park. Delicious English tea in the midst of a host of gorgeous flowers) from Littlington cream tea (£4) to honey roast ham salad (£5), baked potato with Greek yoghurt and fresh herbs (£4.50). They even have a licence.

The Mermaid Inn

Rye
01797 223065

Gorgeous ancient pub with good food and four posters in five of the 31 bedrooms (£75pp). A pricey treat for a romantic weekend away.

The Ram Inn

Firle
01273 858222

Classic cars and open tops crowd the carpark in this otherwise sleepy village on Sunday lunchtimes and misty evenings when the food is hot, the music is live, and the fires roar. Since it was taken over by the landlord's offspring, it's hopping with parents and their kids on a weekend. Something to do with the piles of toys in the family room, the large spaces, the toddler loo seats, the children's playground complete with pirate ship and secret garden perhaps?

For a weekend walk, follow signs from the pub to Firle Beacon, and make sure you've got your kite. If it's too windy for the top of the hill, follow the mass of ramblers around the back of the village.

Sussex Ox

Milton Street,
Alfriston
01323 870840

Great for kids with fantastic adventure playground. Perfect for a huge lunch before a walk to the Long Man of Wilmington.

Tiger Inn

East Dean

01323 423209

A long summer afternoon treat: lunch at the Tiger Inn, then visit the Seven Sisters Sheep Farm before walking through the woods and down the wiggly path to the beach.

The Trevor Arms

The Street, Glynde

01273 858208

Dogs, hiking boots and green wellies are littered around this delightful proper country pub. The food is good too - Sunday roasts are hearty and no nonsense.

Others we've heard about but haven't reviewed (please send us your opinion via the website: www.juicyguides.co.uk

The White Horse at Ditchling

01273 842006

The Smuggler's Inn at Alfriston

6 Market Cross,

Waterloo Square

01323 870241

The Bell Inn at Burwash

01435 882304

The Bear at Burwash

01435 882540

The Anchor Inn at Hartfield

01892 770424

The Rose and Crown at Mayfield

01435 872200

The Giant's Rest at Wilmington

01323 870207

The Cat Inn at West Hoathly

01342 810369

The New Inn at Winchelsea

01797 226252

● FOR KIDS

Ashdown Forest

www.ashdownforest.co.uk

Reputedly the place which inspired AA Milne's Pooh sticks episode. It's a beautiful place, and a lovely dog walk.

Bluebell Railway

www.bluebell-railway.co.uk

01825 722370

Well, not just for kids, but for the thousands of Thomas the Tank Engine fans, a must. Run by volunteers, the Bluebell railway is a beautiful old steam train that gently trundles along an old line from Sheffield Park to near East Grinstead, visiting old stations as it goes. Go to The Griffin around the corner in Fletching for lunch before or for a perfect end to the day.

Bockets Farm

Leatherhead 01372 363764

Working farm with cows, pigs, sheep,

water buffaloes and llamas, lambing, tractor rides and play area. At Christmas, it's the best Santa's grotto around.

Borde Hill
Haywards Heath
01444 450326.
200 acres of parkland, bluebell woods and pirates adventure play area, walks, lake and wood.

Butlins
OK, OK, but your kids are not going to have the same snobbish pre-conceptions as you have when they see Noddyland and the dome covered flumes and sub tropical swimming pool.

A family ticket at Bognor is £16.50 for the day (10am-8pm). You can stay at the resort for more and do the Red Coat thing after the kids have gone to bed, or stay in some lovely little B&B in Arundel and come back the next day. The Jubilee Guest House (01243 863016) is bang opposite Butlins for weekend visitors who can't get onto the resort itself.

Chessington World of Adventures
01372 727227
Fun for all the family as long as you can afford the themepark price of £19.50 for adults and a staggering £15.50 for the 4-13's.

It's only open from April to October but kids love Cartoonland and Dragon Falls.

Devils Dyke
Heritage open top bus from Brighton
01273 886200

Drusillas Zoo Park
Alfriston (on the A26)
01323 870234
Fantastic small animal zoo with creative workshops, train, and huge picnic area with play apparatus for bigger kids and playbarn for toddlers.

Herstmonceux Science Centre
Herstmonceux, nr Eastbourne
01323 832731
Originally the home of the Royal Greenwich Observatory, this is just the job for budding scientists.

Llama Trekking
Walk with llamas and picnic lunches are provided in the summer.
Phone 01273 835656 for details.

Middle Farm
Firle
(on the A26)
01323 811411
£1 entry fee to see small animals, and watch the milking of the Jersey herd at 3.30pm. Kids wooden play area. Tea shop, cider barn, organic food store and craft shop with picnic tables outside. The Apple Festival in mid October has live music, hot mulled cider, a fairground, horse and cart races, toffee apple dunking and all things British and attracts about 3,500 people. (See also Organics)

Paradise Park

Avis Road, Newhaven
01273 512123
Garden centre with botanic gardens and water gardens as well a fossil collection, dinosaur exhibition and rides for the kids. Café.

Rye Heritage Centre

Strand Quay, Rye
01797 226696
Ghosts and smugglers in Rye's walking, talking tour of the history of gorgeous old Rye.

Sheffield Park Gardens

01825 790231
Blissful landscaped gardens just opposite the Bluebell Railway laid out in the 18th century by Capability Brown. The centrepiece is the original four lakes, and gorgeous shows of stunning flowers throughout the seasons are worth the 40 minute trek out of Brighton.

Washbrook Farm

Hurstpierpoint
01273 832201
500 yards from Hurstpierpoint, there are animals in barns to feed, a playground, tractor rides, a tea room and seasonal excitement like Easter egg hunts.

Wish Tower Puppet Museum

Martello Tower, 73 Edward's Parade
Eastbourne
01323 410440
Puppets from east and west, present and past.

● A BIT OF CULTURE

Anne of Cleves House Museum

52 Southover Street, Lewes
01273 474610

Bentley Wildfowl and Motor Museum

Halland, Nr Lewes
01825 840573

Bateman's

Burwash, nr Tunbridge Wells
01435 882302
Rudyard Kipling's home after he left Rottingdean in 1902 until 1936. Corn grinding on Saturdays in the water-driven turbines

Battle Abbey and 1066 Battle of Hastings Battlefield

Battle
01424 773792
Guided tour through one of history's bloodiest moments, and abbey ruins. Children's play area.

Chartwell

Westerham,
Kent
01732 868381
Home to Winston Churchill for more than 40 years.

Fishbourne Roman Palace

Salthill Road, Fishbourne
Nr Chichester
01243 785859

Foredown Tower Countryside Centre
Foredown Road, Hove
01273 292092

Glynde Place
Glynde 01273 858224
16th century house in lovely little village near Lewes. Lunch at the Trevor Arms

Kipling Gardens
Rottingdean
The home of *The Jungle Book* and *If* fame. Rudyard lived here from 1897 to 1902. Summon his spirit in the wild garden or by playing croquet on the gorgeous lawns.

Lewes Castle and Barbican House Museum
169 High Street, Lewes
01273 486290

Michelham Priory
Upper Dicker,
Hailsham
01323 844224
Gorgeous Tudor mansion and medieval priory with moat

Regency Town House
Brunswick Square,
Hove
01273 206306
Grade 1 listed building and heritage centre which transports its visitors into the heart of urban 1820's life in Hove. Note that this is not a kiddie friendly kind of place.

Wakehurst Place
near Haywards Heath
1444 894066
Country estate of the world-famous Kew Gardens and home to the new 80 million pound Millennium Seed Bank project which aims to save thousands of endangered plant species from extinction. It features an interactive exhibition to explain the project and the chance to look into the laboratories and see the scientists at work. Wakehurst also has 180 acres of formal botanical gardens and woodland. There is also the Elizabethan mansion, a gift shop, and restaurant.

West Blatchington Windmill
North of Holmes Ave, Hove
Last open to millers in 1897, this lovely old windmill is almost in full working order with much of the original bits and bobs still there. Take the kids to see what life was like in a rural milling town (such as Hove?) and then treat them to tea in the barn.

● WALKS IN THE CITY

The Beach
From Rottingdean right through to Hove, The beach is the best walk in the city - unless you've got a dog and it's between May and October. The dog-free zone runs from the Naturist Beach at Kemp Town to Hove Lawns so keep to East of The Marina where there's sand and rock pools to frolic in or head down past Hove lagoon.

Brighton Racecourse

Warren Road,

Brighton

The race track runs across the top of East Brighton Park, and the sight of horses being exercised in the early morning mists against the backdrop of the English Channel makes getting up early worthwhile.

East Brighton Park

Wilson Avenue,

Kemp Town

One of the best open spaces in all Brighton. A park that backs onto both the South Downs and Brighton Racecourse with options for long walks over to Ovingdean and Rottingdean Windmill. The park can be unpoopscooped and the playground area is one of the shabbiest, but The Friends of Sheepcote Valley - a noble body - do their best and have done a fantastic job cleaning and planting and encouraging local pride. Beyond the park into the hills, you'll get the best view in town. The Pavilion Café, with its clock stuck on teatime, is almost always closed, except for the summer months when the local campsite uses it for its breakfast.

Hollingbury Golf Course

Ditchling Road,

Brighton

Keep to the edges, dodge the golf balls and head to the woods overlooking Wild Park. The permanent breeze makes it the perfect walk on hot summer days.

Hove Park

off Old Shoreham Road,

Hove

Circular, large, and filled with squirrels. Children's playground, café with Victorian balcony, bowling green and miniature railway.

Ovingdean Farm

OK, so it's just out of the city, but only just. Take a left at St Dunstans' roundabout and it's just past the 11th century church. Walk past the cowsheds up into the Downs.

St Ann's Well Gardens

Sommerhill Road, Hove

Small but perfectly formed little park in the middle of Hove with a scented garden for the blind, enormous playground for kids of all ages, and squirrels and conkers everywhere. Café, toilets and a relaxed community spirit.

The Upper Lodges

first right off the road to Ditchling from A27

A myriad of forest walks linking up with Stanmer Park below.

Stanmer Park

Lewes Road (just behind the Brighton by-pass A27, near Falmer)

Picturesque village turned park with café, toilets, plenty of open space for running around, tree climbing, picnicking, kite flying and cycling. Dairy farm (with calves all year round), duck pond and woods.

The Undercliff

The severe weather conditions this year have almost destroyed one of Brighton's favourite treats with part of the cliff above the Undercliff collapsing unexpectedly over Christmas. The Undercliff walk which leads from Asda at the Marina to Rottingdean and beyond normally takes walkers, joggers and cyclists past some of the best and sandiest beaches in town; let's hope the Council can make it safe in time for summer.

Wild Park

off the Lewes Road, just past Moulsecoomb

Shortish circular walk unless you're going to climb the steep hill up to Hollingbury Golf Course, but stacked with rabbits.

Withdean Park

off London Road, just past Preston Park

Not much more than a glorified dog exercise area, except for its national collection of lilac trees. Surrounded by rabbit and squirrel filled woods.

● *We love living in Brighton because it's full of people who think they are living in Spain! There's nowhere else in England where you would nip to the shops for a pint of milk and end up on the beach (having just signed up for guitar/yoga/Spanish lessons), a cocktail in one hand with three new friends and a fabulous new outfit! It's the first place ever where we've actually hung out with our neighbours, been on first name terms with our newsagent, deli-man, postwoman, greengrocer etc (we even know the name of the local traffic warden, but you couldn't print it!) Fabulously funky little hotels so we can still have our 'dirty weekends' here, where else is there? You could eat in a different place and drink in a different bar every day of the year - and believe me we've tried!!! And we couldn't live without Pussy our favourite shop and love being verbally abused by Gwen otherwise Gwen and Nikki will never forgive us. The calm of the sea, the drama of the Downs, the weird, wonderful, colourful, glitteringly wild population (and that's just our neighbourhood). Only the truly boring could ever be bored by Brighton!*

Julie Graham, *actress*

09

● It's a weird old place to work, this city of culture in which the creative industries, the biggest growing sector at 5% a year, are often forced up to London to earn their daily bread. It's a city known for its innovation and engineering excellence, its New Media industry which is so integral to the local economy that it's been dubbed Silicon Beach, where companies like The Sussex Innovation Centre are set up specifically to give free advice to entrepreneurs so that they'll keep their ideas, staff and spending local. But try to break through the invisible barriers between old and new Brighton and you'll be queuing up for the Laptop Express before you can say "mine's a latte".

Simon Fanshawe, champion of Brighton and Hove business, Chair of the Hub 100 project and also of the Brighton & Hove Economic partnership, a forum for the exchange of ideas on regeneration, is set on addressing the problem. "The partnership is focussing on how we can help the creative industries within the economic development of the city. Compared to most cities, Brighton and Hove is very receptive to new ideas; it's been famous for its entrepreneurial spirit since Dr Russell reinvented sea bathing as a health tonic. Its two most famous exports are The Body Shop, a business whose idea of making shampoo out of banana skins was never laughed out of town, and Stomp, a show that took the idea of making music out of dustbin lids all over the world. Our biggest export this year could well be Fatboy Slim".

Richard Daws, chairman of Victoria Real, the award-winning digital media company that blew the broadcast industry into a different century with its web coverage of Big Brother, agrees that there's innovation in the air in Brighton. "There's a general acceptance about people doing things differently here," he says. "Every waiter you come across down here is writing a novel. There's a feeling that if you don't try, you don't get what you want from your life. Not many places are like that".

Rupert Loman, 18, and his 23-year-old brother Nick won the Place To Be award at the Juicy Awards back in 2000 for their extraordinarily successful online games technology and content company, Eurogamer.net. It sounds like he could have made his millions anywhere, but the boy from Varndean College still lives with his parents in Preston Park. "The first 18 months were pretty difficult but in the last year things really kicked off and are looking good," he says. "We developed some great technology products which we sold to Telewest, Electronics Boutique and British Telecom.

"A lot of our competitors went out of business after they attracted venture capital back in 1999/2000 - even though their businesses couldn't sustain it. We're now working in partnership for Telewest and Sony on technology that allows the PlayStation2 to be played online against others across the world." It was mainly parental influence, which helped the Lomans, although his teachers at Varndean College helped where they could. "They took an interest in what I was doing and didn't penalise me if my business affected my attendance or my homework was late" Rupert laughs.

One of Fanshawe's ideas has already been given the go-ahead by South East Arts. SEA has allocated £450,000 over three years and will raise the rest to make a fund of £1m which will allow Brighton to collaborate with some of the best theatrical talent in the world, radically increasing the city's capacity to produce new theatre. "It's part of a plan to raise the game" he says, "and we should be seeing this across all areas of industry". Another of the forum's initiatives is the creation of Hub100, a web resource centre for high growth and aspiring high growth companies, which should, in time, affect every freelancer currently waiting for the 8.57 to Blackfriars.

But if ideas are the lifeblood of new industry, they are also maverick beasts. The difference between having good ideas and making money from them can be down to working the system. Bureaucracy and civil servants, the arbiters of your future even in this city of enterprise, can be a major problem. Try fitting the multisided shapes of your ideas into the round hole of public, bank or venture capital funding and you'll be bashing your creative head against every brick in the wall. South East Arts, the body that was set up to support the artist in their garret, applies such strict criteria that an idea can have lost its soul by the time it gets the green light for lottery funding. Fanshawe (who sits on the SEA board) thinks this sorts the wheat from the chaff. "The bureaucratic processes are often so onerous that most people give up. They just can't be bothered to see a good idea through after years of trying to persuade the various funding bodies to support them. But if the faint hearted give up, the rest of us do plough on and the most committed will always find a way to make their ideas work."

● NETWORKING

As always, if you need a job doing, then you've got to do it yourself and networking is the answer for many of the freelancers and sole traders who make up so much of the local industry. Once a hideous American dream of making friends with a plastic grin and a handful of business cards, networking has made it into the new century with a caring sharing kind of vision. There are some very successful groups which operate a paid up membership scheme in which members meet every week during business hours and build up a support group as well as a wider network of contacts. Most networking is done in industry oriented groups over a drink after hours, and once you've found your way in, you'll find that there's a different networking meeting every night of the week.

The Arts Club was set up as a response to creative Juicy readers' needs to build relationships, swap stories and find ways of avoiding the London commute. Brighton Underground has developed into a forum for New Media and the Performing Arts and invites key speakers from some of the more interesting companies in the city. This is where you'll find Richard Daws and his industry rival, Donald Clark of Epic; "I see most of the companies I'd expect down there. There are no really mysterious companies here, at least not in the world of New Media".

SWAN is for women from big and small businesses and is building into one of the most well attended girls' nights out in the city. There were more than 200 members at the time of going to press and after a year of meetings, is passing genuine recommendations between women who want to do business together.

Some of the networks are better organised than others and Wired Sussex is an example of how a network can build a community of freelancers and small to medium enterprises. A subsidiary of Sussex Enterprise, it was originally a response to the needs of the mass of university graduates leaving Sussex and Brighton with dollar signs in their eyes and no real desire to leave town. For the 400 new media companies currently in Brighton and Hove, Emily Aitken and her colleagues in the Old Steine, are a focal point of contact, helping them to secure finance, coaching them to pitch for investment and then putting them in front of real investors.

Wired Sussex has an extensive database and like most of the good networks, it's free to join it. It's a good place to look for employment in new media or its related services with between 25 and 50 jobs advertised at any one time. Finance, ecommerce and legal issues are all featured there too.

The key to the success of networking is the joining together of small and informal and big and weighty. Sussex Enterprise, the new style Chamber of Commerce and the winner of the Small Business Service franchise for Sussex could be the link. Its new business portal should be up and running this year and its website will provide information on local businesses which will allow us all to do a spot of window shopping before we call. Check the Juicy Website for news on developments and this all important linking of big and little, fat and lean.

● HELP, ADVICE AND FUNDING

Sussex Enterprise (0845 67 888 67) provides a subsidised range of business services from mailing lists to business counselling; export development to a free 24-hour tax and legal help line to anyone who joins. There are no specific criteria you need to meet for joining Sussex Enterprise, but if you're identified by any of their partners as a high growth start up, you could be in for some support. It's all about encouraging the right people to get the right help. Bobbie Scragg, one of Sussex Enterprise's Business Advisors offered us her top tips for success:

- Always have a current business plan. It should be a live document, which is regularly updated to see whether you're on target with your own plans and objectives.
- Cash is king; are you keeping an eye on your debtors?
- Keep your overheads down and put stock controls in place
- Continuously monitor your finances and don't ignore the Tax and Vat men; you can always talk through your options with them.
- Look after your customers. Communicate up and down the supply chain and don't forget that yesterday's secretary could be tomorrow's head of marketing.
- Have a caring culture for your staff and keep them informed. Look at training their needs to help them grow which will in turn make your company grow too.
- Network and keep your ear to the ground.
- Make sure you're in touch with the agencies that are there to help your business grow.

One of the first ports of call for new businesses should be The Sussex Innovation Centre, which was set up in May 1996 as a response to the enormous potential for wealth creation in the area. With the universities of Sussex and Brighton among the leading institutions producing around 40,000 students in further and higher education in the academic corridor leading up the Lewes Road from Brighton to Lewes, there was a real need to harness their potential in Sussex. Many students decide not to leave Brighton and Hove when they graduate, figuring that it's a pretty good place to live and work, but they need help in setting up their business. Others move here and can't find their way around or access the infrastructure - all of which can make the difference between make and break.

The Sussex Innovation Centre (SINC - 01273 678244) offers free advice to help people develop their business idea and also has a networking arm (www.SINC.net). Business incubation, is what Mike Herd, Sussex Businessman of the Year in 2001, calls it. Come to him or the team with an idea, and they'll either show you how to get to the next stage or send you home to think again.

The SINC team offers market research, market sizing, business planning, and subscriptions to excellent workshops under its Know-how Exchange service. Most importantly, SINC knows its way around the professionals and professional operations that can take your idea to the next step. With academic resources as a back up and those 50 companies on site - most of them new businesses that have grown under SINC's banner - the place provides a focus of activity where people can share ideas, technology and experience.

How much it costs depends on how much you use it; initial consultancy is free and welcome as long as it looks like your idea can grow. "There's nothing that's not appropriate. We're looking for high growth, million pound ideas which might not be earning anything at all yet", says Mike HerdWith 30% revenue growth every six months and a handful of floatation's in the companies under SINC's wings at the Centre itself, it's worth giving them a call "We will charge sometimes for a consultancy fee, but in many cases we simply offer support and hope to share in the company's success in whichever way we can."

SINC is one of the many partners Sussex Enterprise has teamed up with to encourage businesses both new and established to grow. The six Enterprise Agencies around Sussex are also partners of Sussex Enterprise, and are the first port of call for small businesses looking for advice on the early needs from writing business plans and accounting to market research. Once you've grabbed one of the Sussex Enterprise tentacles, you'll find lots of information on where to go next, from the banks that are helpful to Business Angels, both of which could provide financial support or investment.

CITY ART

There's a long tradition of art playing a big part in Brighton and Hove life. From the Open House groups who show their work in their own homes during the Festival in May to the informal artists who work out of Fabrica, there are plenty of networks to lure the artist away from his easel.

For artists, South East Arts is the first point of contact. It gives professional advice to new and established artists across Kent, Surrey and East and West Sussex with information on funding and support. It is also the distributor for the Regional Arts Lottery Programme (RALP).

VIRTUAL ASSISTANTS

Sussex has an unusually high number of people working from home who need as much organising and assistance as an office worker but don't have the space or a desire for an assistant in their sitting room. Virtual assistants work from their own homes, communicating with their clients by e-mail and phone, filing on their own computers and delivering by disc, CD or e-mail. Some even do telesales for a higher fee. It's a perfect job for someone wants to work for themselves in their own hours and from home.

RECRUITMENT

If working for yourself sounds too much like hard work, Juicy has teamed up with Escape Hatch Recruitment to put you in touch with some of the best companies in the area. Set up by London escapees, you'll get more than you'd normally find in the High Street and is a first port of call for anyone looking for a good job. See their details in the directory.

The companies featured in this directory have been handpicked - many from the networking groups. Their doors tend to be open a little wider than most businesses and their bosses are often to be seen at the networks, making contacts and building relationships. The list will grow on our website (www.juicyguides.co.uk) and link with other networks and directories, giving anyone interested in making the best out of life in Brighton and Hove a real head start.

● *Why do I live in Kemp Town? From the train I can ring Paul at Brampton's the butchers and order a leg of lamb before he closes. He'll take it to Protos, the fruit and veg shop opposite, who'll pay for it for me until I pay them back. Then I go for a drink in the Polar bar, which rescued the old Burlington from sub-Victoriana chintz and cheese by creating a modern pub where you can have a pint without getting stuck to the carpet. Then I can wander back home along the front past one of the great Regency seafronts in the world. Part village, part city grandeur where the sea and the buildings square up to each other, creating a frontier of unending ambition on which to live. So why would I ever move? Kemp Town. The World.*

Simon Fanshawe, *writer and broadcaster*

10

● NETWORKS

There are more networks in Brighton and Hove and across Sussex than there are houses for sale, and with such a high proportion of people working for themselves, it's a vital part of the business connection. Some are membership only and charge for their weekly group; Yap! (01903 871030) is an example of the kind of network that has groups across the county and is a good support to those working on their own. But there's absolutely no point in joining one network group and hoping that work will pour in; the more you network, the more contacts you can pass on to others and the more you will get back yourself. Reap and sow, give and gain, that's the secret of effective networking.

All the networks listed below are actively involved with each other and are working with The Council and Sussex Enterprise to represent the views of the creative industries, small to medium enterprises and sole traders. If you're working for yourself, it's in your interest to be a part of it all - not just because it will boost your social life and build your business, but because if we can gather information and feed it to the right people, there will be more support, more money in the pot and more opportunities to create a better working environment for us all. To keep up to date with who's doing what, check the websites. The newsletter at www.juicyguides.co.uk will keep you in touch with it all.

Sussex Enterprise has asked Juicy to gather information about its readers in order to make better working opportunities for the creative industries and SME's in the city and surrounds. We'll be working on this over the next year with questionnaires on the website, focus groups and networking events all designed to feed information about who we are to the organisation which can directly affect how we work.

● FREE NETWORKS

The Arts Club

www.juicyguides.co.uk

A response to the hundreds of e-mails from Juicy readers new to Brighton and Hove about how to make contacts in the creative industries, this aims to be a series of smaller groups with core members and invited guests. The meetings are held once a month at The Sussex Arts Club and the idea is to swap stories and exchange contacts. Compared to the bigger groups like Swan and Underground, The Arts Club is a more intimate opportunity to get to know people from across the creative industries.

Brighton in Regeneration
The Enterprise Agency Brighton,
Hove & Lewes, 23 Old Steine
01273 666800
A free directory of Business Associations 2002, representing small businesses in the City. Call the agency for a copy.

Brighton Underground
www.BrightonUnderground.com.
Brighton Underground is the network for creative artists in Brighton and Hove. They meet every week for a drink and invite local movers and shakers to talk about who, why and how they move and shake. The membership is free and members set the evening's agenda. Visit the website and give them your comments, and then pop down to their evenings at the Sanctuary Café and other venues.

Midweek Social
www.midweeksocial.co.uk
Brighton Underground's new media network group has similar ideas and ways of doing business. They meet weekly downstairs at the Sanctuary Café.

SWAN
www.theswangroup.co.uk
Sussex Women's Alternative Network is

an alternative to the endless grey suited breakfasts where business women can build relationships with future clients. After a year of meeting once a month, the membership is now a solid 200 or so and the website is an invaluable resource.

Brighton Media Centre Information Point
9-12 Middle Street, The Lanes
info@mediacentre.org
www.mediacentre.org
01273 201100
The BMC Information Point is the public face of the Brighton Media Centre which supports 50 small and medium sized media and new media companies with accommodation, facilities and business advice. The Information Point includes:
• Information and promotional material on 50 BMC companies.
• Display area for both artists and new media practitioners.
• Information on creative media industry both locally and nationally.
• Links to both local universities and other media careers agencies.
• Access to business development and support.
• Access to BMC facilities and PhotoMedia photographic studio.
• Retail facility for magazines, books and computer consumables.

Fabrica
Holy Trinity Church, 40 Duke Street,
The Lanes 01273 778646
www.fabrica.co.uk

Art gallery, artists resource centre and network, Fabrica is supported by South East Arts to help artists of all disciplines find their feet.

Wired Sussex

www.wiredsussex.co.uk

See The Business chapter for information on their extremely successful New Media Network.

EMPLOYMENT

Escape Hatch

65 Middle Street,
The Lanes
01273 384276
www.escapehatchmedia.co.uk

Specialist recruitment services to the city's flourishing new media and traditional media sector. Escape Hatch also have a specific section for relocators, so if you're new to the city and looking for a proper job, this should be your first call.

Stridepool

www.stridepool.com

An online diary service for creative freelancers (designers, writers, photographers, Marketing & PR specialists, etc). A £10 monthly subscription fee provides freelancers with an online work calendar and a personal portfolio to showcase work examples.

Stride Recruitment

36 Robertson Road,

Preston Park
01273 560455/429
fax: 01273 560445
www.striderecruitment.com

Well known by companies and candidates alike as the first point of contact for permanent requirements in sales, marketing & PR, new media, and design & development. Stride's sister company, Thinkwell provides employment opportunities for those aged 45 and over.www.wethinkwell.com

● BUSINESS START UP COURSES AND AGENCIES

Sussex Enterprise

0845 6788867
www.sussexenterprise.co.uk

The role of Sussex Enterprise is to help the local economy grow by providing a comprehensive range of business support and employee development services. It aims to bring together networks of people through membership and sector groups to work together and achieve business success. The membership is nearly 3000, but you don't have to be a member to go to anyone of their network events - last year, they held 170 events attended by nearly 1000 delegates.

The Enterprise Agency Brighton, Hove & Lewes

23 Old Steine
01273 666800

Heavily subsidised professional business training and networking opportunities.

Sussex Innovation Centre

01273 678244

www.sinc.co.uk

The Sussex Innovation Centre (SInC) opened in May 1996 to provide support for the creation and growth of technology and knowledge based companies in Sussex. The Centre is a now thriving business environment for nearly 30 high growth companies. It provides advice and networking opportunities for members. Sincnet is its on-line network and members can receive information about courses, funding, research and business development opportunities.

● BIG BUSINESS

Babel Media

01273 764100

www.babelmedia.com

If you've got language skills, give this company a shout. They specialise in direct online communication with international youth markets testing web games, developing educational software and guerrilla marketing for a global audience.

Design Revolution

Queens Park Villas,

30 West Drive, Hove

01273 676151

www.design-revolution.co.uk

Fifteen years of design and marketing for clients like Dorling Kindersley make Design Revolution one of the old school in Brighton and Hove. They're always looking for quality freelance writers, designers and editors.

Midnight Communications

Tower Point,

North Road,

North Laine

01273 666200

www.midnight.co.uk

Since 1995, Midnight has been providing PR services to the UK's leading technology companies. Today, their clients include Adobe, Think Natural, Affinity, Guernsey Board of industry, Brighton & Hove's bid to become City of Culture and, of course, the Juicy Awards. They offer a network of partner PR companies around the world and have previously won the award for Best International PR campaign. They were also named Best Small PR consultancy of the Year by PR Week and Sussex Company of the Year 2000. Most of their projects are staffed in-house but they do employ freelance copywriters.

Victoria Real

International House,

Queens Road,

Brighton

01273 702007

www.victoriareal.com

Award winning digital media company with strong freelance base in Brighton and Hove.

Around 30% of their staff tend to be freelance from designers to project managers and producers.

● BUSINESS COACHING AND DEVELOPMENT

Accept and Act
3 Cavendish Street, Kemp Town
tine@acceptandact.co.uk
www.acceptandact.co
Tine Maria Beÿer coaches ambitious people to get out of the rat race and upgrade their career or business for a more balanced life.

Development Unlimited
Koreen Le Page
01903 810077
info@developmentunlimited.com
Development Unlimited specialises in 'transformational change and innovation' which in a nutshell means personal development and training for organisations, teams and individuals. Leadership, team building, life coaching and change management are among the things on offer.

Henderson Marketing Consultants
01273 227426
Henderson helps companies formulate their business development strategy, and provide a range of services such as project and event management, public relations and hospitality.

Human Interventions
01273 702266
suetye@humaninterventions.com
Sue Tye helps businesses get the most out of their people. Her company tackles one-off projects and on-going consultancy for human resource issues such as employee relations, training, recruitment advice and change management.

Ideamakers
Suzanne
01273 551657 / 07979 692884
suzanne@ideamakers.co.uk
If you're stuck for inspiration, Ideamakers helps identify new business opportunities, then steers you towards developing and implementing your ideas successfully.

QED
Julia Miles
01273 720100
helen@qedcoaching.co.uk
Juicy's own coach and one of the most inspiring women in town, Julia uses sensible planning strategies while unblocking hidden potential. E-mail for information on 12 month business coaching programme for business owners and business retreat programmes which start in the summer. Larger organisations can also take advantage of her extensive business training programmes

● DESIGN, PRINTING, EDITING

Mole Design
01273 271565
moledesign@ntlworld.com
Juicy Guide designer, Adrian Sensicle

comes from a background in publishing (Collins, Simon and Schuster). Simple and stylish, his designs convey information without clutter.

Dawn Clenton

0704 401 6626

Graphic designer from Neville Brody's stable who loves nothing better than playing with a bit typography. Business cards and corporate brochures, magazine design and company newsletters are her favourite jobs.

Andus Printing

47 Highcroft Villas, Preston Park
01273 558880
andus@mistral.co.uk

The most accommodating, flexible and professional printers we've come across in B&H.

Jed Novick

Jed.novick@virgin.net
07930 400798

The finest writer and editor we know. But then again, I'm the editor of this book so I can say anything I like.

Anna Dewis copywriting

anna@annadewis.com
01273 262339

Juicy Guide's own copywriter, Anna came to us through the network and delivered her perfect copy on the dot of deadline. Solid, professional and always up for a restaurant review at late notice, she's the kind of girl we like to work with.

Feng Shui

Diane Elsey
01903 505878

Before you go to a designer for your new business cards, have a chat with Diane. She offers traditional and intuitive feng shui services including advising businesses on their logos, colours and stationery.

ODM

Steve Morris
01273 203100
odm@odm-uk.com

All things stationery from desks to paperclips via printing and computer consumables, ODM is well-known for its personal service, competitive rates, and free delivery, no matter how small the order.

Spectrum

Unit 10, Hove Business Centre,
Fonthill Road, Hove
01273 708222
sales@spectrumphoto.co.uk

Right behind Hove train station, this is where the increasing number of professional photographers who move here are taking their work. They offer a range of traditional photographic and digital services including E6 processing, hand printing and high res scanning. Unlike some of the other labs, the staff here are passionate about photography and happy to offer help and advice.

Shorer's Workshop

01323 894140

www.big-gems.co.uk

Mike Shorer's family has been designing and making unique and exquisite items of jewellery, trophies and objets d'art for over 250 years. And he can remodel old items too so don't get rid of the family jewels.

● EVENTS

LGM Consultancy Ltd

Lucy McCrickard

01273 779508 / 07941 062229

lucy@lgmconsulting.co.uk

Lucy McCrickard has 16 years' experience in sports marketing and sponsorship management so she knows the secret of a successful event. She's the brains behind the Flora London Marathon for one.

WMPlus

contact Diana Horner on 0845 0531647

diana@wmplus.co.uk.

www.wmplus.co.uk

WM Plus create and manage events (such as The Juicy Awards this year) with style and efficiency. They specialise in business events, from training days to exhibitions, conferences and awards ceremonies. Diana is the woman behind the SWAN network so is particularly well connected in the Sussex area.

Harmony in the Community

Unit 2, 95A St. James's Street,

Kemp Town

01273 676057 / 0777 3396792

danny@dharmony.freeserve.co.uk

A unique organisation dedicated to enabling social development through a community production group which designs, plans and co-ordinates cultural and educational events. Danny Horwood is the ambassador for 'cultural arts' and is the man behind The Peace Festival on Hove Lawns.

● INDEPENDENT FINANCIAL ADVICE

Charcol

Ground Floor, Aspect House,

84-87 Queen's Road,

Brighton

01273 712200

wxg@charcol.co.uk

With over 27 years of experience, Charcol is of the UK's leading independent mortgage and financial advisers, offering advice on mortgages, pensions, investments and insurance.

Whatever your needs why not find out if Charcol can help you.

● FINANCIAL

Barton Pryor

Barton House,

73 Southwick View,

Southwick

01273 870089 / 07976 314490

www.thebpa.co.uk

ifa@thebpa.co.uk

More than just a surfing, jiving, networking uber-personality financial advisor, Lee Pryor also gave us the mortgage of our dreams.

Edward Jones Investments

Tim Waite

01273 419224

tim.waite@edwardjones.com

Well-known for their ability to 'debunk' financial jargon, Edward Jones Investments will tailor a portfolio to meet individual client needs. Established in 1871, the company offers the added benefit of access to the American markets.

● NEW MEDIA

Fearless Computing

Ash House, 26 Tongdean Lane, Tongdean

01273 547600

www.fearless.co.uk

Fearless builds PCs to your own specifications, fixes them when they go wrong (coming to your home or office at the drop of a mouse), removes viruses, designs websites and advises on e-commerce solutions. And all without making you feel like a complete idiot for not knowing your broadband from your waistband.

Wicked Web Design

Sarah Gore

01273 383234

A small, local company which specialises in helping businesses get results from their web presence. They can construct new sites but also offer a consultancy service to improve existing sites.

THE JUICY SELECTION – HOUSE STUFF

● EXTERIORS AND INTERIORS

ACW Services

13 Park Street,
Queen's Park
01273 570491 / 07971 101474
adam@acollierwoods.demon.co.uk

Carpenter & Joiner with a penchant for building wardrobes, shelves and storage areas in sympathy with the existing styles of décor. He particularly enjoys a challenge - like the installation of our new kitchen.

Beech and Jarvis

01273 562500

French polishing and furniture restoration.

Blue Door Living Solutions Ltd

tel/fax: 01273 267925 /
07879 897993
www.bluedoorliving.com
info@bluedoorliving.com

Project management service for people who want to take the stress out of doing up their home - and without it costing an arm and a leg. For people commuting every day who want to come back to a house they can live in.

Fred Brewster

01273 517598

Plasterer.

Brian Coomber

07889 407533

Floor Sanding.

Ty Cracker

01273 626919

As you'd imagine from a man called 'Ty the Tiler', Ty is our top tiler.

John Garrett

07970 073145

Painter and decorator.

Susan Kennewell

60 Byron Street, Hove
01273 720231
Alkenmad@talk21.com

Take a blank wall, some original, exotic, stitched textile and Susan Kennewell and you've got one of the hottest interior designs in Brighton.

Kitchen Marvel

01273 220822
www.kitchenmarvel.co.uk

Think of your ideal kitchen or bathroom, tell Kitchen Marvel and they'll design and fit it. This friendly, independent specialist has an extensive range to suit all budgets and will supply only or supply and fit .

L & J Fabrics

Lesley Mole
01273 701812

Roman blinds are the number one request for Lesley Mole, but she can run up just about any blind or curtain design. And if you're moving house, she'll save you money by altering your curtains to fit.

Nic Miller

0787 0533675

Decorative Paint effects and bespoke decorating. Marbling, woodgraining, colourwashing for both commercial and private jobs. Nic also teaches these techniques and has a top portfolio.

Helen Paine Smith

07985 466786

Your own personal shopper. Helen wrote the Juicy Guide shopping chapter and knows where to find the most glamorous chaises longues, the rarest antique fabrics, original retro wallpapers, and all at the best prices. She'll cut out your legwork and provide you with a list of the best buys in town.

John Roberts

01273 889220

Plasterer.

Richard Scott

07813 779753

01903 767774

bushbyvillagera@btinternet.com

Our man at MFI who designed our astonishingly good value kitchen recommended Richard Scott to us. If you're installing a kitchen, planning a conservatory or installing double glazing, these guys will take the entire job off your hands. Project management sounds a bit posh, they say, but with their list of electricians, plumbers, carpenters and odd jobbers, they can take on your whole house. (see also under conservatories)

Feng Shui

Diane Elsey

01903 505878

The whole gamut of traditional and intuitive feng shui services for private and commercial clients including personal profiling, total house rebalance, space clearing and relocating services. Diane even advises businesses on their logos, colours and stationery.

● PLUMBERS, HEATING ENGINEERS, ELECTRICIANS

Kemco

01273 671617

Colin at Kemco has over 20 years' of heating installation and servicing and plumbing experience, offers competitive rates, a reliable, flexible service to suit you and will even refurbish your bathroom.

U Benders

01273 579704

Jane, the plumber with attitude, has moved to the countryside (well, Peacehaven) but is still available in B&H with her rod and smile.

Malcolm Parkes

01237 700074

Plumber.

Bernie Bird

01273 696580

Plumber.

Steve Chapman

01903 212626

07966 401914

Steve will undertake any types of electrical work for both domestic and commercial clients, but he specialises in audio installation and lighting design and installation. City & Guilds qualified, he provides a personal service and free estimates.

● LOFTS & CONSERVATORIES

Nigel Bamford

St Johns Buildings,

76 Hollingdean Terrace,

01273 298344 / 07956 247392

Loft conversion specialist.

Richard Scott

07813 779753 / 01903 767774

bushbyvillagera@btinternet.com

Scott Holder and Richard Charles take on planning, supply and installation of any kind of glazing and conservatory construction.

All these conservatory companies come recommended by Bluedoor Living who use them regularly:

R N Shields Joinery Manufactuers

01530 412786

contact: Robert Shields

Castle House Joinery

01491 642123

07968 261204

contact: Derry Anstiss

Stockbridge Designs

01264 359355

contact: Ian Pickernell

Durabuild

0247663 9696

contact: Fred Halligan

Town and Country

01328 700565

contact: A W Lake

● GARDENS

Eden by Design

01273 604705

Landscape garden designer Tony Mackay provides detailed drawing and planting plans, builds and renovates brickwork, patios and fencing and keeps your garden looking lovely all year round.

● SECURITY

Keyhole Security

01273 601100

Keyhole Security provides a wide range of security needs for both private and commercial clients. Services include supply and fit of locks and safes, CCTV installation, access control systems, master key suites.

● PROPERTY

Barrie Alderton

73 Southover Street, Hanover
01273 570242 Fax: 01273 693560
alderton@btconnect.co.uk
The man who knows more about Hanover, Elm Grove and Lewes Road than anyone else in town.

Bonett's Estate Agents

89 St George's Road, Kemp Town
01273 677365
kemptown@bonetts.co.uk
Paul Bonnet is to Kemp Town and Hove what Barrie Alderton is to Hanover, matching house to client like few others.

Tanat Jones

01273 207207
lettings@tanat-jones.com
Serving Brighton, Hove and the surrounding area, Tanat-Jones is one of Brighton's most established and respected letting agencies. Check out their website. Unlike a lot of letting agency sites, it's updated everyday

● FINANCE

Barton Pryor

Barton House, 73 Southwick View,
Southwick
01273870089 / 07976 314490

www.thebpa.co.uk
ifa@thebpa.co.uk
More than a surfing, jiving, networking uber-personality financial advisor, Lee Pryor also gave us the mortgage of our dreams.

Charcol

Ground Floor, Aspect House, 84-87
Queen's Road, Central Brighton
01273 712200
wxg@charcol.co.uk
With over 27 years of experience, Charcol is one of the UK's leading independent mortgage and financial advisers, offering advice on mortgages, pensions, investments and insurance.

Homestead Mortgages ltd

15 Goodwood Road, Worthing
01903 263516 / 0870 1348798
Directors, Cliff Kallend and Bob Dengate have over 35 years experience with a high street mortgage lender and have spent much of this time dealing with people who were self-employed or who had adverse credit records. Because of this they now specialise in finding the right mortgage for people who do not meet the normal lending criteria and therefore would not be considered by many well-known mortgage lenders.

Sussex Accountancy Services

67 Church Road, Hove
01273 325522
Hand holding, small business management, payroll and general accountancy.

● MECHANICS

ADH Autos
01273 207997
07885 213302
Popular with Brighton taxi drivers, this garage repair workshop does the usual MOTs, welding, tyres etc for both petrol and diesel vehicles.

Mark Bayley
01273 327609
Apparently 30% of Brighton and Hove's taxis are serviced by this guy so he must be good.

J&J Elmes
01273 607926
Juicy's own mechanic in Kemp Town.

Kingpin Autos
Cambridge Grove, Hove
01273 723896
One of the many little ones down this road, Kingpin came recommended by a Juicy reader who reports that their mechanics will fix anything, and explain exactly what you're paying for - and

before they do the work.

John Micklan
01273 607808
The Jaguar Man, people bring their Jags to John from all over the country.

Beverley Turner Insurance
33 Falmer Avenue, Saltdean
01273 308227
beverleyturnerinsurance@ic24.net
The fastest insurance broker in town with deals to beat most quotes from the Big Boys. Mostly done by e-mail, she's as conscientious as she's quick.

● IF ALL ELSE FAILS...

Nigel Dengate Funeral Services
01273 204410
Hopefully you won't need them but if you do, Nigel Dengate's family firm offers the full range of funeral services including burial, cremation, memorial and horse drawn carriages. Their service is discreet and personalised.

● *After the removals van goes, we peer out of the front window of our new house near St Anne's Well Gardens. At a quarter past three the schools chuck out and the pavements are filled with children. This is good: like so many others we have moved here because, with two small kids, London becomes less and less like the place we feel like calling home. And then, the grown-ups: one skids down the pavement on a skateboard. Another has vivid, pink-dyed hair. They are... well, groovy. We have fallen into a neighbourhood of cool-looking couples. People we want to know. Brighton has become a geography of choice. We like-minded people flock to this wild colourful city because we are the kind of grown-ups who like to still play at being 18, and this is the perfect place to do that. Looking through where our curtains will one day hang, we are suddenly a little scared. We move here because we believed it was a smaller version of London. But in London you inevitably rub up against strangers from all corners, from any class. This is going to be an altogether different adventure. The people in our neighbourhood look oddly like us.*

William Shaw

11

● Brighton and Hove has been a centre of well-being since Dr Richard Russell declared sea bathing the new black in the 1700s, and is now an internationally famous centre of alternative therapies. And there's a million reasons why it should be such a honeypot for therapists; ley lines, the biggest witch coven in the South, something in the water? Whatever; the bottom line is that anyone who is vaguely enlightened will seek out the place where they're going to be happiest. And even if right now, you're skimming through this section because you're deeply unhappy, you've got to admit that it's still better here than most places.

But if Brighton is brimming with therapists, it doesn't make it any easier to find a good one. If you're going to entrust your inner self to a third party, you're not likely to look for him or her in The Yellow Pages. You're going to ask a friend, or, if you haven't got a friend, you're going to need a guide. As users of alternative therapies for everyone in the family -even the kittens were given homeopathic nosodes instead of vaccinations - we've put together a list of some of the best therapists that we've come across. This isn't an authoritative document, it's a list of people we've used and who've been recommended to us.

Passing on a name of a cranial osteopath every time you see a child with a snotty nose is not always the best way of promoting complementary therapy to the wider community. If your child is really ill, it could be too much of a leap of faith to take him to the homeopath rather than the doctor, so we've tried to explain why and when you might use the various kinds of therapies on offer.

Embracing complementary health care is about learning to trust that your body is more than able to see you through your life, that it was designed to be perfect, and most of the time it's the choices that you make that disturbs the balance, and puts it out of ease with itself into the dis-ease that could destroy your life.

Much as you'll value the fact that you've got this list - not to mention on-line at the Juicy website where it will grow over the year - when your child is really ill, it could be too much of a leap of faith to take him to the homeopath rather than the doctor.

"It's about finding the middle way", says acupuncturist, Dave Bennett from the Marine Clinic in Rottingdean. "A lot of people come to complementary therapies for something like a frozen shoulder. Once they've found a cure for the pain, they become more sensitive and start to make better decisions about the way they're living their lives.

A lot of them will have been abusing their bodies - either through substances like alcohol or drugs or simply by doing jobs their bodies were not designed for - sound recordists who stand for 17 hours at a time holding a boom above their shoulder. That's mad if you think about it".

Massage therapist, Philippa King agrees that it's about getting to grips with the source of the problem. "It's like taking jumpers off. Most people come to me because they need to be touched, but the more they relax, the more open they become and then they start to realise what they need to do to look after themselves. They realise that by choosing to come for a massage they've taken an important step towards taking responsibility for their own emotional health. That's very empowering for a person who has felt that they couldn't cope".

The mind-body-spirit triumvirate is a powerful force to be reckoned with. For the body to close down and say "Right, that's it. Sort yourself out cos I'm not playing anymore" is a wake up call. Most people flop through their lives complaining that they're tired and miserable, but don't get quite stressed/ill/needy enough to have to do anything about it. By opening the can and examining the worms you might get more than you bargained for, but you'll be much healthier in the end.

So what do you choose and when? Most of the therapists listed will refer you to the right kind of treatment, and as most work in multi-disciplinary clinics, you'll find that you won't have to go too far to find what you're looking for.

● WHO, WHAT, WHEN, WHY

With no mental blocks to get in the way of the healing process, kids respond brilliantly to complementary health care. Many of the seemingly inevitable birth traumas that affect 99% of the population can be cured by the hands of a good cranial osteopath. You can even avoid the horrors of colic in the first 10 weeks of life. Cranial osteopathy is so gentle that it seems that the therapist is doing nothing other than laying hands on the body. But the effect is literally mind-blowing with the release of the spinal fluid flowing down the natural irrigation channels to get everything running smoothly again.

Sinus problems - particularly glue ear, tonsils and adenoids which can mean grommets and a night in hospital for a sickly child - can be avoided by a trip to a cranial. Jonathon Hutson, cranial osteopath at the Dyke Road's Arden House Clinic, says "It's perfect for children, but 90% of our adult clients are also treated cranially rather than with the more traditional manipulation techniques osteopathy has always been associated with. Over the years, patients have found they prefer the gentler, less invasive techniques and have found it just as effective".

Cranial osteopaths are trained in osteopathy first and specialise further to work with the more subtle rhythmical shape changes in the tissues all over the body and particularly in the cranium. They pick up on trauma, repetitive strain and poor lifestyle that lead to ill health so headaches and migraines, mild asthma, digestive problems as well as the more traditional lower back and neck pain and sports injuries can be healed.

Homeopathy is also a must for any parent. From chamomilla for tension to pulsatilla for tantrums, arnica for bruises and shock, argent nit for nerves (as you confront your child's head teacher) and thuja for those modern day verucas, the molluscum warts, homeopathic remedies can make up most of the first aid in your medical box.

Acupuncture, homeopathy and osteopathy (including cranial) work particularly well together and a good osteopath will often refer clients to his or her preferred homeopath. A good homeopath is essential to maintaining the health of everyone in the household and a top tip is to book a session at the beginning of each season for a constitutional boost.

Aromatherapy is something that many people can and do use at home, but it's wise to find a qualified therapist to teach you the ropes. "There are many oils that are contraindicated with various conditions and medicines" says Philippa King. "Rosemary for example, should never be used with hypertension (high blood pressure) and Lavender which can reduce blood pressure, can also become a dangerous stimulant if more than the therapeutic dose is used. Some oils can also nullify the effects of homoeopathic treatment."

Unqualified therapists are also nullifying their massage insurance if they practise with essential oils, leaving them vulnerable should there be any claim against them, either massage or oil related. Clients should see the qualification up on the wall.

Reflexology, particularly using the hands rather than the feet, is another skill which a qualified therapist can teach you to use on yourself. It works on the basis that the body is mapped out in the feet and hands, and by learning what part of the toe or the thumb correlates with the neck and shoulders, you can get instant gentle relief. It's a good booster and something you can do on your hands or feet while you're watching telly, but nothing beats an hour's session with someone as experienced as Kathy Chapman who brings the skill to the workplace as well as into the home. Her number is in the directory below.

On-site massage is an excellent way of getting what some people see as an alternative therapy into the mainstream by setting up a massage chair right in the middle of the office. "People want to watch" says on-site Indian head massage therapist, Mary Mussett. "We give anything from 15 to 30 minute massages which are a great alternative to a coffee break and give someone who's been hunched over a computer all day a tremendous release." Marina Banks does on-site acupressure chair massage which is an opportunity to get your head down and forget about the world around you for 15 minutes. It's an upper body rebalancing and health check that energises as well as calms the recipient. "RSI is a big problem in the work place" Marina says "and sometimes just touching the hands and wrists makes people aware of what could become a serious problem". Stress management is possibly the most effective way of keeping your staff well, working to their potential and most importantly, in the office.

Mary Mussett also practices shiatsu at The Dolphin House Clinic and assists at The Shiatsu College in Brighton. "Shiatsu is about using finger pressure on the meridians, the classical Chinese channels of energy or Chi". Where acupuncture is more specific to blockages and uses needles, shiatsu is about an hour's worth of relaxation, takes place on a futon on the floor and is fully clothed. If you're frightened of needles, shiatsu is less invasive than acupuncture and for those with chronic back pain, it can be a gentler and more effective therapy than something like osteopathy or chiropractic.

Yoga, tai chi, qigong and other energy raisers (including tantric sex) are part of the holistic life complementary health care will steer you towards. If you can't manage to get to classes, make sure you find some way of raising your chi in the morning if your energy is to get you back in balance and healing yourself. Therapies can be expensive if you need too many of them, but the best therapists will be able to get the body into a position to heal itself within very few sessions.

● RECOMMENDED CLINICS

Ayurvedic Health Clinic
01273 563340
Ayurveda is one of the most ancient and most holistic sciences. A detox is an essential precursor to any treatment that is going to work but if done properly, can sort out anything from skin problems to infertility.

Dolphin House Clinic
14 New Road, Central Brighton
01273 324790
Dolphin House is a registered charity and has a sliding scale of donations, providing homeopaths, acupuncturists, nutritionists, auric healing, osteopathy and herbal treatments. The same practitioners also run an adult clinic at normal prices. The Dolphin House Clinic is planning to build a new environmentally friendly new centre, and as charitable beneficiary of The Juicy Awards this year, we hope that the injection of cash will speed the process.

Dyke Road Natural Health Clinic
274 Dyke Road, Preston Park
01273 561844

Holistic Health Clinic
53 Beaconsfield Road, Preston Circus
01273 696295

Marine Clinic
12 Marine Drive, Rottingdean
01273 307001

The Ardern Foot and Health Clinic
123 St James's Street,
Kemp Town
01273 673964
Treatments get really holistic here; it's not just chiropody and reflexology, Indian Head Massage and Shiatsu but also Geopathic stress and Allergy testing, Earth Bound Energy checks and removal (that's ghosts and lost souls to you).

● **ACUPUNCTURE**

Dave Bennet @ Marine Clinic
12 Marine Drive,
Rottingdean
01273 307001
Juicy's own acupuncturist, Dave's non-white coat approach and lack of judgement marks him out among acupuncturists. He uses Japanese Toyohari acupuncture which barely penetrates the skin but has maximum effect.

Steve Guthrie @ Dyke Road Natural Health Clinic
274 Dyke Road,
Preston Park
01273 561844
Head honcho at Dolphin House too, you'll have to wait weeks before getting a session with Steve.

Elaine Cook @ Dyke Road Natural Health Clinic
274 Dyke Road,
Preston Park
01273 561844

Elaine Gibbons
01273 562676
Specialises in pregnancy.

Anne Marie Urbanowicz
72 The Drive, Hove
01273 203820

Thomas Sydenham @ The Crescent Clinic
37 Vernon Terrace, Seven Dials
01273 202221

Nina J Kirby @ Dyke Road Natural Health Clinic
274 Dyke Road, Preston Park
01273 561844
Nina direct: 01903 884244/07790 681669

● **AROMATHERAPY MASSAGE**

Philippa King @ The Clinic
69 Gordon Road, Preston Park
01273 232629

Ruth Smith
02173 699470

Sarah Calderbank @ Holistic Health Clinic
53 Beaconsfield Road, Preston Circus
01273 696295

● BABY MASSAGE

Sally Cranfield
01273 279691

● CHINESE MEDICINE

The Chinese Medicine Centre
122 St James's Street, Kemp Town
01273 699852
Chinese medicine boosts the immune system and gets the body back of track, thinning blood and correcting disorders in the vital organs.

Vahida Starcevich @ Holistic Health Clinic
53 Beaconsfield Road,
Preston Circus
01273 696295
Chinese acupuncture and herbal therapy.

● CHIROPRACTIC

Brighton Chiropractic Clinic
34 Brunswick Square, Hove
01273 733469

● CLAIRVOYANT & HEALER

Ruth Farber Nathan
01273 305664
Discreet and spookily accurate with a celebrity clientele.

● COACHING & COUNSELLING

Ariana Gorrill, The Relationship Coach
Heartbeat Coaching - Relating 2 Life
01273 772045
www.HeartbeatCoaching.com
"Life isn't over until your last heartbeat" said the writer Joseph J Mazzella. Ariana's coaching and workshops are about getting out there again after divorce, separation or infertility, and finding out how to live the life you've always wanted to live.

Paul Burley @ Holistic Health Clinic
53 Beaconsfield Road, Preston Circus
01273 696295

● CRANIAL SACRAL THERAPY

Dawn Pearson
079617 1567
Dawn works with super-homeopath, Kate Diamantopoulo who is frighteningly choosy about her fellow therapists.

Judy Lewis @ Holistic Health Clinic
53 Beaconsfield Road, Preston Circus
01273 696295

● HOMEOPATHY

For general advice and orders, call Helios Pharmacy on 01892 537254. For consultations contact the following:

The Diamantopoulo Practice

57 Bates Road, Preston Park
01273 563787
Kate Diamantopoulo RGN SCM HV
RsHom, Jane Prisley RGN ONC LCPH
MARH, Dawn Pearson ITEC LCH HMA
RCST

Kate, the mother of all homeopaths, was the founder of the Dolphin House Clinic 18 years ago and has been one of the most important figures in alternative health in Brighton. Now she's in Australia, she continues to work with her old clients by e-mail - which is surprisingly efficient. She trained Jane and Dawn to take over her practice for new clients and those who prefer a face consultation. She remains Juicy's own homepath.

Sohani Gonzalez

01273 689194
or Dyke Rd Natural health Clinic
274 Dyke Road, Preston Park
01273 561844

Jan Matthew

Fiveways
01273 388857

Pemma Saunders

Kemp Town
01273 699775

AK-Bicom Clinic - Eaton Medical Centre

3 Eaton Gardens, Hove
(entrance in Eaton Villas)
01273 733620 www.healthaccess.co.uk

Andrew & Myriam use a combination of Applied Kinesiology, Bioresonance Therapy, Nutrition, Vibrational remedies to meet the individual needs of the client. They specialise in smoking (one session is good enough for most people), allergies, eczema, emotional trauma, preventive treatment of Anaphylaxis and pain reduction. The machine that they use looks like something out of a Brave New World, but the effects are exceptional.

Ambient Health

Surrenden Crescent (opp Varndean 6th
Form College), Preston Park
01273 262559 www.ambient-health.co.uk

Homeopathic treatment is complemented with the QXCI, a state-of-the-art quantum energetic bio-resonance device. As part of their gentle and stress-free approach, Ambient Health can provide clinics at your workplace, or appointments outside regular working hours.

● HYPNOTHERAPY

Michael Martin @ Holistic Health Clinic

53 Beaconsfield Road,
Preston Circus
01273 696295

Adrian Stather @ Holistic Health Clinic

53 Beaconsfield Road,
Preston Circus
01273 696295

● INDIAN HEAD MASSAGE

Dr Asmita Jani @ Ayurvedic Health Clinic

01273 563340

Linda Thaper @ Sundial House Clinic

North Road, Central Brighton

01273 774114

Reflexology, Swedish massage, aromatherapy and deep tissue massage

● INTUITIVE HEALING

Sally Roberts RGN @ Holistic Health Clinic

53 Beaconsfield Road, Preston Circus

01273 696295

Sally is a trained nurse who spends half the week healing people on the NHS and the other using colour therapies, Reiki and the most astonishing intuition we've ever witnessed to heal her more holistic clients. She's also extremely effective with children, using angels and colours to heal their night fears, communication blocks and other imbalances.

● MEDITATION

Bodhi Garden Dharma Centre

7a Ship Street Gardens, The Lanes

01903 218963 or 01273 235367

Osho Meditation

01273 602965/607374

Osho meditations are physical and cathartic for people who think of shopping lists every time they try to meditate. The Aum is a four-hour cathartic experience with a party afterwards held one Sunday in every month. Ring for details

Brighton Buddhist Centre

17 Titchbourne Street, North Laine

01273 772090

Drop-in and courses in yoga and meditation.

● MIDWIFERY

Wisewoman

01273 276288

Crowborough Birthing Centre,

Southview Road, Crowborough

01892 654080

Birthing pool and doulas for those who hate hospitals

● WATERBIRTH

Active Birth Centre

020 7482 5554

Order your birthing pool and they'll deliver and collect.

● MUSIC THERAPY

Wendy Halsted

Flat One, 1-2 Ventnor Villas (side entrance), Hove

01273 329841

A professional music therapist, Wendy uses one to one or group musical improvisation therapy for children and adults, especially those with profound learning difficulties.

● NATUROPATHY & NUTRITION

Lucy Pook @ Holistic Health Clinic
53 Beaconsfield Road, Preston Circus
01273 696295
Lucy uses the five elements of Chinese Medicine to understand how the vital organs might be under-functioning. She also teaches the Gerson Technique which has been proven to be effective in dealing with Cancer

● ON-SITE MASSAGE

Mary Mussett
07951 146469
Marina Banks
07977 079919
Indian head massage and acupressure chair massage in the workplace. Mary and Marina are also fully qualified shiatsu practitioners and work from their own clinics.

● OSTEOPATHY (INCLUDING CRANIAL)

Jonathon Hutson @ Dyke Road Natural Health Clinic
274 Dyke Road, Preston Park
01273 561844
Possibly the best cranial osteopath we've ever come across.

PARTICULARLY FOR KIDS:

Alexandra Luzzato
Dyke Road

Jasmina Cordal @ Holistic Health Clinic
53 Beaconsfield Road,
Preston Circus
01273 696295

Rex Brangwyn
98 The Drive, Hove
01273 775559

● PREGNANCY AND BIRTH

● ACTIVE BIRTH CLASSES

Karel Ironside
365 Ditchling Road,
Preston Park
01273 277309
Not just an opportunity to spend some meditative time with your bump, but a really practical way of getting ready for childbirth. The yoga will make you more supple and Karel's print outs on active labouring are essential when things don't go quite to plan - as we found out ourselves...

● PSYCHOTHERAPY

Manya Goldman @ Dyke Road Natural Heath Centre
274 Dyke Road,
Preston Park
01273 561844

● REBIRTHING

Pat Bennaceur
01273 720853

● REFLEXOLOGY

**Kathryn Chapman,
Association of Reflexologists
(MAR)**
01273 269852; 07044 016484
Grab yourself an hour with Kathy Chapman and bliss out. Kathy specialises in hand and foot reflexology treatments for all sorts of problems. She visits homes and offices.

Yael Jury
01273 390151

● SHIATSU

Mary Mussett @ Dolphin House Clinic
14 New Road, Central Brighton
01273 324790 / 07951 146469
The Dolphin House Clinic operates on a needs must basis with a sliding scale of fees for all its treatments

Paola Campanelli @ Holistic Health Clinic
53 Beaconsfield Road,
Preston Circus
01273 696295

● THAI YOGA MASSAGE

Alexandra Schunemann @

Dyke Road Natural Health Clinic
274 Dyke Road, Preston Park
01273 561844
01273 600726 (home visits)
This ancient form of body work includes massage, acupressure and stretches in the form of yoga-like positions leaving the receiver feeling both relaxed and energised at the same time.

● YOGA

Natural Bodies
01273 711414

Brighton Natural Health Centre
27 Regent Street, North Laine
01273 600010 www.bnhc.co.uk
Yoga, raqs sharqi, qigong, tai chi, meditation, feldenkrais, shiatsu, this is the centre of Brighton's holistic universe.

Andrew Payne @ Dyke Road Natural Health Centre
274 Dyke Road, Preston Park
01273 552766
Viniyoga and Kriya Yoga.

Evolution
2 Sillwood Terrace, Central Brighton
01273 729803

Natural Bodies
18 Bond Street, North Laine
01273 711414
Look out for Liz Warrington's Iyengar

classes(01273 461541) for adults and kids.

Alive
25-27 Castle Street, Central Brighton
01273 739606
Hatha yoga on Monday 8.15pm, Wednesday 6pm, Thursday 11.15am, Sunday 9.30pm.

Southover Community
Southover Street, Hanover
Monday nights (7.30pm) drop in for Iyengar. No phone number available.

● AND FINALLY, A VET

Tim Couzens
01273 558838/01825 840966
Tim holds a surgery one Wednesday a month at Grove Lodge, 104 Preston Drove and offers acupuncture, herbal medicine as well as homeopathic alternatives to vaccinations.

● FURTHER READING

Look in the shopping chapter for some of the better bookshops.

The Game of Life and How to Play It - Florence Scovel-Shinn £4.99

The Complete Homeopathy Handbook - Miranda Castro (Macmillan) £15.99

A Little Light on Angels - Diana Cooper

All the different disciplines have their own websites. Check for qualifications.

● *Dee and I moved from London more or less on a whim in 1975...hard to believe, but there's so much to do in this city, if you have enthusiasm and energy, and suddenly its 25 years on! Looking out the kitchen window on a clear day and seeing the sea in the distance - it's brilliant. One day we'll move and get a full-on sea view...that would be nice. We're at last getting spoilt for choice for restaurants, although years ago it wasn't like that...and of course, just crossing the road for a bottle of wine from The Butlers Wine Cellar - too handy! The worst thing about living here is the number of interesting things you never get to see, because of the other interesting things you do get to see...can't be bad. And what about the mix of people...the world in microcosm; and, I promise, Brightonians are getting more tolerant. Our now grown-up children could hardly think of a better place to be - that says a lot about this unique place. The only other choice for me would be deep in the country - I don't think we're ready for that!*

Paul Bonett, *estate agent*

12

● BRIGHTON & HOVE COUNCIL

01273 290000

● CASHPOINTS

(other than main banks and building societies)

Barclays

Royal Sussex Hospital outside building

Link machine outside main post office, Ship Street

Nat West

Churchill Square: next to Mothercare on Upper Mall, next to Discovery Store on Lower Mall

BP garage on Ditchling Road

Shell garage on Preston Road

Q8 garage on A23/A27 roundabout

● CHEMISTS (LATE)

Ashtons

98 Dyke Road, Seven Dials

01273 325020

9am-10pm.

Westons

6 Coombe Terrace,

Lewes Road

(opposite B&Q)

01273 605354

9am-10pm.

● CITIZENS ADVICE

01273 772277

● CHURCHES, SYNAGOGUES AND PLACES OF WORSHIP

● CHURCHES

St Bartholomews Church

Ann Street, Old Steine

01273 685142

C of E Grade 1 listed building which, say the children of Brighton, is the real Noah's arc upside down.

St Paul's

West Street,

Central Brighton

01273 739639

Astonishingly laid back local church which is packed to the gills every Christmas as families come to show their kids what church-going should be like.

St Peter's

York Place,

Old Steine

01273 682960

Austere Parish church with proper job choir in frilly collars and awesome organ. C of E.

● SYNAGOGUES

Middle Street Synagogue
Middle Street, The Lanes
01273 888855
The oldest and most splendid of synagogues in the area. It's an Orthodox working shul but open to the general public on the first Sunday of every month from March to November. During the May festival, it's open every Sunday. Its sister synagogue is in New Church Road, Hove.

Hove Hebrew Congregation
Holland Road, Hove
01273 732035

Brighton & Hove New Synagogue
Palmeira Avenue, Hove
01273 735343
Reform synagogue.

Brighton & Hove Progressive Synagogue
6 Lansdowne Road, Hove
01273 737223
Rabbi Elizabeth Tikvah Sarah has recently taken over from the progressive Paul Glantz who went out of his way to welcome mixed families into the Jewish community. The religion school is open to children of members of the shul.

● COUNTY COURT
County Court, William Street,
Brighton
01273 674421

● FAMILY PLANNING CLINIC
01273 242091

● GAY BRIGHTON

The Gay switchboard on 01273 204050 is there for counselling and advice, and also helps find rooms in gay-friendly accommodation. There are also some specifically gay hotels/B&Bs in the Accommodation chapter of this book.

Brash
(youth community scheme)
01273 293632

Brighton Relate
01273 697997

● HOSPITALS
These are the only hospitals with A&E facilities:

Royal Sussex
Eastern Road, Kemp Town
01273 696955

Southlands
Upper Shoreham Road, Shoreham
01273 455622

Victoria
Nevill Road, Lewes
01273 474153

For health and dental care for registered NHS patients: 0800 665544

● MAGS AND RAGS

The Argus, the only daily newspaper serving East and West Sussex, comes out twice a day. The Property to let supplement is published on Mondays; Property to buy on Wednesdays; business with Sitsvac on Tuesday; more jobs on Thursday; and cars for sale on Friday. Saturday carries weekend and sports supplements. Its website www.thisisbrightonandhove.co.uk has news and community information if you want to check what's happening in the school holidays. *Limited Edition* is its glossy freebie.

City News is free from the Council and is delivered each month

Friday Ad is the Loot of the South East and comes out every Friday.

The Insight (formerly *New Insight*) is probably the best of the local reads. It's monthly and free from restaurants, pubs and cafes around town. It does take ads, but their reviews, unlike most in this city, don't seem to be from deep in the pocket of their advertisers.

The Leader is the freebie published by Argus and distributed to every home on Fridays. It is particularly good on cars for sale.

G-Scene and *Impact* are both predominantly gay mags for Clubland. Newsquest has just published 360, its first gay magazine.

The Source is Newsquest's student rag, packed with clubs and pubs and listings for anyone who has the energy to wade through its migraine-inducing design.

The Latest Homes is a weekly magazine with listings and features.

ABC is the kiddie guide to Sussex and comes out three times a year in cafes in and around Brighton and Hove. Tel 01273 542257.

Wave is the alternative magazine for Sussex with features and news on what's happening in holistic B&H. Again, it's free and available from shops and cafes which advertise in its pages.

Brighton and Hove Life is a glossy bi-monthly which is about as *OK!* as it gets in this part of Sussex. Available from newsagents.

● POLICE STATIONS

For all non-emergencies, call Sussex Police on 0845 6070999. This is a central number that deals with the whole of Sussex. (Obviously, if things are a little more urgent, you should call 999).

Lost property: 01273 665510

The front desk at Brighton Police Station (John Street, Kemp Town) is open 24-hours.

● POST

The post depot on North Road has a late collection at 8pm.

● RADIO STATIONS

Southern FM - 103FM
Sussex wide pop music.

Juice FM - 107.2FM
Local info and pop culture. Juice are Juicy's broadcaster for the Juicy Awards.

BBC Southern Counties Radio
- 95.0FM, 104.5FM
Now housed in Queen's Road in a newly refurbished building, with state-of-the-art studios (including a remote control TV studio) and free introductory computer courses (run by CSV 01273 720894) and internet café in the shop/reception area.

● TOURIST INFORMATION

10 Bartholomew Square, Brighton
01273 292599
Open Monday to Friday 9am-5pm; Saturday 10am-5pm; Sunday 10am-4pm.

● 24-HOUR HELPLINES

Animal welfare
0870 555 5999

Environment Agency
0800 807060
Childline
80800 1111
Samaritans
0845 7909090
Sussex Police
0845 6070999

● WEBSITES

www.thisisbrightonandhove.co.uk is *The Argus'* website and part of the massive fish4 online shopping emporium for everything from a car to a new home.

www.brighton.co.uk for listings and events. The tourism section is controlled by the Council's city marketing division, so you can also try www.brighton-hove.gov.org and you'll come across the same information.

www.hanovernet.co.uk and *www.kemp town.org* are both community websites for the respective areas.

www.zelnet.com is the website for the Connective, Zel's guide to Brighton from the pub-goer's point of view.

And, of course, *www.juicyguides.co.uk* for reviews and views on the ever changing scene in Brighton & Hove.

13

the juicy guide

the juicy guide

● SHOPS

the juicy guide

● SPORT

● TEEN